Communications and Culture

Communications has been defined as the conveying or exchanging of information and ideas. This wide definition is taken as the starting-point for this series of books, which are not bound by conventional academic divisions. The series aims to document or analyse a broad range of cultural forms and ideas.

It encompasses works from areas as esoteric as linguistics and as exoteric as television. The language of communication may be the written word or the moving picture, the static icon or the living gesture. These means of communicating can at their best blossom into and form an essential part of the other mysterious concept, *culture*.

There is no sharp or intended split in the series between communication and culture. On one definition, culture refers to the organisation of experience shared by members of a community, a process which includes the standards and values for judging or perceiving, for predicting and acting. In this sense, creative communication can make for a better and livelier culture.

The series reaches towards the widest possible audience. Some of the works concern themselves with activities as general as play and games; others offer a narrower focus, such as the ways of understanding the visual image. It is hoped that some moves in the transformation of the artful and the scientific can be achieved, and that both can begin to be understood by a wider and more comprehending community. Some of these books are written by practitioners – broadcasters, journalists and artists; others come from critics, scholars, scientists and historians.

The series has an ancient and laudable, though perhaps untenable, aim – an aim as old as the Greeks and as new as holography: it aspires to help heal the split between cultures, between the practitioners and the thinkers, between science and art, between the academy and life.

PAUL WALTON

Communications and Culture

SERIES EDITORS ROSALIND BRUNT, SIMON FRITH, STUART HALL, ANGELA McROBBIE
FOUNDING EDITOR PAUL WALTON

Published

Tony Bennett and Janet Woollacott BOND AND BEYOND: THE POLITICAL
 CAREER OF A POPULAR HERO
Roy Boyne and Ali Rattansi (eds) POSTMODERNISM AND SOCIETY
Victor Burgin (ed.) THINKING PHOTOGRAPHY
Victor Burgin THE END OF ART THEORY: CRITICISM AND POSTMODERNITY
Iain Chambers URBAN RHYTHMS: POP MUSIC AND POPULAR CULTURE
Andrew Davies OTHER THEATRES: THE DEVELOPMENT OF ALTERNATIVE AND
 EXPERIMENTAL THEATRE IN BRITAIN
James Donald (ed.) PSYCHOANALYSIS AND CULTURAL THEORY: THRESHOLDS
Erving Goffman GENDER ADVERTISEMENTS
Stephen Heath QUESTIONS OF CINEMA
Simon Jones BLACK CULTURE, WHITE YOUTH: THE REGGAE TRADITION
 FROM JA TO UK
Peter M. Lewis and Jerry Booth THE INVISIBLE MEDIUM: PUBLIC,
 COMMERCIAL AND COMMUNITY RADIO
Herbert Marcuse THE AESTHETIC DIMENSION: TOWARDS A CRITIQUE OF
 MARXIST AESTHETICS
Cary Nelson and Lawrence Grossberg (eds) MARXISM AND THE
 INTERPRETATION OF CULTURE
John Tagg THE BURDEN OF REPRESENTATION
John Tulloch and Manuel Alvarado DOCTOR WHO: THE UNFOLDING TEXT
Janet Wolff THE SOCIAL PRODUCTION OF ART

Forthcoming

Steven Best and Douglas Kellner POSTMODERNISM AND SOCIAL THEORY:
 INTRODUCTION AND CRITIQUE
Philip Corrigan CULTURE AND CONTROL
Lidia Curti GENDER AND GENRE
Stuart Hall REPRODUCING IDEOLOGIES
Dick Hebdige THE MEANING OF SUBCULTURES
John Tagg MAPS OF MODERNITY: ART HISTORIES AND CULTURAL THEORIES

Contents

Contents

Preface

This volume is the fruit of a series of talks delivered at the Institute of Contemporary Arts in London between January and March 1987. It turned out to be an opportune moment to present work from the intersections between psychoanalysis and cultural theory, for positions entrenched in the 1970s were becoming more fluid and self-critical. I would therefore like to thank all the contributors: not only those whose papers are published here (some very much as delivered, some in more revised form) but also the first four speakers in the series – Stephen Frosh, Stuart Hall, Mandy Merck, and Jeffrey Weeks – whose contributions were extremely important to its continuing success.

The original idea for the project came from Lisa Appignanesi of the ICA, Brian Finney from the Department of Extra-mural Studies at the University of London, the co-sponsors of the event, and Steven Kennedy, editor of Macmillan's 'Culture and Communication' series. I am grateful to them all for trusting me to organise and chair the talks.

I would also like to thank Erica Carter and Katy Sender of the ICA's Talks Department not only for their efficiency and intellectual input, but also for making the series so enjoyable and unstressful.

The frame stills from *Underworld USA* (pp. 120–6 and 130–1) are reproduced with the permission of Columbia Pictures.

References to Freud's works are to *The Standard Edition of the Complete Psychological Works of Sigmund Freud*, 24 volumes, ed. J. Strachey (Hogarth Press, London, 1953–74), given as *SE* in the notes, and/ or to *The Pelican Freud Library*, 15 volumes, ed. A. Richards (1973–82) and A. Dickson (1982–6) (Penguin, Harmondsworth, 1973–86), given as *PFL*.

JAMES DONALD

1

On the Threshold: Psychoanalysis and Cultural Studies

James Donald

I would not say that an attempt of this kind to carry psycho-analysis over to the cultural community was absurd or doomed to be fruitless. But we should have to be very cautious and not forget that, after all, we are only dealing with analogies and that it is dangerous, not only with men but also with concepts, to tear them from the sphere in which they have originated and been evolved.

(Freud, *Civilization and its Discontents*)

Well, the attempt had succeeded. Without trouble or noise, journalist and detective had made their way into the house.

(Marcel Allain and Pierre Souvestre, *Fantômas: The Silent Executioner*)

When I was invited to organise and chair a series of talks on psychoanalysis and cultural theory at the Institute of Contemporary Arts in London, my first reaction was to reach for my address book and suggest better qualified alternatives. Then I hesitated. After all, wasn't the folk hero of this Thatcherite age the ill-starred brickie Yosser Hughes in the television series *Boys from the Blackstuff*, for whom one of life's great mysteries was that ignorance or incompetence should be a bar to employment? 'I can do that,' he'd have said, 'Gi'us the job'. Hastily translating that into an academic justification, I recalled a question I had come across in Shoshana Felman's essay on 'Psychoanalysis and education': 'How can I interpret *out of* the dynamic ignorance I analytically encounter, both in others and in myself? How can I turn ignorance into an instrument of teaching?'[1]

So I accepted the invitation, primarily in the hope that I might learn something, that I might finally come to grips with the issues raised by psychoanalysis for the sorts of cultural and educational studies in which I work. That may mean I end up here as the editor presumed to know, but, even so, don't expect in this introduction a masterly exegesis of all the arguments raised in the essays that follow. They, in any case, require neither explanation nor apology from me. What you will find in them is neither a comprehensive introduction to the often fraught engagements between psychoanalysis and cultural theory,[2] nor a definitive new line, but rather a 'snapshot' of a range of work in progress at a particular moment and in a particular context – work that shares certain priorities, problems and points of reference.

Of course, my involvement in the talks and the book has not been altogether innocent. I had my own polemical reasons for wanting to stage the series in the spring of 1987. Negatively, I sensed then that the perennial suspicion endemic among the British intellectual left towards psychoanalysis – and specifically towards the types of psychoanalysis that I find interesting – might be erupting, as it periodically does, into overt hostility. More positively, I also felt that this was a transitional moment, that established ways of yoking together concepts around 'psychoanalysis' and 'culture' were being subjected to a self-critical re-examination. (This is exemplified here in Elizabeth Cowie's review of 1970s film theory, and in the different estimations of the possible relations between psychoanalysis and literary theory by Robert Young and Elizabeth Wright.) Given this starting point, it is important to be clear about *which* psychoanalysis it is that we are talking about, and so also about what claims are and are not being made for psychoanalysis in relation to cultural theory.

However dissimilar their intellectual approaches, I was struck by the remarkably similar way in which Stuart Hall, in his contribution to the introductory session at the ICA, and Robert Young (p. 144) characterised this psychoanalytic field. It is, they agreed, psychoanalysis after the feminist rereading of Lacan's rereading of Freud.[3] This is, in other words, the psychoanalysis that emerged (in Britain at least) as part of an attempt in the 1960s and 1970s to pose cultural and social questions in new ways, to see things differently. This impulse clearly lay behind such projects as Juliet Mitchell's heretical rehabilitation, or reclamation, of Freud in *Psychoanalysis and Feminism*, or the journal *Screen*'s attempt to establish film theory in Britain with its heady cocktail of Lacanian psychoanalysis, Althusserian Marxism, radical semiotics and a Brechtian aesthetic. Since then, those formulations have been criticised, contested, rethought and refined – not least by their first begetters. A feminist engagement with psychoanalysis, drawing also on Foucauldian work in its critique of Althusser, was a consistent and central theme in the journal *m/f* (of which Parveen Adams and Elizabeth Cowie were editors) – despite a sometimes quite hostile rejection of the claims for the importance of subjectivity for cultural and social life in the name of a class-based feminism.[4] On the other hand, a key figure in the development of cultural studies like Stuart Hall, although remaining sceptical in some ways, has increasingly incorporated psychoanalytic *questions* into his attempts to understand the significance of identity, ethnicity and desire in the dynamics of political mobilisation.[5] That impulse to interrogate cultural issues in the light of psychoanalytic insights continues to be evident in this book.

This formulation has a number of implications. It means that these essays do not treat psychoanalysis as just another technique for reading through the phenomenal forms of culture to unmask their 'real' meaning – though substituting the operations of the unconscious for the determining 'reality' of economic relations proposed by some Marxist cultural theory. In considering the visual arts, cinema, literary theory, questions of perception and identity, and also (in John Forrester's essay) psychoanalysis itself, the authors do not simply *apply* psychoanalysis to a reading of cultural forms. The question they raise is, how do you analyse the dynamics of culture differently once you recognise the centrality of the unconscious?

This entails neither incorporating psychoanalysis into cultural theory, nor claiming that either is a metadiscourse able to explain and resolve the lacunae in the other, nor creating a new synthetic theoretical field which might accommodate them both. Any such attempt to merge the two bodies of theory blunts their specific insights and ignores their incompatibilities and contradictions. What seems potentially more fruitful is the dialogue in which, although the two discourses remain distinct – they are always to some extent talking past each other – the questions untranslatably specific to each can provoke new thinking and insights in the other. (It is worth noting that this dialogue has not been limited to the conventional terms of academic discourse, but has generated new forms of art practice. These are exemplified by Mary Kelly's contribution to this book; Victor Burgin in his photography-based art works and Laura Mulvey in her films similarly cross and recross the thresholds of theory and aesthetics.)

It follows from the refusal to collapse psychoanalysis and cultural theory into each other that the essays in this collection do not attempt a pathology of contemporary British culture – Freud quite properly warned us off that path. It is cultural *analysis* not cultural therapy that is at issue here. Nor are they primarily concerned with individual psychological health, with the more or less successful and more or less painful processes of psychic maturation, nor with the scars left on the psyche by its adaptation to the social and the cultural. Their focus on questions of culture distinguishes them not only from psychological notions of development, but also from sociological assumptions about the construction of individual identity through the internalisation of social norms. They take it as axiomatic that, as Jacqueline Rose observes, the psychoanalytic concept of the un-conscious 'constantly reveals the "failure" of identity'. By this she does not mean a passing blip in a process of socialisation: ' "failure" is something endlessly repeated and relived moment by moment throughout our in-dividual histories. It appears not only in the symptom, but also in dreams, in slips of the tongue and in forms of sexual pleasure which are pushed to the sidelines of the norm.'

For Rose, it is this recognition that 'there is a resistance to identity at the very heart of psychic life' that suggests the affinity between feminism and psychoanalysis.[6] To me, it also suggests why it is impossible to stage the dialogue between psychoanalysis and cultural theory in terms of what I think of as the Polyfilla model – remember the time when we all got terribly worried that Marxism and/or cultural studies did not have a theory of the subject, and hoped that (following Althusser's appropriation of Lacan) psychoanalysis might provide it? Fill that gap, ran the argument, and we would finally have a complete picture of the complex unity of 'reality', or at least of ideology and social relations.

One reason this was never going to work is that even if cultural studies lacked a fully developed theory of the subject, a concern with – indeed, a *commitment to* – a certain conception of identity lay at its very heart. Its original project (at least in the institutional form that began to emerge in Britain in the post-1956 period) was, in large part, to make the experiences of ordinary people and the texture of everyday life, previously ignored within most academic discourse, a legitimate and necessary focus of concern. This principle had two corollaries. One was a new attention to the historical importance of collective subjects like 'the people' or 'the working class'. The other was the assertion that individual consciousness is social in the sense that it derives from the shared experiences that produce these collective identities. E. P. Thompson spelt out his version of the link between them in his definition of class in *The Making of the English Working Class* in 1963:

> Class happens when some men, as a result of common experiences (inherited or shared), feel and articulate the identity of their interests as between themselves, and as against other men whose interests are different from (and usually opposed to) theirs. The class experience is largely determined by the productive relations into which men are born – or enter involuntarily. Class consciousness is the way in which the experiences are handled in cultural terms: embodied in traditions, value-systems, ideas and institutional forms.[7]

Although Raymond Williams's conception of a 'structure of feeling' stresses generational as well as class determinations, it shares this dual focus. In *The Long Revolution*, he characterised it in terms of 'a particular sense of life, a particular community of experience'. Later, in *Marxism and*

Literature, he again defined it in terms of 'meanings and values as they are actively lived and felt', but now underlined the inherently social nature of experience even when it appears 'private, idiosyncratic and even isolating'. It is just that its structuring characteristics may only become recognisable retrospectively as they become 'formalised, classified, and in many cases built into institutions and formations'.[8]

A central proposition of the cultural studies of Thompson and Williams, then, was that a shared social and historical experience produces a common sensibility which is the stuff of individual consciousness; hence its concern with questions of identity and that apparent tautology 'lived experience'. How does psychoanalysis subvert this model? It is not – despite some of Williams's remarks[9] – by denying the social nature of subjectivity or by proposing a purely individualist account. (What, after all, is the Oedipus scenario if not an account of the psychic incorporation of patriarchal social relations?) Rather, it is by revealing that the *lived* in 'lived experience' begs the question of how the 'outside' of collective experience is supposed to become the 'inside' of individual consciousness. The insistence on the fact of the unconscious, far from plugging any holes in this model, explodes the very idea of a complete or achieved identity to which Thompson and Williams ascribe such ethical and political import-ance. In contrast to their knitting together of social being and individual consciousness in a largely seamless unity, psychoanalysis focuses on the caesura between the *structure* of social determination and the psychic affect of *feeling*. It introduces '*die Idee einer anderer Lokalität*, the idea of another locality, another space, another scene, *the between perception and consciousness*'.[10] This space of psychic reality presents a less sanitised version of how we exist in the world than Thompson or Williams. Here rumour, gossip, prohibition and lack bubble away. Here fantasy stages its *mise en scène* of desire, presenting those disgracefully novelettish scenarios that are both a symptom of, and perhaps a compensation for, the failure of ideology ever to get the full measure of subjectivity.[11]

This is not, it is true, how the theory was developed in much 'second-generation' cultural studies.[12] Rather, this took from Althusser's theory of ideology as the production of subjects the idea of *interpellation* as the mechanism whereby the subject recognises (misrecognises) itself in the address of the symbolic as it is embodied in cultural forms. This allowed a move from the notion of ideology as false beliefs or illusions – or Thompson's notion of culture as the expression of shared experiences and collective consciousness – to an understanding of ideology as a system of *representation* which shapes our perception and experience of the world:

> In truth, ideology has very little to do with 'consciousness', even supposing this term to have an unambiguous meaning. It is profoundly *unconscious*. . . Ideology is indeed a system of representations, but in the

majority of cases these representations have nothing to do with 'consciousness': they are usually images and occasionally concepts, but it is above all as *structures* that they impose on the vast majority of men, not via their 'consciousness'. They are perceived-accepted-suffered cultural objects and they act functionally on men via a process that escapes them.[13]

Hence cultural studies in this mode were often characterised by the meticulous analysis of the textual organisation and collusive pleasures of novels, films, advertisements, women's magazines, seaside resorts and whatever. Often, though, some notion of false consciousness seemed to linger on in the background. The assumption still seemed to be that ideology *works*, that the symbolic forms succeed in recruiting people to their allotted slot in the social relations of production even if they remain unconscious of them. By stressing the symbolic at the expense of the processes of imaginary identification, these analyses tended to slip back into a model of individual adaptation to cultural norms. They underestimated the structural resistance to identity (whether consensual or oppositional), the splitting of the ego and the inevitable mismatch of subject and culture that were the Lacanian contribution to Althusser's theory – not to mention those aspects of subjectivity 'beyond interpellation' that Althusser himself left out of account.

For example, their focus was still on sociological categories like 'gender' and 'race', rather than on the performative dynamics of sexual difference and ethnicity. The analysis of the latter has generally been developed outside Cultural Studies as it took on capital letters and found itself a precarious niche within the academy. In her sequence of studies on the formation of femininity, for example, Jacqueline Rose draws centrally on psychoanalysis but always pulls it both 'towards a recognition of the fully social constitution of identity and norms, and then back again to that point of tension between ego and unconscious where they are endlessly remodelled and endlessly break'.[14] (The critical exploration of the formation of femininity and masculinity is continued in this volume in Parveen Adams's discussion of hysterical identification.) And Homi Bhabha too moves decisively 'beyond interpellation' in his explanation of the emergence of social collectivities and of cultural difference. (In his contribution to this book, for instance, in rethinking Benedict Anderson's influential account of the nation as imagined community in terms that derive from Derridean deconstruction as well as post-Lacanian psychoanalysis, he develops an alternative view of the communality of 'the people' as an *enunciation* which produces not an imaginary identity so much as a positionality that is always split and therefore also uncanny.)

In cultural theory like this, we've come a long way from E. P. Thompson's 'class consciousness' or Raymond Williams's 'structures of feeling' – and not just by recognising their failure to integrate the consideration of sexual and cultural difference into their analysis. They offered 'culture' as an explanatory category into which the social relationships of production, the collective actors – like 'the English working class' – that appeared on the stage of history, and individual consciousness could all be fitted. Although post-Althusserian cultural studies offered a different account of subject formation, in terms of symbolic and imaginary identification, it too failed to acknowledge the excess beyond these processes. Now, in contrast to that claim that ideology can get the measure of subjectivity, the key question for any cultural theory (including psychoanalysis and/or cultural studies) is the *failure* of ideology. The starting point for investigation is that a perfect fit between culture and subject, between social relations and psychic reality, is an impossibility.

This 'lack of fit' is perhaps the most disconcerting question that psychoanalysis poses to cultural studies. It does not entail any denial of the specific operations and effectivity of the social: it does, however, suggest the need to rethink the social as itself open and unsutured (to use Ernesto Laclau and Chantal Mouffe's terms[15]). Their axiom that 'society doesn't exist' is a corollary of the psychoanalytic critique of the subject. It suggests an attempt within cultural theory to rethink a concept like hegemony in a way that takes into account *both* the operations of the unconscious *and* the opacity of the social. It acknowledges that this opacity is in one sense a symptom of the alienation that is an effect of the mechanisms of identification studied by psychoanalysis: social reality always exists for a subject. But it also recognises that there is a social *real*, whose sheer complexity, heterogeneity and contradictoriness generate dynamics which can only be apprehended symptomatically.

This formulation resists the temptation to leave the last word with psychoanalysis, and so to gloss over the questions and problems that cultural theory might raise for it in return. Possibly the most testing and salutary of these is the irreducibly heterogeneous and contradictory nature of the social antagonisms around which the play of desire, fantasy and identification is organised. The openness and its organisation can no more be explained solely in terms of the 'same difference' of castration than in terms of the fundamental class antagonism of Marxist cultural theory. (Hence the theoretical as well as the political importance of questions around ethnicity and racism. Here both spheres of determination are clearly in play, but neither discourse can offer a wholly adequate explanation.) Also, the centrality ascribed to ideology in the dialogue between cultural studies and psychoanalysis is called into question by Michel Foucault's work. This offers quite a different account of the techniques of subjectification and individuation through which power has come to operate in the modernity of the West, and so demands/promises a different account of individual interiority. Although he acknowledges the achievement of Freud and Lacan in exposing and exploring 'the logic of the unconscious', Foucault argues – *contra* the Althusserian view as well as the Thompson/Williams model – that 'power relations can materially penetrate the body in depth, without depending even on the mediation of the subject's own representations. If power takes hold in the body, this isn't through its having first to be interiorised in people's consciousness.'[16] Derrida too questions the emphasis on the organisation of representation and the symbolic in psychoanalysis – although his insistence on the endless free play of *différance* means that it is not any particular tying down of meaning and identity that is the issue so much as the possibility of *any* organisation.

In these various competing ways, it is as they address the perennial, irreconcilable tension in both subjectivity and culture between the push to identity and the structural resistances to any such closure that psychoanalysis and cultural theory come to occupy the same troublesome terrain. And in doing so, they begin to displace the old imagery of *the individual* being determined by and/or adapting to *society* – including 'structure of feeling' and 'lived experience' – in favour of notions of fantasy, enunciation, cultural technologies and translation.

This dialogue between the discourses of psychoanalysis and cultural theory is one referent of the image of *thresholds* in the title of this book. But a threshold is a boundary as well as an interchange. The image is thus a reminder too of the impossibility of any easy synthesis between them, or of any final answers to the enigmatic transactions between subject and culture, between the psychic and the social. Paradoxically, it may be this *impossibility*, on which Freud insisted in his final text, that is of particular interest and importance.

> It almost looks as if analysis were the third of those 'impossible' professions in which one can be sure beforehand of achieving unsatisfying results. The other two, which have been known much longer, are education and government.[17]

As it happens, my own interest in psychoanalysis was originally prompted by a prior concern with education and politics. But whereas I may have first turned to it in the hope of finding some clues to ways of overcoming their frustrating failure to produce desired social outcomes, what I learned was that this 'impossibility' is less a malfunction than a sign of the *necessary* failure of identity in the psyche and of closure in the social that I have begun to sketch here. This, of course, has profound implications for how one thinks about the dynamics of culture, not least by alerting one to the need to hang onto to both the operations of the unconscious and the opacity of the social at the same time. By teaching us not to be satisfied with explanations that are easily accepted (because narcissistically desired)

or already known (the comfort of repeating the same),[18] it also underlines
the value of psychoanalysis as a pedagogy – Shoshana Felman character-
ises Lacan's view of it as 'an invention that, in its practice, *teaches people
how to think beyond their means*'.[19] The dialogue between psychoanalysis
and cultural theory may thus do more than teach us to accept the
impossibility of the perfection or completion of either subjectivity or of
culture. It can also teach us to learn from the limitations of theory, and (to
end at the beginning) from our ignorance. In different styles and from
different perspectives, the essays in this collection are a contribution to this
dialogic attempt to 'think beyond our means'.

Notes

1. Shoshana Felman, 'Psychoanalysis and Education: Teaching Terminable and
    Interminable', in *Jacques Lacan and the Adventure of Insight: Psychoanalysis
    in Contemporary Culture* (Harvard University Press, Cambridge, Mass. &
    London, 1987), p. 80.
2. On the debates about psychoanalysis and anthropology between Ernest
    Jones and Bronislaw Malinowski in the 1930s, for example, see Paul Hirst
    and Penny Woolley, *Social Relations and Human Attributes* (Tavistock,
    London, 1982), ch. 8, and Rosalind Coward, *Patriarchal Precedents: Sexual-
    ity and Social Relations* (London: Routledge & Kegan Paul, 1983), ch. 8. On
    some of the recent debates between psychoanalysis and both the British left
    and British feminism, see Jacqueline Rose, *Sexuality in the Field of Vision*
    (Verso, London, 1986). A key text in contemporary psychoanalytic literary
    theory is Shoshana Felman (ed.), *'Literature and Psychoanalysis. The
    Question of Reading: Otherwise'*, *Yale French Studies*, nos 55/56 (1977).
3. For examples of this feminist rereading, see Juliet Mitchell, *Psychoanalysis
    and Feminism* (Allen Lane, London, 1974); Juliet Mitchell and Jacqueline
    Rose (eds), *Feminine Sexuality: Jacques Lacan and the école freudienne*
    (Macmillan, London, 1982); Rose, *Sexuality in the Field of Vision*; Felman,
    Jacques Lacan...; Jane Gallop, *The Daughter's Seduction: Feminism and
    Psychoanalysis* (Macmillan, London, 1982) and *Reading Lacan* (Cornell
    University Press, Ithaca, 1985).
4. On these see 'Feminism and the Psychic' and 'Femininity and its Discon-
    tents' in Rose, *Sexuality in the Field of Vision*.
5. Stuart Hall, *The Hard Road to Renewal: Thatcherism and the Crisis of the
    Left* (Verso, London, 1988), esp. chs 18 & 19; also his 'Minimal Selves', in
    Lisa Appignanesi (ed.), *Identity: The Real Me* (ICA, London, 1987) and
    'New Ethnicities', in Kobena Mercer (ed.), *Black Film, British Cinema*
    (ICA, London, 1988).
6. Rose, *Sexuality in the Field of Vision*, pp. 90–1 (see note 2).
7. E. P. Thompson, *The Making of the English Working Class* (Penguin,
    Harmondsworth, 1968 [1963]), pp. 9–10.
8. Raymond Williams, *The Long Revolution* (Penguin, Harmondsworth,
    1965), p. 64; *Marxism and Literature* (Oxford University Press, Oxford,
    1977), p. 132.
9. See, for example, Williams, 'Crisis in English Studies', in *Writing in Society*

THE LIBRARY
West Surrey College of Art and Design \

(Verso, London, n.d.) p. 210; 'The Uses of Cultural Theory', *New Left Review*, no. 158 (1986), p. 26.

10.   Jacques Lacan, *The Four Fundamental Concepts of Psychoanalysis* (Hogarth Press, London, 1977), p. 56.

11.   This argument is made by Slavoj Žižek in his essay 'Identity, Identification and its Beyond', in Ernesto Laclau (ed.), *New Reflections on the Revolution of Our Time* (Verso, London, forthcoming).

12.   I am thinking mainly of the work associated with the Centre for Contemporary Cultural Studies at the University of Birmingham. For a representative collection, see Stuart Hall, Dorothy Hobson, Andrew Lowe and Paul Willis (eds), *Culture, Media, Language* (Hutchinson, London, 1980).

13.   Louis Althusser, *For Marx* (New Left Books, London, 1977), p. 233.

14.   Rose, *Sexuality in the Field of Vision*, p. 7 (see note 2).

15.   Ernesto Laclau and Chantal Mouffe, *Hegemony and Socialist Strategy: Towards a Radical Democratic Politics* (Verso, London, 1985).

16.   Michel Foucault, *Power/Knowledge*, Colin Gordon (ed.) (Harvester, Brighton, 1980), pp. 196, 213.

17.   *SE*, XXIII, p. 248, quoted in Felman, *Jacques Lacan...*, p. 70 (see note 1).

18.   I have taken this formulation from Constance Penley, 'Introduction', in *Feminism and Film Theory* (Routledge, New York: BFI Publishing, London, 1988), p. 2.

19.   Felman, *Jacques Lacan...*, p. 15 (see note 1).

2

Geometry and Abjection

Victor Burgin

'simple geometrical opposition becomes tinged with aggressivity'
(Bachelard, *The Poetics of Space*)

Although it makes no direct reference to Althusser's essay of 1970, 'Ideology and Ideological State Apparatuses',[1] Roland Barthes's essay of 1973, 'Diderot, Brecht, Eisenstein', had the effect of spatialising the Althusserian concept of ideology as representation: 'there will still be representation for so long as a subject (author, reader, spectator or voyeur) casts his gaze towards a horizon on which he cuts out the base of a triangle, his eye (or his mind) forming the apex'.[2] Laura Mulvey's essay of 1975, 'Visual Pleasure and Narrative Cinema',[3] subsequently theorised the voyeuristic subject of Barthes's theatrical space in terms of Freudian psychoanalysis. The change across this five-year period is profound. Instead of a contingent set of ideas which might be dissipated by reason, 'ideology' was now conceived of in terms of a space of representations which the subject inhabits, a limitless space which the desiring subject negotiates by predominantly unconscious transactions.

For all these innovations, however, there remained significant ties with tradition. Barthes's optical triangle is, after all, one-half of the diagram of the camera obscura – a metaphor not unfamiliar to students of Marx. Furthermore, 1975 was also the year of publication, in French, of Foucault's *Discipline and Punish*.[4] Barthes's 'eye at the apex' was therefore easily conflated with that of the jailor, actual or virtual, in the tower at the centre of the panopticon. For all that Foucault himself would have opposed it, this further contributed to the survival of that strand of theory according to which ideology is an instrument of domination wielded by one

11

section of a society and imposed upon another – 'the dominant ideas are the ideas of those who dominate'. In this context, then – and given the urgent exigencies of a feminist *Realpolitik* – it is not so surprising that one effect of Laura Mulvey's essay was that all man-made images of women were henceforth viewed, without discrimination, as instruments of sadistic objectification, and were therefore proscribed.

I believe that the metaphor of the 'cone of vision', predominant in theories of representation during the past twelve years, is itself responsible for a reductive and simplistic equation of looking with objectification. In so far as this metaphor is drawn from physiological optics, it is inappropriate to the description of psychological functions. In so far as it is drawn from Euclidean geometry, it is inadequate to describe the changed apprehension of space which is an attribute of so-called 'postmodern' culture.

I

Space has a history. In the cosmology of classical Greece, as F. M. Cornford writes, 'the universe of being was finite and spherical, with no endless stretch of emptiness beyond. Space had the form of . . . a sphere with centre and circumference'.[5] This classical space essentially survived the biblically-derived 'flat earth' of early Christian doctrine, to re-emerge in the late Middle Ages. In medieval cosmology, supercelestial and celestial spheres encompassed, but did not touch, a terrestrial sphere – the scene of human action – in which every being, and each thing, had a place pre-ordained by God and was subject to his omnivoyant gaze. Foucault has termed this medieval space the 'space of emplacement'; this space, he observes, was effectively destroyed by Galileo:

> For the real scandal of Galileo's work lay not so much in his discovery, or rediscovery, that the earth revolved around the sun, but in his constitution of an infinite, and infinitely open space. In such a space the place of the Middle Ages turned out to be dissolved . . . starting with Galileo and the seventeenth century, extension was substituted for localisation.[6]

The vehicle of this changed cosmology was Euclidean geometry. Euclid wrote the *Elements of Geometry* around 300 BC. Husserl, in *The Origin of Geometry*, supposes that this system arose out of practical activities, such as building. However, the classical conception of space seems to have been based upon visual evidence rather than technique – the horizon appears to encircle us, and the heavens appear to be vaulted above us.[7] In the Renaissance this conflict between observation and intellection, between hyperbolic and Euclidean space, was played out during the early stages of the invention of perspective. The absence of a necessary connection between knowledge of Euclidean geometry and the development of perspective is evident from the example of the Islamic world. In the West, the primacy of geometry over perception was stressed by St Augustine, who wrote: 'reason advanced to the province of the eyes... It found ... that nothing which the eyes beheld, could in any way be compared with what the mind discerned. These distinct and separate realities it also reduced to a branch of learning, and called it geometry.'[8]

Although dependent upon Euclid's *Elements*, Renaissance perspective took its most fundamental concept from Euclid's *Optics*. The concept is that of the 'cone of vision'. Some two thousand years after Euclid, Brunelleschi conceives of this same cone as intersected by a plane surface – the picture-plane. By means of this model, something of the pre-modern worldview passes into the Copernican universe – a universe which is no longer geocentric, but which is nevertheless homocentric and egocentric. A basic principle of Euclidean geometry is that space extends infinitely in three dimensions. The effect of monocular perspective, however, is to maintain the idea that this space does nevertheless have a centre – the observer. By degrees the sovereign gaze is transferred from God to Man. With the 'emplacement' of the medieval world now dissolved, this ocular subject of perspective, and of mercantile capitalism, is free to pursue its entrepreneurial ambitions wherever trade winds blow.

Entrepreneurial humanism first took liberties with, then eventually replaced, theocentric determinism according to a model which is implicitly Aristotelian, and in a manner which exemplifies the way in which spatial conceptions are projected into the representation of political relationships. In Aristotle's cosmological physics it was assumed that the preponderance of one or other of the four elements first posited by Empedocles (earth, water, air and fire) would determine the place of that body within a continuum from the centre to the periphery of the universe. This continuum of actual and potential 'places' constituted space. Analogously, the idea that a human being will find his or her 'natural' resting place within the social space of differential privileges according to his or her 'inherent' qualities has remained a cornerstone of humanist-derived political philosophies. Newton disengaged space *per se* from Aristotelian 'place',[9] and Newtonian physics was in turn overtaken by the physics of Einstein, in which, in the words of Minkowski, 'space by itself, and time by itself, are doomed to fade away into mere shadows, and only a kind of union of the two will preserve an independent reality'.[10] More recently, the precepts of general relativity have themselves come into question in 'quantum theory'.[11] The cosmology of modern physics has nevertheless had little impact on the commonly held world view in the West, which is still predominantly an amalgam of Newton and Aristotelianism – 'places in space', a system of centres of human affairs (homes, workplaces, cities) deployed within a uniformly regular and vaguely endless 'space in itself'.

In the modernist avant-garde in art, references to a mutation in the apprehension of space and time brought about by modern physics and mathematics are not unusual. Thus, for example, in 1925 El Lissitsky wrote: 'Perspective bounded and enclosed space, but science has since brought about a fundamental revision. The rigidity of Euclidean space has been annihilated by Lobachevsky, Gauss, and Riemann'.[12] Nevertheless, modernists more commonly ascribed a changed apprehension of space not to scientific concepts *per se*, but rather to technology. Thus Vertov wrote: 'I am the cinema-eye. I am a mechanical eye. I, a machine, can show you the world as only I can see it ... I ascend with aeroplanes, I fall and rise together with falling and rising bodies'.[13] Constrained by mechanical metaphors, Russian futurism, like cubism, ultimately failed – notwithstanding El Lissitsky's pronouncement – to abandon Euclidian geometry. The mirror of perspectival representation was broken only in order that its fragments, each representing a distinct point-of-view, be reassembled according to classical geometric principles – to be returned, finally, to the frame and the proscenium arch.[14]

In the modern period, space was predominantly space traversed (by this token we judge that the prisoner has little of it). In the 'postmodern' period, the speed with which space is traversed is no longer governed by the mechanical speed of machines such as aeroplanes, but rather by the electronic speed of machines such as computers and video links, which operate at nearly the speed of light. A mutation in technology therefore has, arguably, brought the technolog*ism* inherited from the spatial perceptions of modernist aesthetics into line with the perceptions of modern physics. Thus, for example, Paul Virilio writes that, 'technological space ... is not a geographical space, but a space of time'.[15] In this space-time of electronic communications, operating at the speed of light, we see things, he observes, 'in a different light' – the 'light of speed'.[16] Moreover, this space seems to be moving, once again, towards self-enclosure. For example, David Bolter, a classics professor writing about computer programming, concludes, 'In sum, electronic space has the feel of ancient geometric space'.[17] One of the phenomenological effects of the public applications of new electronic technologies is to cause space to be apprehended as 'folding back' upon itself. Spaces once conceived of as separated, segregated, now overlap: live pictures from Voyager II, as it passes through the rings of Saturn, may appear on television sandwiched between equally 'live' pictures of internal organs, transmitted by surgical probes, and footage from Soweto. A counterpart in the political sphere of the fold-over spaces of information technologies is terrorism. In the economic sphere it is the tendency of multinational capitalism to produce First World irruptions in Third World countries, while creating Second World pockets in the developed nations. To contemplate such phenomena is no longer to inhabit an imaginary space ordered by the subject–object 'stand-off' of Euclidean perspective. The analogies which fit best are now to be found in non-Euclidean geometries – the topologist's Möbius strip, for example, where the apparently opposing sides prove to be formed from a single, continuous surface.

Space, then, has a history. It is not, as Kant would have it, the product of a priori, inherently Euclidean, categories of mind. It is a product of representations. Premodern space is bounded; things within it are assigned a place along a predominantly vertical axis – 'heaven-earth-hell', or the 'chain of being', extending from God down to stones. Modern space (inaugurated in the Renaissance) is Euclidean, horizontal, infinitely extensible, and therefore, in principle, boundless. In the early modern period it is the space of the humanist subject in its mercantile entrepreneurial incarnation. In the late modern period it is the space of industrial capitalism, the space of an exponentially increased pace of dispersal, displacement and dissemination, of people and things. In the 'postmodern' period it is the space of financial capitalism – the former space in the process of imploding, or 'infolding' – to appropriate a Derridean term, it is a space in the process of 'intravagination'. Twenty years ago Guy Debord wrote about the unified space of capitalist production, 'which is no longer bounded by external societies', the abstract space of the market which 'had to destroy the autonomy and quality of places', and he commented: 'This society which eliminates geographical distance reproduces distance internally as spectacular separation.'[18] Such 'internal distance' is that of psychical space. Nevertheless, as I have already remarked, psychoanalytically inspired theories of representation have tended in recent years to remain faithful to the Euclidean geometrical–*optical* metaphors of the modern period.

II

At the head of her 1975 exposition of Lacan's concept of 'The Imaginary',[19] Jacqueline Rose places a quotation from Lacan's first seminar (1953–54): 'I cannot urge you too strongly to meditate on the science of optics . . . peculiar in that it attempts by means of instruments to produce that strange phenomenon known as images'.[20] As already observed, 1975 was also the year of publication of Laura Mulvey's essay 'Visual Pleasure and Narrative Cinema', with its own emphasis on, in Mulvey's words, 'the voyeuristic-scopophilic look that is a crucial part of traditional filmic pleasure'. If we re-read these two papers today we should read them in tandem, as the one is an essential, albeit somewhat contradictory, complement of the other.

In terms of theories of visual representation (at least, in Britain and the US) Laura Mulvey's essay is, arguably, the single most influential article of the 1970s, and it is worth remembering the context in which it first

appeared.[21] The observation that there is a fundamental difference between 'classic' semiology, which reached its apogee in the mid-1960s, and
semiotics since about 1970 has become a commonplace. The difference,
which in principal affects not only semiotics but all theoretical disciplines,
is that the classical subject–object dichotomy has been 'deconstructed' –
the interpreter is no longer outside the act of interpretation; the subject is
now part of the object. As I have remarked, the metaphor of the 'cone of
vision', inherited from classical perspective, has been used to clarify this
insight. If the theme of 'the look' dominated Anglophone theories of film
and photography during the 1970s, and entered theories of painting in the
1980s, it is perhaps because, apart from the urgent sexual-political questions it could address, the cone of vision metaphor also functioned as an
aide-mémoire in a crucial epistemological break with Western tradition.

   In the 1970s the cone of vision model was often conjoined with Lacan's
concept of the 'mirror-stage'. In Laura Mulvey's essay, for example,
Lacan's early geometric perspective version of 'the imaginary' provides a
model of cinematic 'identification' in opposition to identification's own
'mirror image' – scopophilic objectification. However, as Jacqueline
Rose's article on 'the imaginary' is at pains to point out, 'it is precisely at
the moment when those drives most relevant to the cinematic experience
as such start to take precedence in the Lacanian schema [she refers to the
scopic and invocatory drives] that the notion of an imaginary plenitude, or
of an identification with a demand sufficient to its object, begins to be
undermined'.[22] On the one hand, the model of the cone of vision was
valuable in reinstating the ideologically elided presence of the observer in
the space of representation. On the other hand, it was complicit in
preserving what was most central to the ideology it sought to subvert – that
punctual ego which Lacan identifies, in his later extended critique of the
geometric perspective model of vision, as assuming that it can 'see itself
seeing itself'. That much of the point of the Lacanian critique of vision had
been lost is nowhere better indicated than in the debates which followed
Mulvey's influential paper, which so often revolved around the objection
that Mulvey had said nothing about the position of the women in the
audience.

   We see here precisely what Rose identifies as the 'confusion at the basis
of an "ego psychology"', which is 'to emphasise the relationship of the ego
to *the perception-consciousness system* over and against its role as fabrica-
tor and fabrication, designed to preserve the subject's precarious pleasure
from an impossible and non-compliant real'[23] (my emphasis). This confusion is supported and compounded by the cone of vision model.
Certainly, as already noted, the model incorporates the subject as an
intrinsic part of the system of representation, in so far as the image projects
its sightlines to an ideal point where that subject is supposed to be;
nevertheless, the object in this case is quite clearly maintained as external

to the subject, existing in a relation of 'outside' to the subject's 'inside'. The object of psychoanalysis, the lost object, may thus easily be confused with some real object. As Rose indicates, it is precisely for this reason that Lacan subsequently abandons the geometric perspective model.

'The idea of another locality', writes Freud, in a famous phrase. 'The idea of another space', adds Lacan, 'another scene, the *between perception and consciousness*'[24] (my emphasis). Pscyhoanalysis reveals unconscious wishes – and the fantasies they engender – to be as immutable a force in our lives as any material circumstance. They do not, however, belong to material reality, but to what Freud termed 'psychical reality'. The space where they 'take place' – 'between perception and consciousness' – is not a material space. In so far, therefore, as Freud speaks of 'psychical reality', we are perhaps justified in speaking of 'psychical space'.[25] In the passage I have quoted, Barthes speaks of representation as taking place whenever the subject 'cuts out the base of a triangle, his eye (or his mind) forming the apex'. 'His eye or his mind': clearly, Barthes conflates psychical space with the space of visual perception, which in turn is modelled on Euclid. But why should we suppose that the condensations and displacements of desire show any more regard for Euclidean geometry than they do for Aristotelian logic? Some of the peculiar spatial properties of the theatre of desire are indicated by Freud in his paper 'A Child is Being Beaten'.[26] Here the subject is positioned in the audience *and* on stage – where it is both aggressor *and* aggressed. The spatial qualities of the psychical *mise-en-scène* are clearly non-Euclidean: different objects may occupy the same space at the same (non)instant, as in condensation in dreams; or subject and object may collapse into each other. As Rose observes, what this paper most fundamentally reveals is 'the splitting of subjectivity in the process of being held to a sexual representation (male or female)'.[27]

'Author, reader, spectator or voyeur', writes Barthes, identifying his subject of representation. All of these subjects desire, but none more *visibly* than the voyeur. In the chapter of *Being and Nothingness* which bears the title 'The Look', and to which Lacan refers in his own extended discussion of the look as conceived in terms of geometric perspective, Sartre chooses to describe his 'being-as-object for the Other' from the position of the voyeur: 'Here I am, bent over the keyhole; suddenly I hear a footstep. I shudder as a wave of shame sweeps over me. Somebody has seen me. I straighten up. My eyes run over the deserted corridor. It was a false alarm. I breathe a sigh of relief.' But, Sartre continues, if he now persists in his voyeuristic enterprise, 'I shall feel my heart beat fast, and I shall detect the slightest noise, the slightest creaking of the stairs. Far from disappearing with my first alarm, the Other is present everywhere, below me, above me, in the neighbouring rooms, and I continue to feel profoundly my being-for-others.'[28] As Lacan puts it, 'I am a picture' (just as 'I' was God's picture in the medieval space of emplacement).

If Sartre had been less hostile to the concept of the unconscious he might not have excluded the condition of 'being-for-others' from his relation to the object of his scopophilic interest. Merleau-Ponty's phenomenology moved towards a *rapprochement* with psychoanalysis (in a preface he contributed in 1960 to a book on Freud he spoke of a 'consonance' between the two disciplines). Chapter IV of Merleau-Ponty's final, unfinished, work, *The Visible and the Invisible*, is titled 'The Intertwining – The Chiasm'. (*Chiasm*, an anatomical term for the crossing over of two physiological structures, is derived from a Greek root which means 'to mark with a cross'. A cross usually consists of one line placed 'across' another, but it might also be perceived as two right-angles – each the reflection of its inverse other, and only barely touching each other. Appropriately, then, the same Greek root has also given us *chiasmus* – the rhetorical term for the trope of 'mirroring'.) The emphasis upon the alienation of subject and object, so often found in readings of Lacan's paper of 1936 on the mirror-stage,[29] is absent from this essay by a man whose work so impressed Lacan (an essay in which we rediscover the 'chiasm' in *chiasmus*). Merleau-Ponty writes:

> since the seer is caught up in what he sees, it is still himself he sees: there is a fundamental narcissism of all vision. And thus, for the same reason, the vision he exercises, he also undergoes from the things, such that, as many painters have said, I feel myself looked at by the things, my activity is equally passivity – which is the second and more profound sense of the narcissism: not to see in the outside, as the others see it, the contour of a body one inhabits, but especially to be seen by the outside, to exist within it, to emigrate into it, to be seduced, captivated, alienated by the phantom, so that the seer and the visible reciprocate one another and we no longer know which sees and which is seen.[30]

Fenichel begins his paper of 1935, 'The Scoptophilic Instinct and Identification', by remarking on the ubiquity of references to the incorporative aspects of looking – for example folk tales in which 'the eye plays a double part. It is not only actively sadistic (the person gazing puts a spell on his victim) but also passively receptive (the person who looks is fascinated by that which he sees)'.[31] He adds to this observation a reference to a book by G. Roheim on 'looking-glass magic'; the mirror, Fenichel observes, by confronting the subject with its own ego in external bodily form, obliterates 'the dividing-line between ego and non-ego'. We should remember that Lacan's paper on the mirror-stage concerns a *dialectic* between alienation and identification, an identification not only with the self, but also, by extension, with other beings of whom the reflected image is a simulacrum – as in the early phenomenon of transitivism. Fenichel writes: 'one looks at an object in order to *share in* its experience ... Anyone who desires to witness the sexual activities of a man and woman really always desires to share their experience by a process of empathy, generally in a homosexual sense, i.e. *by empathy in the experience of the partner of the opposite sex*[32] (my emphasis).

As I have remarked, as far as is known, it never occurred to Euclid to intersect his cone of vision with a plane surface. This idea, which gave birth to perspective, is attributed to Brunelleschi, who gave a famous practical demonstration of his invention. Using his perspective system, Brunelleschi painted a picture of a church upon a panel. In order that the viewer see the image from the correct position – the true apex of the cone of vision – Brunelleschi made a small hole in the panel. The viewer, from a position behind the panel, looked through the hole into a mirror. What the viewer then saw was not him or herself, nor the reversed image of the screen behind which he or she was concealed. What they saw was the church of Santo Giovanni de Firenze, and the Piazza del Duomo.[33] In the description of a contemporary:

> he had made a hole in the panel on which there was this painting . . . which hole was as small as a lentil on the side of the painting, and on the back it opened out pyramidally, like a woman's straw hat, to the size of a ducat or a little more. And he wished the eye to be placed at the back, where it was large, by whoever had it to see . . . it seemed as if the real thing was seen: and I have had it in my hand, and I can give testimony.[34]

To my knowledge, and surprise, Lacan never spoke of Brunelleschi's experiment. But this hole in the panel, 'like a woman's straw hat', is the same hole through which Norman Bates peers in Hitchcock's *Psycho*. Had we been able, there and then, to arrest this eye in the name of a moral certainty, we might have saved Janet Leigh. In reality there would have been no choice. We should not, however, confuse policework with psychoanalysis, or with art criticism, or with art. It is a mistake to believe that the truth of psychological states may be derived from observable behaviour. The cone of vision model, however, encourages precisely such misrecognitions. As Sarah Kofman writes in her book on the model of the camera obscura, 'All these specular metaphors imply the same postulate: the existence of an originary sense . . . the "real" and the "true" pre-exist our knowledge of them.'[35]

The model of the cone of vision in 1970s theory, has both a positive and a negative aspect. On the positive side, it reinstates the subject in the space of representation; on the negative side, it maintains a subject–object dichotomy as a relation of inside/outside, underwriting that familiar confusion in which the psychical becomes a mere annexe to the space of the social. Thanks to such positivism, certain critics pay lip service to psycho-analytic theory while speaking of scopophilia as if there were nothing more to say about it than that it is a morally reprehensible form of behaviour of men.

Catherine Clément has described Lacan's 'era of models' as falling into two distinct periods. The first was a time of points, lines, arrows and symbols – two-dimensional representations. The second 'began when he realised that two dimensions were not enough to make his audience understand the theory of the unconscious as he conceived of it: specifically, he wanted to show that the unconscious is a structure with neither an outside nor an inside'.[36] To this second period belong the topological models – the torus, the Möbius strip, the Klein bottle – which 'gave him the means to represent forms without insides or outsides, forms without boundaries or simple separations, forms of which a hole is a constitutive part'.[37] Clément concludes that such geometrical models 'merely complicated the exposition of his ideas'. However, in the special case of the application of psychoanalytic theory to 'visual' art, I believe this metamorphosis of models provides a necessary corrective to a too-easy confluence of psychoanalytic concepts with some familiar prejudices of positivist-intuitionist art theory and criticism – a discourse too ready to collapse sexuality into gender, psychology into sociology, and too ready to take for granted precisely that sexual *difference* which psychoanalysis puts into question.

III

No space of representation without a subject, and no subject without a space it is not. No subject, therefore, without a boundary. This, of course, is precisely the import of the mirror stage: the founding *Gestalt*, the matrix within which the ego will take place. For Kristeva, however, there is a necessary gesture anterior to this first formation of an uncertain frontier in the mirror stage, a prior demarcation of space. In so far as geometry is a science of boundaries, and in a certain interpretation of Kristeva, we might say that the origin of geometry is in *abjection*.[38]

As a concept, the 'abject' might fall into the gap between 'subject' and 'object'. The abject, however, is in the history of the subject, prior to this dichotomy; it is the means by which the subject is first impelled towards the possibility of constituting itself as such – in an act of revulsion, of expulsion of that which can no longer be contained. Significantly, the first object of abjection is the pre-Oedipal mother – prefiguring that positioning of the woman in society which Kristeva locates, in the patriarchal scheme, as perpetually at the boundary, the borderline, the edge, the 'outer limit' – the place where order shades into chaos, light into darkness. This peripheral and ambivalent position allocated to woman, says Kristeva, has led to that familiar division of the field of representations in which women are viewed as either saintly or demonic – according to whether they are seen as bringing the darkness, or as keeping it out. Certainly, in Kristeva's

work the 'feminine' – in the wider sense she has given this term – is seen as
marginalised by the symbolic, patriarchal, order; but it is biological woman
– the procreative body – that this order abjects. In *The Revolution of
Poetic Language*, Kristeva writes: 'It is not the "woman" in general who is
refused all symbolic activity and all social representativity . . . That which is
. . . under the sign of interdiction is the reproductive woman, through
whom the species does not stop at the "imaginative producer" and his
mother, but continues beyond, according to a natural and social law.'[39]
The woman's body, that is to say, reminds men of their own mortality.
When Narcissus looks into this abjected pool, of milk and blood, he sees
the pale form at the feet of Holbein's ambassadors. Thus in *Powers of
Horror* Kristeva reiterates: 'Fear of the archaic mother proves essentially
to be a fear of her generative power. It is this power, dreaded, that
patrilineal filiation is charged with subduing.'[40] Thus, in the rites with
which certain tribal peoples surround menstruation, Kristeva identifies a
fear of what she calls the 'power of pollution'.[41]

There is an extraordinary passage in Plotinus[42] in which this particular
apparition of the abject is allowed to reveal itself in a discourse created
precisely to conceal it. Plotinus has been speaking of beauty; he continues:

> But let us leave the arts and consider those works produced by Nature
> and admitted to be naturally beautiful which the creations of art are
> charged with imitating, all reasoning life and unreasoning things alike,
> but especially the consummate among them, where the moulder and
> maker has subdued the material and given the form he desired. Now
> what is the beauty here? *It has nothing to do with the blood or the
> menstrual process*: either there is also a colour and form apart from all
> this or there is nothing unless sheer ugliness or (at best) a bare recipient,
> as it were the mere matter of beauty . . . Whence shone forth the beauty
> of Helen, battle-sought; or of all those women like in loveliness to
> Aphrodite; or of Aphrodite herself; or of any human being that has been
> perfect in beauty; or of any of these gods manifest to sight, or unseen but
> carrying what would be beauty if we saw?[43] (my emphasis)

Plotinus' Platonic answer to his own question is, of course, the 'Idea'.
What is abjected here – distanced by that trope of *accumulation*, that wave
of perfect beings which carries the speaker away – is the body itself, as the
mere 'matter' of beauty. The abjected matter of which Kristeva speaks,
from fingernail clippings to faeces – all that which we must shed, and from
which we must distance ourselves, in order to be (in order, as we say, to
'clear a space for ourselves'). 'It has nothing to do with. . .', writes Plotinus,
using a device similar to that which classical rhetoric named 'preterition',
but which must wait another fifteen hundred years for Freud to conceptual-
ise as 'negation' – for, of course, it has everything to do with Plotinus'

desire. We have only to view the abject from a certain angle to see a category which might have been known to Plotinus, from a text by Longinus – the 'sublime'. Thus, in its eighteenth-century incarnation, at the edge of Romanticism, in Shaftesbury: 'the rude rocks, the mossy caverns, the irregular unwrought grottos and broken falls of waters, with all the horrid graces of the wilderness itself ... these solitary places ... beauties which strike a sort of melancholy'.[44] For all the discussions recently devoted to the sublime, I still see in it a simple displacement, a banal metaphorical transference of affect from the woman's body to these caverns and chasms, falls and oceans, which inspire such fervent ambivalence, such a swooning of identity, in these Romantic men.

'Beauties which strike a sort of melancholy' – in *Soleil Noir*, Julia Kristeva shows me the path which leads from beauty to an object I have lost, or which has abandoned me;[45] I also know that depression may be the mask which anger wears – the concept of the sublime may be the sublimation of a more violent fear. Adopting the voice of the fascism he describes, here is Klaus Theweleit in, *Male Fantasies*:

> If that stream reaches me, touches me, spills over me, then I will dissolve, sink, explode with nausea, disintegrate in fear, turn horrified into slime that will suffocate me, a pulp that will swallow me like quicksand. *I'll be in a state where everything is the same, inextricably mixed together.*[46] (my emphasis)

It proves, finally, to be not woman *as such* who is abjected, but rather woman as privileged signifier of that which man both fears and desires: the extinction of identity itself. In the terms of the thermodynamic model which informs Freud's concept of the death-drive, what is feared is the 'entropy' at work at the heart of all organisation, all differentiation. In religious terms, it is the indifferent 'dust' to which we must all return. The transient matter of the woman's body, however, is doubly abjected, in that it is chronically organised to remind us of our common condition as brief events in the life of the species. By this same token, however, the woman also signifies precisely that desired 'state where everything is the same': the pre-Oedipal bliss of the fusion of bodies in which infant and mother are, 'inextricably mixed'; that absence of the pain of differing, condition of identity and meaning, whose extinction is deferred until death.

IV

Apropos of looking, Sartre writes: 'it appears that the world has a sort of drain hole in the middle of its being and that it is perpetually flowing off through this hole'.[47] It is perhaps this same intimation of loss in the register of the visual which the *quattrocento* defended itself against by fetishistically turning the intuition into a system: 'perspective' – built not only upon a founding subject, the 'point of view', but also upon the disappearance of all things in the 'vanishing point'. Previously, there was no *sign* of absence – the *horror vacui* was central to Aristotelianism. In classical cosmologies, space was a plenum. Similarly, in the medieval world, God's creation was a fullness without gap. In *quattrocento* perspective the subject first confronts an absence in the field of vision, but an absence disavowed: the vanishing-point is not an integral part of the space of representation; situated on the horizon, it is perpetually pushed ahead as the subject expands its own boundary. The void remains abjected. In later, non-Euclidean, geometry we find the spherical plenum of classical cosmologies collapsed upon itself to enfold a central void. For Lacan, this figure, the 'torus', can represent a psychical space in which the subject repetitively comes into being, in a procession which circumscribes a central void – locus of the lost object, and of the subject's death.

Much has been made of the insecurity of the 'postmodern condition', and of its attendant 'crisis of representation'. There is nothing new in insecurity; it is the very condition of subjectivity, just as it is the condition of representation to be in crisis. This is not to say, however, that nothing changes. I have argued that our space has changed, and that our optical models for negotiating it are now out of their time. In 'Women's Time' Kristeva describes a mutation of space, a new 'generation' of 'corporeal and desiring mental space', in which 'the very dichotomy man/woman as an opposition between two rival entities may be understood as belonging to metaphysics'. She asks, 'What can "identity", even "sexual identity", mean in a new theoretical and scientific space where the very notion of identity is challenged?'[48]

In this changed space, this new geometry, the abject can no longer be banished beyond some charmed, perfectly Euclidean, circle. The postmodern space of our 'changing places' can now barely accommodate the old ghettos, which are going the way of the walled city-state. Perhaps we are again at a moment in history when we need to define the changing geometries of our changing places. I do not believe that it is a time when an art/theory which thinks of itself as 'political' should admonish, or exhort, or proffer 'solutions'. I believe it is a time when it should simply describe. Perhaps it is again, in this time of post-industrial revolution, the moment for a realist project. It cannot, of course, be what it was at the time of Courbet, or even of Brecht. Attention to psychical reality calls for a *psychical realism* – impossible, but nevertheless. . .

Notes

1. Louis Althusser, 'Ideology and Ideological State Apparatuses (Notes Towards an Investigation)', in *Lenin and Philosophy and Other Essays* (New Left Books, London, 1971).
2. Roland Barthes, 'Diderot, Brecht, Eisenstein', in *Image-Music-Text* (Hill & Wang, New York, 1977), p. 69.

3.   Laura Mulvey, 'Visual Pleasure and Narrative Cinema', *Screen*, vol. 16, no. 3, Autumn, 1975.
4.   Michel Foucault, *Discipline and Punish* (Penguin, Harmondsworth, 1977).
5.   F. M. Cornford, *Plato's Cosmology* (Harcourt Brace, New York, 1937).
6.   M. Foucault, 'Of Other Spaces', *Diacritics*, vol. 16, no. 1 (Spring, 1986), pp. 22–27.
7.   This remark is prompted by Panofsky's essay, 'Die Perspektive als "symbolische Form"' – today an unpopular article. For a summary of the debates, see, Samuel Y. Edgerton, Jr., *The Renaissance Rediscovery of Linear Perspective* (Harper & Row, New York, 1976), pp. 153ff.
8.   Augustine, *De Ordine*, ch. 15, 42; in, A. Hofstadter and R. Kuhns, *Philosophies of Art and Beauty* (University of Chicago Press, Chicago, 1976), p. 180.
9.   'Absolute space in its own nature, without relation to anything external, remains always similar and immovable. Relative space is some movable dimension or measure of the absolute spaces; which our senses determine by its position to bodies; and which is commonly taken for immovable space' – Isaac Newton, *Mathematical Principles of Natural Philosophy*, quoted in F. Durham and R. Purrington, *Frame of the Universe* (Columbia University Press, New York, 1983), p. 156.
10.   H. Minkowski, 'Space and Time', in, A. Sommerfeld (ed.), *The Principle of Relativity* (Dodd, Mead & Co., New York, 1923).
11.   'For example, at extremely short distances, on the order of 10^{-33}.cm, the geometry of space is subject to *quantum fluctuations*, and even the concepts of space and space-time have only approximate validity' – Durham and Purrington, *Frame of the Universe*, p. 191 (see note 9).
12.   El Lissitsky, 'K. und Pangeometrie', quoted in P. Descargues, *Perspective: History, Evolution, Techniques* (Van Nostrand Reinhold, New York, 1982), p. 9. It is necessary to distinguish between 'Non-Euclidean geometry' (or *metageometry*), and 'n-dimensional geometry' (or *hypergeometry*). The former, initiated in the nineteenth century by Gauss and Lobachevsky, and developed by Riemann, is a geometry of curved surfaces – spaces which are boundless and yet finite; the latter, also developed in the nineteenth century, is the geometry of 'hyperspace' – a hypothetical space of more than three dimensions. The idea of a fourth dimension as a *literal* fact gained much popularity from the close of the nineteenth century and into the 1930s, and exerted some considerable influence on the early modern movement in painting, not least in its more mystical formulations (the fourth dimension as 'higher reality' – for example, in the Theosophism of Kandinsky and Mondrian). Beyond the 1920s, however, after the popular dissemination of the ideas of Einstein and Minkowski, the idea of a fourth dimension of space largely gave way to the idea of a four-dimensional spatio-temporal continuum – with *time* as the fourth dimension. See, L. D. Henderson, *The Fourth Dimension and Non-Euclidean Geometry in Modern Art* (Princeton University Press, Princeton, 1983).
13.   Dziga Vertov, 'Film Directors, A Revolution', *Lef*, vol. 3, in *Screen Reader 1* (SEFT, London, 1977), p. 286.
14.   At this point, the necessary simplicity of my outline risks an injustice to Vertov. The industrial-materialist emphasis of some Russian Formalism was asserted against the mysticism which had entered early Russian Futurist art, primarily from the philosophy of P. D. Ouspensky. In *Tertium Organum* (1911), Ouspensky identifies the 'fourth dimension' (see note 11) as that of the Kantian 'noumena', and allocates to the artist the function of revealing

that 'higher' world, 'beyond' phenomena. When, in 1913, the Futurist Matyushin translated extracts from Gleizes and Metzinger's *Du Cubism* (1912) for the journal *Union of Youth*, he accompanied them with passages from *Tertium Organum*. In the same year, Mayakovsky published, 'The "New Art" and the "Fourth Dimension"', in which he counters the notion of a higher, non-material, reality with the assertion that the 'fourth dimension' is simply that of *time*: 'There is in every three-dimensional object the possibility of numberless positions in space. But to perceive this series of positions ad infinitum the artist can only conform to the various moments of time (for example, going around an object or setting it in motion)', (quoted in, C. Douglas, *Swans of Other Worlds: Kazimir Malevich and the Origins of Abstraction in Russia* (UMI Research Press, Ann Arbor, 1980, p. 31). Mayakovsky's observations adequately describe the programme of French Cubism (which, in today's terms, we might say 'shatters the object', rather than deconstructs the subject-object dichotomy); further, his observations are in agreement with Eisenstein's subsequent thought: 'the fourth dimension (time added to the three dimensions)' ('The Filmic Fourth Dimension' (1929), in, Jay Leyda (ed.), *Film Form: Essays on Film Theory* (Harcourt Brace, New York, 1949, p. 69). Vertov's 'unmotivated camera mischief' (Eisenstein), on the other hand, often seems to point outside such accommodation of ideas from 'n-dimensional geometry', and towards the 'wraparound' spaces of Non-Euclidean geometry. (Information in this note derived from L. D. Henderson, *The Fourth Dimension and Non-Euclidean Geometry in Modern Art* (Princeton University Press, Princeton, 1983).)

15.   Paul Virilio, *L'Espace Critique* (Christian Bourgeois, Paris, 1984).
16.   P. Virilio, *Speed and Politics*, Semiotext(e), (New York, 1986).
17.   David Bolter, *Turing's Man* (Raleigh, University of North Carolina, 1984), p. 98.
18.   Guy Debord, *Society of the Spectacle* (Black & Red, Detroit, 1983), paragraph 167.
19.   Jacqueline Rose, 'The Imaginary', in *Sexuality in the Field of Vision* (Verso, London, 1986).
20.   Jacques Lacan, *Le Séminaire, livre I: Les écrits techniques de Freud* (Seuil, Paris, 1975), p. 90.
21.   We should also, incidentally, bear in mind that Mulvey herself has continually denounced the widespread attempt to freeze her evolving argument – an argument to be traced through her film-making, as well as through her writing – at that particular, 1975, frame.
22.   Rose, 'The Imaginary', p. 182 (see note 19).
23.   Ibid., p. 171.
24.   J. Lacan, *The Four Fundamental Concepts of Psycho-Analysis* (Hogarth, London, 1977), p. 56.
25.   Since writing this paper, I have come across the following notes by Freud: 'Space may be the projection of the extension of the psychical apparatus. No other derivation is probable. Instead of Kant's *a priori* determinants of our psychical apparatus. Psyche is extended; knows nothing about it.' *SE*, XXIII, p. 300.
26.   S. Freud, '"A Child is Being Beaten": A Contribution to the Study of the Origin of Sexual Perversions', *SE*, XVII, pp. 175–204.
27.   Rose, 'The Imaginary', p. 210 (see note 19).
28.   Jean-Paul Sartre, *Being and Nothingness* (Washington Square Press, New York, 1966), pp. 369–70.
29.   Laura Mulvey's article is clear in its insistence on the narcissistic, identificatory,

aspect of looking (see section II.B). However, in this article, identification is seen uniquely as, 'that of the spectator fascinated with the image of his like . . ., and through him gaining control and possession of the woman within the diegesis' (p. 13).

30.   Maurice Merleau-Ponty, *The Visible and the Invisible* (Northwestern University Press, Evanston, Ill., 1968), p. 139.

31.   Otto Fenichel, 'The Scoptophilic Instinct and Identification', in H. Fenichel and D. Rapaport (eds), *The Collected Papers of Otto Fenichel*, First Series (Norton, New York, 1953), p. 375.

32.   Ibid., p. 377.

33.   It has been proposed that the purpose of this experiment was to demonstrate that the vanishing point is equal in distance 'behind' the picture-plane to the distance of the point-of-view in front of it. A little 'reflection' will reveal that the viewer of Brunelleschi's panel was, in effect, positioned 'looking back at herself' from the 'other' building at which she was looking.

34.   A. Manetti, *Vita di Filippo di Ser Brunellesco*, Elana Tosca (ed.) (Roma, 1927), pp. 11 ff.; quoted in, John White, *The Birth and Rebirth of Pictorial Space* (Faber, London, 1971), p. 116.

35.   Sarah Kofman, *Camera Obscura de l'Idéologie* (Galilée, Paris, 1973).

36.   Catherine Clément, *The Lives and Legends of Jacques Lacan* (Columbia University Press, New York, 1973), p. 160.

37.   Ibid., p. 161.

38.   In a response to this paper (at a conference at the University of Warwick, May, 1987) Julia Kristeva said she would 'more cautiously' prefer the word 'precondition', rather than 'origin' here; she referred to abjection as the 'degree zero of spatialisation', adding, 'abjection is to geometry what intonation is to speech'.

39.   Julia Kristeva, *La révolution du langage poétique* (Seuil, Paris, 1974), p. 453.

40.   J. Kristeva, *Pouvoirs de l'horreur* (Seuil, Paris, 1980), p. 92.

41.   Ibid., p. 93.

42.   My thanks to Francette Pacteau for having shown this passage to me.

43.   Plotinus, *Ennead I,* Eighth Tractate, Beauty; quoted in, A. Hofstadter, and R. Kuhns, *Philosophies of Art and Beauty* (University of Chicago Press, Chicago, 1964), p. 152.

44.   Shaftesbury, 'The Moralists', Part III, Section II, in Hofstadter and Kuhns, *Philosophies of Art . . .*, pp. 245–46.

45.   J. Kristeva, *Soleil Noir: Dépression et Mélancolie* (Gallimard, Paris, 1987), 107ff.

46.   Klaus Theweleit, *Male Fantasies* (Polity, Cambridge, 1987).

47.   Sartre, *Being and Nothingness*, p. 343.

48.   J. Kristeva, 'Women's Time', in Toril Moi (ed.), *The Kristeva Reader* (Basil Blackwell, Oxford, 1986), p. 209.

3

The Oedipus Myth: Beyond the Riddles of the Sphinx

Laura Mulvey

Riddles of the Sphinx was made in 1976–7. The film used the Sphinx as an emblem through which to hang a question mark over the Oedipus complex, to investigate the extent to which it represents a riddle for women committed to Freudian theory but still determined to think about psychoanalysis radically or with poetic licence. *Riddles of the Sphinx* and *Penthesilea*, my previous film with Peter Wollen, used ancient Greece to invoke a mythic point of origin for Western civilisation, that had been reiterated by high culture throughout our history. Both the history of the Oedipus Complex and the history of antiquity suggest a movement from an earlier 'maternal' stage to a later 'paternal' or 'patriarchal' order. For me, as someone whose interest in psychoanalytic theory was a direct off-shoot of fascination with the origins of women's oppression, this dual temporality was exciting. Perhaps there was an original moment in the chronology of our civilisation that was repeated in the chronology of each individual consciousness. Leaving aside the temptation to make speculative connections and an analogy between the earlier culture of mother goddesses and the pre-Oedipal, the idea of a founding moment of civilisation, repeated in consciousness, suggested that it might be possible to modify or change the terms on which civilisation is founded within the psyche and thus challenge the origins of patriarchal power through psychoanalytic politics and theory.

These Utopian dreams now belong to more than ten years ago. In the meantime, the relation between feminism and psychoanalysis has become infinitely more complex and less instrumental. But some primitive attraction to the fantasy of origins, a Gordian knot that would suddenly unravel, persisted for me. My interest then concentrated on breaking down the binarism of the before/after opposition, by considering the Oedipus story as a passage through time, a journey that could metaphorically open out or stretch the Oedipal trajectory through significant details and through its formal, narrational, properties.

In 1986–87, I returned to the Oedipus story.[1] My intention was to consider the story in the light of different disciplines and from different angles. Whereas in *Riddles of the Sphinx*, our intention had been to shift narrative perspective to the mother in the Oedipal triangle, this time my intention was rather to discover things that the story itself suggested through its mode of telling and then through the theoretical work on narrative that could be brought to bear on its narrative structures; and to consider whether the signifiers of narration were linked to its signified, whether, that is, certain kinds of material demanded certain modes of telling. The first part of the paper (in two sections) is about the core Oedipus story. Then there is a digression about the metaphors of space and time that negotiate shifts between the poetics of psychoanalysis and narrativity. The final part (also in two sections) stretches out the core of the Oedipus story to the moment of his death and the pre-history before his birth.

OEDIPUS: THE CORE STORY

Freud re-tells the Oedipus myth in the following manner:

> Oedipus, son of Laius, king of Thebes, and of Jocasta, was exposed as an infant because an oracle had warned Laius that the still unborn infant would be his father's murderer. The child was rescued and grew up as a prince in an alien court, until, in doubt as to his origin, he too questioned the oracle and was warned to avoid his home since he was destined to murder his father and take his mother in marriage. On the road leading away from what he believed to be his home, he met King Laius and slew him in a sudden quarrel. He came next to Thebes and solved the riddle set him by the Sphinx who barred his way. Out of gratitude the Thebans made him their king and gave him Jocasta's hand in marriage. He reigned long in peace and honour and she, who unknown to him, was his mother, bore him two sons and two daughters. Then, at last a plague broke out and the Thebans made inquiry once more of the oracle. It is at this point that the Sophocles tragedy opens. The messenger brings back the reply that the plague will cease when the murderer of Laius has been driven from the land.
>
> 　　　　　But he, where is he? Where shall now be read
> 　　　　　The fading record of this ancient guilt?

The action of this play consists of nothing other than the process of revealing, with cunning delays and ever mounting excitement – a process that can be likened to the work of psychoanalysis – that Oedipus himself is the murderer of Laius, but further that he is the son of the murdered man and of Jocasta. Appalled by the abomination which he himself has unwittingly perpetrated, Oedipus blinds himself and forsakes his home. The oracle has been fulfilled.[2]

From a structural point of view, the story, as it is told above, is separated into two parts according to two codes of narration. This formal division implies that the story is a hybrid; or rather, its hybrid form indicates that it has come into being across transitional material that cannot be contained within a unified narrational system. It functions as a pivot. Roland Barthes, in *S/Z*, analyses the codes of narrative and distinguishes two as irreversible in time, propelling the story forward point by point, from its beginning to its end. The proairetic is the code of action. It governs events in sequence, on a cause and effect basis. It is, in Barthes's words, the voice of empirics. The hermeneutic is the code of enquiry. It sets up an enigma, formulates the questions that ensue and holds an answer in suspense until the moment of its solution. It is, again, in Barthes's words, the voice of truth. Whereas the proairetic code functions on a single, linear temporal level, the hermeneutic folds back on the past and contains two levels of temporality. Although the two codes are very commonly interwoven, the chronological split in the Oedipus story according to these two codes is striking.

1 The Proairetic Code

The structure of the first part of the story conforms in broad outline to Vladimir Propp's analysis of a type of folk narrative in *The Morphology of the Folktale*. The dramatis personae perform a series of fixed and given actions as the hero travels along the course of a journey from home, arriving unknown at a new and future home where he performs a difficult task (for instance, he rescues the people or the princess from a monster or a dragon). He is then rewarded with the kingdom and the hand of the princess in marriage. His actions, and those of the helpers or enemies that he meets on the way, take the story forward within a chronologically linear time. The linearity of the narrative is reflected in the linearity of the journey as it moves through time and space; the journey space of the road the hero takes also represents a passage through time, from departure to arrival. Thus the formal aspect of the story is materialised in its serial events and its imagery or *mise-en-scène*. The journey also represents a social space. The hero is transformed from one status to another, as though the story reflected, in narrative form, a rite of passage. The hero, Oedipus, leaves the security of his home in Corinth as an exceptional but untried young man, to encounter hurdles and cross boundaries as an adventurer in a liminal space and without recognised name or identity. His journey takes him out of youth into maturity, out of anonymity into recognition, from unmarried to married status, from lone individual in doubt as to his name and parentage into the possession of property and power. The spatial metaphor of the journey as transition is joined by the spatial metaphor of the social pyramid: the hero ascends the apex and becomes king.

Freud recounts a similar series of events in his essay 'On Creative Writing and Day-dreaming', in which he condenses the 'erotic and ambitious' aspirations of the ego (as hero of the psyche) with the presence of the invulnerable hero of popular fiction. The day-dream also tells of a transition in space and time and social status, but in Freud's example the hero's upward mobility takes place in an urban, bourgeois milieu.

> He is given a job, finds favour with his new employer, makes himself indispensable in the business, is taken into the employer's family, marries the charming young daughter of the house, and then becomes a director of the business, first as his employer's partner and then as his successor.

In this fantasy, the dreamer has regained what he possessed in his happy childhood, the protecting house, the loving parents, the first objects of his affectionate feelings. 'It seems to me, that through this revealing character-istic of invulnerability, we can immediately recognise His Majesty the Ego, the hero alike of every day-dream and every story.'[3] (Perhaps Dick Whittington mediates between the peasant hero of the Proppian folk-tale and Freud's bourgeois scenario.)

However, the Oedipus story has a different twist. Oedipus arrives at Thebes only apparently as an unknown outsider. With a deeper symmetry, he has arrived at his own true home, and, instead of inheriting through marriage and from his father-in-law, he inherits the kingdom to which he is patrilinearly entitled. At the simplest level, the folk tale pattern celebrates a transition to maturity similar to that of a rite of passage; on another level it reflects day-dreams of social aspiration in a society in which wide separations of wealth and power divide the propertied from the dispossessed. Both levels together condense family relations and property relations, as though the word 'possession' were a key that could turn either way between the psychoanalytic and the social.

Concentrating on the 'ambitious and erotic' aspects of the day-dreaming ego's consciousness, Freud overlooks the Oedipal, unconscious aspects of his paradigm day-dream. The hero recognises by leaving home that to 'become the father' he must avoid his own Oedipal set-up, which invites rivalry and desire, but particularly rivalry with the father. If the journey then represents escape into exogamous kinship relations, *kingship* and possession bring back a memory of Oedipal rivalry. With its Oedipal twist, the repressed returns. The day-dreaming ego's consciousness is faced with the ultimate horror, and hope beyond expression, that the poor parents you leave will return in the form of the king or king substitute and his daughter who are waiting for you to rescue them at the end of your journey. There are also echoes here of the social complexity of family romance. In a footnote about his own Revolutionary Dream[4] Freud notes: 'A prince is known as the father of his country; the father is the oldest, first, and for children the only authority. And, indeed, the whole rebellious content of the dream, with its *lèse-majesté* and its derision of higher authorities went back to rebellion against my father.' This quotation carries the question of property and social status, the desire to *become* the father by avoiding conflict with him, to possibly radical undertones to Oedipal rivalry. The son is the dispossessed and thus liable to identify with rebellion against the possessing powers that be,[5] an aspect, perhaps, of the short term radicalism of youth.

For Propp, the Oedipus story is a symptom of a social and historical transition that determines the transitional or hybrid content of the narrative material itself. The early folk-tale structure is a reflection of an ancient marriage pattern.

> The usual order of events in the fairy tale reflects matrilocal marriage, the entry of the bridegroom into the bride's family . . . Now let us see what happens to Oedipus. Just like the fairy tale hero, he is sent away from home. But after his upbringing he does not go to the country of his future wife. Rather, unbeknownst to himself, he returns to the home of his father. As a hero of the new patriarchal order he heads for his father's family, the family where he belongs, rather than his wife's family. This shift in Oedipus' destination represents a turning-point in the history of the tale. At this point Oedipus diverges from the fairy tale and forms a new offshoot, a new tale within the framework of the same compositional scheme.[6]

Propp then points out that Oedipus goes through the same three adventures as the fairy tale hero. He kills the old king, he solves the riddle of the Sphinx and rids the city of distress, he receives the hand of the queen.

> According to patriarchal ideas, the heir could not ascend the throne during the life time of the old king . . . Under the matriarchal system, on the contrary, the heir appears as the daughter's husband first, and then the old king is removed, or as the fairy tale has it, shares the kingdom with his son-in-law. Hence in the fairy tale the proclamation comes from the old king himself, while in the Oedipus it comes from the citizens of Thebes who have lost their king.

In Propp's terms, the change of sequence whereby the old king is killed, by his own son, before the difficult task is performed, is one mark of the transitional, historical nature of the Oedipus story. Writing in the Soviet

Union, as a scholar of folk tale and anthropology, Propp was looking for a historical materialist explanation of the Oedipus story. But he, too, comes up with a story of *origins*, the origin of patriarchal inheritance. And it is revealing that he is *only* interested in the part of the story that is under the aegis of the proairetic code.

In Freudian terms, Propp's explanation takes the story inexorably back, in its transitional mode, to father–son rivalry and the incest taboo which lie at the core of the Oedipus complex. The question of property and inheritance is of primary importance to Propp, confirming the story's grounding in the social. But the father's attempt at infanticide has disordered the true line of inheritance, and opened up the way for incest to return by an oblique route, the old folk tale pattern. Heroism and apotheosis through achievements coalesce with blood legitimacy, so that the hero is bound to commit incest in order to reclaim his patrimony in this hybrid or pivotal story. Although Propp's emphasis on the matrilocal is clearly at several moves from Bachofen's *Mutterrecht* or Engels's *Origins of Private Property and the Family*, there is a residual, suggestive link with forms of social organisation in which patriarchy was not supremely in command. The misty, forgotten epochs of time and mythology in which things might have been other for women return as a ghostly presence. Propp's interpretation acknowledges the coming of an era in which the exchange of women as signifier of relations between men takes on a new inflection in relation to property and inheritance. Teresa de Lauretis,[7] in her powerful narrative and topological analysis of the Oedipus story (to which these observations are indebted) emphasises the essential masculinity of its folk-tale structure. The hero spans the space of the story and commands the action (the proairetic code). The feminine principle is static, represented either by the Sphinx or the Princess, Jocasta. She is a resistance, a boundary to be crossed, a space of enclosure. It is clear that the hero represents an active force of masculinity, or perhaps, the *rite de passage* of *mensch* and thus *man* as the universal point of reference under patriarchy, and the subject position is definitely that of the male child. However both the parent functions are *other*, that of the father as much as that of the mother. And in the Oedipus story, it is the father's response to the oracle's prophecy, 'your son shall kill you' that disorders the family structure and generates his son's future trajectory as hero and its tragic consequences. The social-historical problem of inheritance, the narrative structure of myth, and the trajectory of the individual psyche meet at a crossroads.

2   The Hermeneutic Code

At a particular point in his narration of the Oedipus story, Freud says: 'Here Sophocles' tragedy begins'. The aesthetics of Greek drama, its commitment to the unities of time, place and action as well as the constraints of performance, would all influence the placing of the first part of the myth within a containing formal structure. Sophocles folds the horizontal, chronologically linear materialisation of that narrative, realised in the spatial pattern of a journey (also a journey through time and a rite of passage through the social space and time of liminality) within another narrative code, the hermeneutic. However, this is not a simply story-teller's decision, or a purely formal device. The unravelling of the enigma is essential to the Oedipus story in its own right; and the formal narrational pattern that the hermeneutic code generates is a key to the ultimate meaning of the play. Not only does the old mystery of Oedipus's true parentage remain unsolved between the two parts of the story but a murder has been committed and the criminal must be revealed. The play proceeds to follow through a sequence of enigmas, in which the actions of the first part of the story are transformed into clues or bits of evidence out of which the truth will ultimately be disclosed. In this process Oedipus takes on the role of investigator. But it only gradually emerges that he is telling his own story, revealing, as detective hero, the hidden meaning behind his actions as the hero of the folk-tale.

The play opens with a generative enigma that activates all the sub-sequent inquiries. Thebes is inflicted with a plague and Oedipus under-takes to find out why. He is confident of his abilities; he has become king as a result of his intelligence, his riddle-solving powers. This fact, too, pre-figured his future and separates him from heroes who depend on physical strength to conquer a monster.

> But I came by. Oedipus the ignorant, I stopped the Sphinx!
> with no help from the birds, the flight of my own intelligence
> hit the mark.[8]

The oracle offers a clue to the mystery and sets up another. The murderer of Laius must be found.

> 'No! I'll start again – I'll bring it all to light myself!'[9]

At the beginning of the play Teiresias, the seer gives the true answer to the murder mystery. Oedipus responds bitterly, in an excess of anger that speaks simultaneously of the necessity for delay within the hermeneutic code, the processes of resistance and negation in psychoanalysis, and the quick temper Oedipus inherited from his father. In order to reassure him, Jocasta recounts the old prophecy, that Laius would be killed by his son, and describes the circumstances of his death 'where the three roads meet'. Oedipus recognises the description, and knows he is himself the murderer. From that moment on, he is not so much a regal, or legal, investigator as a man desperately seeking the truth of his own family origins and the meaning of his actions. But as the evidence accumulates inexorably, Oedipus still resists, bearing out Teiresias's warning.

> You with your precious eyes
> you're blind to the corruption of your life,
> to the house you live in, those who love with –
> who *are* your parents? Do you know? All unknowing
> you are the scourge of your own flesh and blood....[10]

After Jocasta's suicide he sees the meaning of his life for the first time, in all its unwitting horror and perversity. He blinds himself and leaves the city. The second part of the story thus strips away the folk-tale's happy ending; the hero's material apotheosis, marriage, power and property are revealed to be worthless illusions.

The second part of the story is thus necessarily posited on the code of mystery and investigation. The *locus classicus* of the hermeneutic code, the detective story, only developed formally as a genre comparatively recently. Oedipus, ahead of the genre, acts as a detective faced with a murder to solve, and the hybrid, two-part story acquires another formal duality, that of time.

According to Tzvetan Todorov, the detective story, and particularly its 'whodunit' mode, is always based on a double time structure. There are two stories to be told. The first precedes the opening of the narrative and is the story of the crime. This story is gradually unfolded in the course of the second which is the story of the investigation. The first story cannot be completed until the identity of the criminal is revealed by the process of detection. As Michel Butor, cited both by Todorov and by Peter Wollen, has his detective story writer say in *Passing Time*: 'The narrative superimposes two temporal levels: the days of investigation that begin with the crime, the days of drama that lead up to it.' The two levels of time entail a metaphysical shift from action to thought that is foreshadowed, in Oedipus's case, by the nature of his encounter with the riddling Sphinx, a monster, but one that can only be defeated by intelligence. The power of the hero's actions in the proairetically dominated folk-tale pattern is replaced by the power of law. The struggle between hero and monster is replaced by a struggle between a criminal and the law's representative. The heroic adventure is replaced by the inexorable process of justice. The rite of passage is replaced by the theme of morality. And whereas the folk-tale type story is about the acquisition of power and property the second part of the story is about the acquisition of self-knowledge. The popular, oral, folk-tale tradition, with its emphasis on function (in Propp's terms) gives way to a literary genre that depends on the decipherment of clues and suspense for its mode of narration. Todorov describes the work done by narrational codes within detective fiction. Thus, he says, story A tells what really happened and story B tells how the narrator, and so the reader, gets to know about it. He invokes the distinction made by Russian formalist critics between story (fable) and plot (subject): 'In the story there is no inversion of time, actions follow their natural order; in the plot the author can present results before their causes, the end before the beginning.'[11]

The plot consists of the orchestrated accumulation of evidence, of clues that have to be found and interpreted, remnants and traces of past action. Memory and the testimony of witnesses must play a crucial part in this process. In *Oedipus Rex*, Oedipus is shown to be a determined investigator, armed at first with the righteousness and the responsibilities of kingship. Later, as a desperate man in a position of power, he investigates with anger and cruelty, especially when his witnesses are poor and defenceless, like the shepherd who rescued him in his infancy. Class position plays ironically with our foreknowledge of Oedipus's own ultimate fate. But it is still the process of his investigation and his knowledge that control narrative development. The act of narration is inseparable from the detective form itself, and the writer, the ultimate literary narrator, controls the reader's knowledge or suspense through the process of the hero's investigation and discovery. It is here that the Oedipus story, once again, both works within a given narrative code and represents a twist, a deviation from a particular compositional scheme (Propp's term). In this case, the detective is himself the criminal. Propp argues that the shift in the chronology of functions in the Oedipus story transforms the tale into a transitional model within the folk-tale and the proairetic code; *Oedipus Rex* takes the detective genre into wider questions of the unconscious. What is at stake on this level of narration is not just the ability of an exceptional man to interpret clues and evidence, but the ability of man to understand the truth of his own history. As Freud says, the play unfolds 'like the process of psychoanalysis itself'. The relationship between the Oedipus myth and psychoanalysis, therefore, lies in its narrative methodology and the metaphysical implications of its narrative form, in addition to the overt content of the story (rivalry with the father and desire for the mother) that first attracted Freud's attention.

I have emphasised the popular, detective structure of the narrative pattern in *Oedipus Rex* rather than its place as literary tragedy to highlight the importance of clues, riddles and enigmas that link Oedipus figuratively with the clues, riddles and enigmas of the unconscious that psychoanalysis deciphers. Teiresias is also a seer, who deciphers riddles, and is linked as a hybrid, a hermaphrodite, with the Sphinx. Oedipus conquers the Sphinx in the final moments of his heroic story; she 'returns' in the shape of Teiresias at the opening of *Oedipus Rex*. Teiresias 'returns' in the image of the blind Oedipus 'seeing' the truth as he exiles himself from the city he won by his victory over the Sphinx. The folk-tale hero's journey is resolved in the material world with material success; the detective undertakes an investigation in pursuit of knowledge in the name of the Law; the hero of *Oedipus*

Rex finds himself thrown into an inferno of self-discovery through which he will understand his origins, his fate and, ultimately, have the possibility of redemption. The hero's trumphant apotheosis, achieved with the answer 'man', turns sour and the detective's search for a criminal inaugurates a metaphysical journey. The literal space of the road has been replaced by an abstract journey into the self. The horizontal continuum of the proairetic-ally based plot has changed direction into the self which then must precipitate an excavation into the past. The axis of exploration shifts between space and time. But time attracts figures of space: of the layering of history, on top, as it were, of the spatial layers of geological time.

BELOW THE SURFACE: TIME AND SPACE

Freud described the unconscious in terms of topology, using spatial figures and images to evoke the relation between a surface consciousness and the stuff of repression, hidden from consciousness, that could only be investigated or excavated obliquely. Signs and symptoms bear witness to the continuous presence of psychopathology, and to the working of the unconscious in the present tense, as a living monument to the past, the traumatic experiences of childhood. Things that are concealed from surface consciousness have roots in the past. It is perhaps at least of poetic interest that Freud's world, the second half of the nineteenth century, saw the growth of two cultural phenomena that both bear a relation to these two levels and to the structure of the Oedipus myth as we inherit it. These two phenomena are the development of archaeology and the development of the detective story as a popular literary genre. *The Moonstone* by Wilkie Collins, generally considered to be the first example of the detective genre, was published in 1868. During the 1860s Schliemann excavated Troy. (Freud was born in 1856.) Both the detective story and archaeology dig into lost or concealed worlds; in one case it is the mystery of an urban underworld that is revealed, in the other it is the lost cities of antiquity that are brought to light. The two tropes condense in the contemporary connotations of the Oedipus story and also suggest figures for the topology of the unconscious, a concealed layer in the psyche, and the process of investigation, psychoanalysis, which interprets them.

In his reminiscence of Freud, the Wolf Man says:

> Once we happened to speak of Conan Doyle and his creation Sherlock Holmes. I had thought Freud would have no use for this type of light reading matter and was surprised to find that he had read this author attentively. The fact that circumstantial evidence is useful in psycho-analysis when reconstructing a childhood history may explain Freud's interest in this type of literature.[12]

It is tempting to see the detective story as the myth or legend of the newly constituted industrial cities that had grown up *outside* order. The nether world of the city, seething with bars, prostitutes and criminals, also the uncontrollable presence of the working class, could provide a mythic terrain for scenarios of adventure and constitute a modern space of liminality similar to the no man's land through which the heroes of antiquity travelled. But whereas the ancient or the folk-tale heroes embarked on a linear journey outside the city space, the journey of the urban detective is a descent into a hidden world of what is repressed by bourgeois morality and respectability to decode and decipher signs and restore order through the process of reason. This sense of spatial *mise-en-scène* is familiar, too, in the Hollywood movie genre *film noir*, and suggests a link between such a descent into a nether world and the hero's rite of passage that condenses the liminal space of adventure and the abstract journey of self discovery:

> What [*film noir* screen-plays] share in adaptation to the screen is the tendency to organise the unfolding of an enigma as a single character's initiation into an alien world; they present a process of psychological upheaval that is manifest in verbal, behavioural, and physiological signs as well as in certain optical/perceptual changes projected onto the environment. It is the *process* of change, the transition, which constitutes the ground of film-noir narrative. Whether or not the 'first story' is suppressed in favour of a narrating investigator there is a consistent stress on internal transformation – in all its ramifications – incited through participation in a criminal milieu, on the slippage of personal identity and its reassumption in an unintegrated form.[13]

Rites of passage, celebrated in narrative, find an appropriate diegesis, a contemporary scenario for self-discovery and transition. The Oedipus story brings together the two narrative forms to transform achievement through action into self-discovery. This evolution takes the Oedipus model out of a primary emphasis on its immediate content, patricide and incest, and raises formal questions about the way that the signifier of narration affects a story's signified. These images and processes of popular mythology relate, by analogy, to psychoanalysis. The topological space of the city, its dark, after-hours underworld, echoes Freud's topology of the psyche. The journey and its narration parallel the process by which unconscious material is transformed.

The Oedipus story emanated from Mycenae, a civilisation that could barely be discerned beyond the lost years of the Dark Ages (as those centuries would still have seemed to Freud's generation). In its apotheosis as *Oedipus Rex*, the myth became part of the literary legacy of classical, historical Greece, suspended between the timelessness of great literature and remoteness in a historical period that is taken to be the origins of

Western civilisation. Freud is well known to have been fascinated to the point of obsession with the remnants of ancient civilisations. He collected antiquities and his visits to Rome and Athens were crucial experiences in his life. Again, the Wolf-Man tells us:

> In the weeks before the end of my analysis, we often spoke of the danger of the patient's feeling too close a tie to the therapist ... In this connection, Freud was of the opinion that at the end of a treatment, a gift from the patient could contribute, as a symbolic act, to lessening his feeling of gratitude and consequent dependence on the physician. So we agreed that I would give Freud something as a remembrance. As I knew his love for archaeology, the gift I chose for him was a female Egyptian figure, with a mitre-shaped head-dress. Freud placed it on his desk. Twenty years later, looking through a magazine, I saw a picture of Freud at his desk. 'My' Egyptian immediately struck my eye, the figure which for me symbolised my analysis with Freud, who himself called me 'a piece of psychoanalysis'. [14]

Freud used the image provided by the burial of the ancient world as a metaphor for the topology of the unconscious and Pompeii, buried so suddenly by a volcanic eruption, provided him with a particularly vivid example. Analysing Jensen's story *Gradiva*, he was fascinated by the author's use of Pompeii to evoke both the repression and the preservation of childhood desire, its mis-recognition and ultimate excavation. In his notes on his analysis of the Rat Man he says:

> I then made some short observations on the psychological differences between the conscious and the unconscious, and the fact that what was conscious was subject to the process of wearing away, while what was unconscious was relatively unchanging. I illustrated my remarks by pointing at the antiquities standing about in my room. They were, in fact, only objects found in a tomb and their burial had been their preservation. The destruction of Pompeii was only beginning now that it had been dug up. [15]

The detective story is a narrative that carries the hero into another space, a nether world. Exploration of this space depends on a re-telling of events, the investigation of an immediate past that lies within the experience of the characters involved in the drama. This, as argued above, is also the narrative pattern of *Oedipus Rex*. Archaeology depends on the preservation of actual objects in time, and the fossilisation of these objects in a medium that preserves their reality intact. In semiological terms, its signs are indexical. They come to the surface as a challenge to the erosion of time and provide a point of contact with, and traces of, a remote and almost lost epoch. Detection, too, makes use of indexical signs in the traces and clues which have to be interpreted and read to make sense. This leads, once again, to the psychoanalytic process. Lacan takes the analogy with archaeology and its indexical traces one step further:

[The unconscious] is the censored chapter. But the truth can be rediscovered: usually it has been written down elsewhere.
Namely:
– monuments: this is my body. The hysterical nucleus of a neurosis in which the hysterical symptom reveals the structure of a language. Deciphered like an inscription, which once recovered, can without serious loss be destroyed;
– in archival documents: these are my childhood memories, just as impenetrable as are such documents when I do not know their provenance;
– in semantic evolution: this corresponds to the stock of words and acceptations of my own particular vocabulary, as it does to my style of life and to my character;
– in traditions, too, and even in the legends which in a heroicised form, bear my history:
– and, lastly, in the traces that are inevitably preserved by the distortions necessitated by linking the adulterated chapter to the chapters surrounding it, and whose meaning will be established by my exegesis.[16]

There is an interesting coincidence between the indexical signs cited by Lacan and those cited by historians as the only means of retrieving the culture of the Dark Ages of antiquity across cultural amnesia and a total lack of historical records. These were the traces left by objects recovered in archaeology, the dialects, and forms of language that persisted though geographically dispersed, and the legends that were handed on orally through a period of time that had no written language. The exegesis can only come into being in the final historical narration. It is obviously this point that interests Lacan: 'What we teach the subject to recognise as his unconscious is his history – that is to say, we help him to perfect the present historicisation of the facts that have already determined a certain number of the historical turning-points in his existence.'[17]

So, what is specific about Oedipus, the crucial issue that separates him from the simple detectives of the whodunit, is the theme of internal transformation which obliquely relates him to the modern, post-psychoanalytic, heroes-in-crisis of the *film noir*. The story he investigates is his own; he is the criminal in his detective story. The evidence and clues he compiles all pile up against him but also allow him to see his own history, to go through the process of recognition and understand 'the historical turning-points in his existence'.

Lacan then returns again to antiquity, to the Athenian drama which he describes as: 'the original myths of the city state and the "material" through which a nation today learns to read the symbol of destiny on the march'. He moves away from the question of narration in an individual analysis to collective fantasies narrated in culture. He has thus traced a triple relationship: between fossilised indexical evidence left as remnants of the past, the process of psychoanalysis that interprets these traces (as practised in relation to individuals) and the collective construction of history and mythology. In the shift from Freud to these points of Lacan's, another shift is contained. That is, the shift between the matter of the Oedipus story as it relates to the Oedipus complex (the incestuous and murderous fantasies of a small child) and the question of the structure of narration as a process of recognition both in an individual analysis and, then, perhaps, in culture. For Lacan, of course, this is above all an issue of the function of language and the symbolic, which allows raw, indexical, material to be transformed into words, to be narrated, and so transformed into something else. This issue, too, makes a dramatic appearance in Sophocles's second Oedipus play.

BEYOND THE CORE STORY

1 The Ending: The Father's Legacy

After Oedipus left Thebes, the third traumatic departure of his life (he was expelled from Thebes as an infant; he left Corinth in search of his true parentage), he wandered in poverty and great mental and physical suffering, accompanied only by his daughter, Antigone. Sophocles starts the play *Oedipus at Colonus* at the moment when they arrive at a little wood, outside Athens, that is sacred to the Eumenides. Oedipus recognises the place where he is destined to die but is challenged by the local people who see his presence there as sacrilegious. Theseus, the king of Athens, is summoned while the people (the Chorus) question Oedipus and ask his name; it is he who is now subject to investigation and interrogation. When Oedipus finally speaks his name, the people react with the fear and terror combined with fascination that Freud noted in contemporary reactions to *Oedipus Rex*, and that he used as evidence for the universality of the Oedipus complex. Then Ismene arrives, with the news of another oracle, again the third in Oedipus's life (the first predicted his expulsion from Thebes by his father and then, when it was repeated to him, determined his decision to avoid Corinth and travel from Delphi towards Thebes; it was the second that instructed him to find the murderer of Laius and which sets in motion the investigative process of *Oedipus Rex*). This time the oracle promises that Oedipus will achieve a special, transcendent power at the moment of his death, which he will be able to bestow on the people among whom he chooses to die. The Thebans, therefore, want him back, locked as they are in a war between the two sons, Polyneices besieging with a foreign army the city that is now under the control of Eteocles and their maternal uncle, Creon. The Chorus question Oedipus again. They want to hear his story, the most unspeakable story that they already know by hearsay. ('Your name, old stranger, echoes through the world.') As Oedipus tells the story, the events of his life are repeated for a third time, the events that he first enacted, then re-tracted in investigation, he now recounts in his own words.[18] Theseus arrives and Oedipus promises to bestow the 'blessing' of his death on him and his people. Creon arrives and when Oedipus denounces him bitterly, he threatens the two girls until Theseus intervenes to rescue them. Polyneices then arrives also in search of his father's mysterious power and this time Oedipus curses both his sons. Theseus returns and is alone allowed to accompany Oedipus to the moment of his death. He dies in strange circumstances, leaving no body. Finally Antigone takes the decision to go back to Thebes to try to end the fratricidal war between her brothers.

The play has little complex action or narrative structure. It is about death, naming and inheritance. Thebes is falling into primal chaos, torn by fratricidal feud, outside history and lacking government. Athens is at the dawn of civilisation. There is, perhaps, an 'invention of tradition' aspect to Sophocles's last play, written when he was in his nineties, at the end of the glorious fourth century, at a moment when Athens was itself under siege during the Peloponnesian War. Theseus is considered to be the legendary founder of the Athenian state; he organised the legal system, established a constitution and abidcated from the kingship. Oedipus's choice in bestowing his 'blessing' on Athens, in preference to his own tragic city, takes on a particular cultural significance. From a Lacanian perspective, the story of Oedipus at Colonus can be interpreted as the story of the coming into being of the resolution of the Oedipus complex around the Name of the Father, the Law, and the Symbolic Order. Oedipus performed the different roles in the inter-generational drama out of phase by a generation. As a man, in the role of child, he acted out the Oedipal desire; then as a child and father, he performs the act of symbolic castration, blinding himself and stripping himself of all power and possessions (usurped from his father). At Colonus, he arrives to meet his death purged and cleansed by suffering. At the end of *Oedipus Rex* he was polluted but now he has undergone yet another psychic metamorphosis:

> Don't reject me as you look into the horror
> of my face, these sockets raked and blind.
> I come as someone sacred, someone filled
> with piety and power.[19]

His power is no longer the material power of property and possessions or even the abstract power of the king as representative of the law who can solve mysteries in the Name of the Law. His power emanates from his unique identity as the emblematic embodiment of Oedipal desire; action transmuted by narration, the flesh, as it were, made Word. The Athenian legacy, personified by Theseus, confirms that the qualities of culture and civilisation that complement the incest taboo are there in Oedipus's gift of power. Realised by the old man, the child's experience is visibly born into culture and bequeathed to civilisation. This myth of origins, in which the incest taboo is an essential corollary to the law of social organisation, is central to both Lévi-Strauss's and Lacan's concepts of the origins of culture;

> The Oedipus is articulated in the forms of social institutions and of language of which the members themselves are unconscious – unconscious to their meaning and, above all, to their origin. The Oedipal unconscious is homologous with all these symbolic structures. The Oedipus is the drama of the social being who must become a subject and who can only do so by internalising the social rules, by entering on an equal footing into the register of the symbolic, of Culture and of language ... a development which presupposes the transition from nature into culture ... we can say that the Oedipus is the unconscious articulation of a human world of culture and language; it is the very structure of the unconscious forms of society.[20]

In an exquisitely mapped article, to which I cannot do justice here, Shoshana Felman argues a parallel development between *Oedipus Rex/ Oedipus at Colonus* and *The Interpretation of Dreams/Beyond the Pleasure Principle*. In each case, the first work is about sexuality and Oedipal desire and the second is the compulsion to repeat and the death drive. It is the compulsion to repeat lived experience that generates symbolisation and consequently myth and narrative.

> Oedipus *is born*, through the assumption of his death (of his radical self-expropriation) *into the life of his history*. Oedipus at Colonus is about the transformation of Oedipus' story into history: it does not tell the drama, it is *about the telling* and re-telling of the drama. It is, in other words, about the *historicisation* of Oedipus' destiny, through the *symbolisation* – the transformation into speech – of Oedipal desire.[21]

She also argues that there is a third transition in the sequence: the shift from Freud to Lacan in the history of the psychoanalytic movement. All these transitions represent a transmutation of Oedipal desire in which the place of the object of desire is taken by questions of language and symbolisation. (Lacan: 'What we teach the subject to recognise as his unconscious is his history'.) Shoshana Felman argues that the generative force of psychoanalysis is characterised by the compulsion to repeat, itself characteristic of the death drive. In analysis, the analysand repeats, in words and narrative, lived experience and past events: 'What is then, psychoanalysis if not, precisely a life-usage of the death instinct – a practical productive usage of the compulsion to repeat...'.

Peter Brooks has used *Beyond the Pleasure Principle* most illuminatingly to discuss the impact of the compulsion to repeat and the death drive on narrative. Repetition offers mastery over a state of loss and anxiety (as Freud noticed in his famous example of the game that he interpreted as a child's symbolisation, by means of a toy, of his mother's absence and imagined return):

> An event gains meaning by its repetition, which is both a recall of an earlier moment and a variation on it ... Repetition creates a return in the text, a doubling back. We cannot say whether this is a return to, or a return of: for instance, a return to origins or a return of the repressed.[22]

And:

> We have a curious situation in which two principles of forward movement operate upon one another so as to create a retard ... This might be consubstantial with the fact that a repetition can take us both backward and forward because these terms have become reversible: the end is a time before the beginning.[23]

The Oedipus story is punctuated with foretellings, tellings and re-tellings: the oracles foretell, Teiresias tells, at the beginning of *Oedipus Rex*, the story that Oedipus then has to piece together for himself, and that he then re-tells to the Chorus at Colonus. The story itself existed as a myth before its literary re-working by Sophocles, so it would have been well known to the Athenian audience to whom the play would have necessarily seemed a re-telling. The story has since been used and re-told many times. Lévi-Strauss makes this point: 'Not only Sophocles but Freud himself should be included among the recorded versions of the Oedipus myth on a par with earlier or seemingly more authentic versions'.[24] (In the light of Lévi-Strauss's interpretation of the Oedipus myth as about belief in the autochthonous origins of man, he strangely omits the hero's 'rebirth' in the wilderness, shared with many other heroes such as Romulus, Moses, and Cyrus and commented on by Freud in 'Moses and Monotheism'.) The significance of the act of telling and of narrational patterns in the Oedipus story confirms the importance, dismissed by structuralism, of narrative in myth. Terence Turner has criticised Lévi-Strauss's analysis of the Oedipus myth to draw attention to and reinstate the contribution of temporal structures ('the syntactic structures of narrative sequence') to the meaning of myth, alongside the component elements, the 'bundles' that are central to Lévi-Strauss's structural analysis.

Myths do indeed provide synchronic models of diachronic processes, but they do this directly at the level of organisation as temporal sequences, through the correspondence between their sequential patterns and aspects of the diachronic processes they 'model'. The unique mythical relationship between synchrony and diachrony, between historical events and timeless structure, must be sought in the way myth itself patterns time in the syntactic structure of its narrative; that is, in Lévi-Strauss's own words 'in the story which it tells'.[25]

He brings out the link between narrative sequence as a structural element and the alternation between change and stasis in 'traditional narrative genres', in which a synchronic timelessness is disrupted by a sequentially patterned series of events, a diachronic disordering of stasis.

These observations have a bearing on what might be called the politics of narrative closure. Shoshana Felman argues that Lacan identified with the exiled Oedipus, personally because of his expulsion from the International Psychoanalytic Association, and he identified with *Oedipus at Colonus*, theoretically because of its relation to *Beyond the Pleasure Principle* (the text that orthodoxy could not absorb) and because it tells, not a mythic story but the story of the coming into being of a myth. This has some bearing on the openness of the implicit narration in psychoanalytic practice:

> The psychoanalytic myth derives its theoretical effectiveness not from its truth value, but from its truth-encounter with the other; from its capacity for passing through the other; from its openness that is to an expropriating passage of one insight through another; of one story through another; the passage for example of Oedipus the king through Oedipus at Colonus; of the passage of the myth of 'Instinct' through this later and more troubling myth of 'Death'.[26]

Narrative is outside history but related to it. Terence Turner's emphasis on change through disorder in narrative raises the problem of change in lived political narrative. The potential for change in the disordered middle is in dialectical opposition to the timeless stasis of the beginning and end. There is a similar 'political poetics' inherent in Peter Brooks' 'return to', 'return of' and 'the end is before the beginning'; and also in Shoshana Felman's perception of the compulsion to repeat and (what she calls) the 'uncertainty principle' as safeguards against new movements, such as psychoanalysis, fossilising into the timeless stasis of institutional authority. For a final word something of this aesthetic of permanent narration is present in François Roustang's observations on the difficulty of maintaining change within the psychoanalytic institution.

> If one wants to be an analyst, one must analyse one's own transference to Freud, one must question his writings, which are not to be taken as the word of the Gospel but as a place where one's fantasies and desires are caught and projected along with Freud's. In this way, the trust we place in advance (*im Voraus*) in his works should become, through deferred action, both the uncertainty and the strength of our discourse.[27]

One strange aspect of the Oedipus story is its lack of clear resolution in the normal narrative sense. The core story contained in Sophocles's *Oedipus Rex* ends with yet another departure, a return to the journey and liminality, threatening the security of every 'and then they lived happily ever after'. *Oedipus at Colonus* ends with the death of the hero and the birth of his Symbolic Order. It is as if the presence of death, the ultimate point of timeless stasis that Peter Brooks has shown to be lying behind the drive to an ending, must be neutralised by the timeless stasis of paternal authority. There is, perhaps, a fundamental tension between the openness of narrative transformation and the censorship imposed by this authority. Of course, both lie within the Symbolic Order. But the father's place in the Lacanian Oedipus complex tips the balance in the paternal direction; the Symbolic Order is born under his aegis. Or so it seems. Just before Oedipus dies, Sophocles introduces an incident that dramatically raises a ghost from the distant past, the compulsion to repeat comes to the fore in a violent return of the repressed.

2 The Beginning: The Son's Inheritance

Just as he had been cursed, just as his father had tried to murder him, Oedipus curses his own sons and condemns them to kill each other.

> Die!
> Die by your own blood brother's hand – die –
> killing the very man who drove you out!
> So I curse your life out!
> I call on the dark depths of Tartarus brimming hate,
> where all our fathers lie, to hale you home!
> I cry to the great goddesses of this grove!
> I cry to the great god War
> who planted that terrible hatred in your hearts!
> Go! – with all my curses thundering in your ears –
> go and herald them out to every man in Thebes
> and all your loyal comrades under arms! Cry out
> that Oedipus has bequeathed these last rights,
> these royal rights of birth to both his sons![28]

Quite apart from the question of the justice of Oedipus's attitude to his sons, or their previous behaviour to him, two elements return here, at the end of the story, that vividly invoke its beginning. First of all, Oedipus continues the curse on his family line and, second, the curse reminds us that he had previously narrowly escaped being killed by his own father, first as a new born infant, and then, in the fateful encounter with Laius at the crossroad. He claims many times that the old man in the carriage would have killed him outright had he not defended himself ('the man I murdered

– he'd have murdered me!'). Not only, then, does Oedipus's approaching death bring to mind his father's attempts to kill him, thus evoking Laius's presence in the story, but his father's character returns to haunt Oedipus's relation to his own sons.

Oedipus at Colonus is based on the legend that Sophocles's own birthplace, Colonus, was the place where Oedipus had died. The events and narrative structure are more literary than mythic, so that the play, in being less closely tied to pre-existing myth, can be self-conscious about how myth grows and works. In contrast the pre-history of the Oedipus story remains extremely primitive and has been systematically ignored in both classical tragedy and later tradition. Most commentators, including Freud, leave out the question of why Oedipus and Laius and Jocasta were cursed, and Laius's responsibility for bringing the curse down on them.

Laius's father, Labdakos, died during his son's infancy. The throne was usurped, and later usurped again and Laius was driven into exile. He was given hospitality by King Pelops of Sparta, where he fell in love with the King's beautiful young son Chrysippos. He kidnapped the boy, raped him and caused his death. (It is argued that the outrageousness of this act lay, not in the act of homosexuality, but in the violation of hospitality.) King Pelops then cursed Laius, saying that if he should have a son, the son would kill him. Laius made up his mind never to have children, but one night he got drunk, and slept with his wife Jocasta, who conceived. Later Hera sent the Sphinx to ravage Thebes in retribution for Laius's crime and also, no doubt, to set the scene for Oedipus's victorious arrival in the city.

According to this pre-history of the myth, Laius's aggressive and violent homosexual act is the latent cause of the curse and Oedipus's later suffering. Chrysippos's experience with Laius can act as a displacement on to another young boy from a primal anxiety in son-to-father relations; the repression of this aspect of the myth then becomes a repression of the father's fault in the Oedipal scenario. Marie Balmary explains Freud's oversight in terms of his need to repress the Laius-like qualities of his own father Jacob Freud. She argues that the logical consequence of this (personal) repression was the (theoretical) repression of the father's fault and Freud's decision to 'exonerate' the father of seduction and 'incriminate' the child's fantasy of seduction.[29] It is known that Freud adopted the fantasy theory of seduction during the period of mourning over his own father's death.

This scotomisation of the complementary Oedipus complex is probably rooted in the adult's deep-seated need to place all responsibility for the Oedipus Complex on the child, and to ignore wherever possible those parental attitudes which stimulate the infant's Oedipal tendencies. That this deliberate scotoma is rooted in the characteristic authoritarian atmosphere of the nineteenth-century family is suggested by Freud's own thoughts on the aetiology of hysteria.[30]

Without attempting to solve this problem of primary fault or guilt, the narrative and narrational structures that are basic to the Oedipus myth can recast it so as to avoid a direct choice between fact and fiction or between reality and fantasy. Laius's crime is literally pre-Oedipal; it pre-exists the life story of his child whose tragic history transmutes the horror generated by the primal father into the father represented by the Symbolic Order in the person of Theseus.

The Oedipus myth, in its transition from the primal father to the father of the Symbolic Order, also shifts the question of fault or guilt out of the mythic terrain of phylogenesis and places it within the psyche, within fantasy and thus also within culture and the possibility of resolution within culture.

The assumption of guilt on the part of the child is essential to the shift in formal and narrational structure in the Oedipus story. Whereas Laius, the guilty father, exists in a sphere of pure action, outside self-consciousness, the Oedipal trajectory gives Oedipus the metaphysical power to reconstitute his own history through the process of narration. This ability to *tell* and transcend is the crucial constitutive aspect of the myth, and is more important a human attribute than unconscious guilt or innocence. It is here that the process of narration in psychoanalysis and the collective compulsion to repeat, that generates narrative in culture, come together in the Oedipus story.

The story of Oedipus's life moves through stages (from victim to royal child, from wanderer to hero-king, from defilement to catharsis, from sanctification to symbolic authority) that span the chasm separating Laius from Theseus. But Laius represents something that returns like a ghostly apparition when his son curses his own sons. In a criss-cross of time and space, from the lower depths of the mind and out of the mists of the past, the primal father erupts like Dennis Hopper's Frank in *Blue Velvet*. Frank is both the sadistic father of the primal scene, and a fearfully erotic father whose homosexual aggression threatens the hero/child with sexual passivity and death. Frank's world comes into its own at night, with the drugs, alcohol, bars and brothels that make up the criminal underbelly concealed by small town America's homely, law-abiding exterior. Jeffrey's descent into the lower depths is like the hero's journey in the folk-tale or *film-noir* that marks a rite of passage; he emerges on the other side as a mature man who has won the right to marry the daughter of the representative of the law. Frank leaves a legacy to the newly mature initiate into the patriarchal order. The end of the movie suggests that he will live on, a point of repression and attraction and fear, within Jeffrey's psyche, waiting for the moment of return. The lower depths of the psyche are condensed with the imagery of the lower depths of the town, inhabited by personifications that are displaced from childhood traumas, the primal fantasies of the Oedipus complex, the castration complex and the primal scene.

Patriarchy is founded on rites and rights of inheritance and exchange of women that neutralise a neurotic, violent father/son rivalry and establish the basis for a symbolic order. But perhaps this symbolic depends shakily on the repression of the primal, pre-Oedipal father so that culture continues to be tinged with violence and institutions that claim to be guardians of the law and defence against chaos are maintained by the violence that lies behind patriarchal authority. The image of the primal *father* confuses the neat polarisation between pre- and post-Oedipal that reproduces a polarisation between mother and father. Julia Kristeva has discussed the pehnomenon of horror and disgust as a culture returning under the aegis of a pre-Oedipal mother, a body without boundary, 'an unspeakable'. Perhaps even more 'unspeakable', hardly even achieving symbolisation in the collective fantasy of popular culture, is the threat embodied by the primal father. Perhaps even his lack of cultural recognition is significant, returning rather in symptomatic social and sexual anxieties that afflict our society. Perhaps desire for and fear of a powerful mother and the misogyny it generates conceals something even more disturbing, desire for and fear of a violent father. Perhaps it is the 'unspeakable' ghost of Laius that haunts relations between men, generating homophobic anxieties and an attraction bonded by physical violence represented by Frank's relationship to Jeffrey.

Looking at the Oedipal myth in detail it is remarkable to what extent it is about father/son relations and how marginal the feminine is to the story. Even though the incest theme can suggest residual memories of ritual and inheritance that pre-date the fully fledged patriarchal order, desire for the mother is more significant as a symptom of father/son rivalry. However, the story's narrative structure and the importance of investigation and telling in the story itself offers a Utopian promise, a pointer towards the transformative power of telling one's own story and the social function of popular culture as the narrativisation of collective fantasy. Recently, feminism through critical and analytical work has been attempting to inflect the way in which our society narrativises itself. In the process, feminist consciousness can affect the discourse of patriarchy and upset the polarisation between masculinity and feminity that keeps its order in place. Shoshana Felman quotes Lacan:

> To bring the subject to *recognise* and *name* his desire, this is the nature of the efficacious action of analysis. But it is not a question of recognising something that would have been there already – a given – ready to be captured. In naming it the subject creates, gives rise to something new, makes something new present in the world.[31]

Certainty is the other side of the coin to anxiety. Curiosity and the riddling spirit of the Sphinx activate questions that open up the closures of repression and maintain the force of an 'uncertainty principle'. As Teresa de Lauretis points out at the end of her chapter on Oedipus in *Alice Doesn't*, the story is still in the making. The Sphinx and her riddle are still waiting for a 'beyond'.

Notes

1. This chapter has grown out of work initiated and discussed in a graduate seminar in the Department of Cinema Studies, New York University, during the fall semester 1986. I enjoyed and benefited from the seminar enormously. I would like to thank the following students who worked with me: Vicky Abrash, Parag Amladi, Catherine Benamou, Sarah Berry, Leo Charney, Manohla Dargis, John Johnson, Alexandra Juhasz, Barbara Kassen-Taranto, Irma Klein, Fay Plant, Doug Riblet, Vince Rocchio, Annabelle Sheehan, Shelley Stamp, Chuck Stephens, Michael Taslitz, Andreas Timmer, Christie Timms, Doug Troyan, Debbie Wuliger. The chapter has also been reproduced in Laura Mulvey, *Visual and Other Pleasures* (Macmillan, London, 1989).
2. S. Freud, *The Interpretation of Dreams*, *SE* IV (Hogarth Press, London), pp. 261–2.
3. S. Freud, 'On Creative Writing and the Ego', *SE* IX, p. 148.
4. *The Interpretation of Dreams*, p. 217n.
5. Carl Schorske in his book *Fin de Siècle Vienna* (Alfred A. Knopf, New York, 1980) discusses the intricate web of condensation and displacement at work in Freud's dreams about his father, and the political significance they contain: particularly, Freud's reaction to his father's lack of revolutionary spirit in the face of anti-semitism. 'This struck me as unheroic conduct on the part of the big, strong man who was holding the little boy by the hand. I contrasted this scene with one that fitted my feelings better: the scene in which Hannibal's father, Hamilcar Barca, made this boy swear before the household altar to take vengeance on the Romans' ('The Interpretation of Dreams', p. 197). This point brings out the possibility of identification in rebellion between father and son in the face of social, economic and political oppression.
6. Vladimir Propp, 'Oedipus in the Light of Folk-Tale', in Lowell Edmunds and Alan Dundas (eds), *Oedipus, a Folk Lore Case-Book* (Garland, New York and London, 1984).
7. Teresa de Lauretis, *Alice Doesn't* (Indiana University Press, Bloomington, 1984), p. 116.
8. Sophocles, 'Oedipus the King', *The Three Theban Plays*, Robert Fagles (trans) (Penguin Classics, Harmondsworth, 1982), p. 182.
9. Ibid., p. 167.
10. Ibid., p. 183.
11. Tzvetan Todorov, 'Detective Fiction', *Poetics of Prose* (Cornell University Press, Ithaca, 1977).
12. Muriel Gardiner (ed.), *The Wolf-Man and Sigmund Freud* (Hogarth Press, London, 1972), p. 146.
13. Paul Arthur, *Shadows on the Mirror: Film Noir and Cold War America 1945–57* (Praeger, New York, 1989).
14. Gardiner, *The Wolf-Man and Sigmund Freud*, pp. 149–50.
15. S. Freud, 'Two Case Histories', *SE* X, pp. 176–7.

16.   Jacques Lacan, 'The function and field of speech and language in psychoanalysis', *Ecrits. A Selection* (Tavistock Press, London, 1977), p. 50.
17.   Ibid., p. 52.
18.   Sophocles, 'Oedipus at Colonus', *The Three Theban Plays*, pp. 295–7 and pp. 314–17.
19.   Ibid., p. 300.
20.   Anika Lemaire, *Jacques Lacan* (Routledge & Kegan Paul, London, 1970), pp. 91–2.
21.   Shoshana Felman, 'Beyond Oedipus. The Specimen Story of Psychoanalysis', *MLN Comparative Literature*, vol. 98, no. 5 (Johns Hopkins University Press, Baltimore, 1983), pp. 1029–30.
22.   Peter Brooks, *Reading for the Plot* (Vintage, New York, 1985), pp. 99–100.
23.   Ibid., p. 103.
24.   Claude Lévi-Strauss, 'The Structural Study of Myth', in *Structural Anthropology* (Penguin, Harmondsworth, 1963).
25.   Terence Turner, 'Oedipus: Time and Structure in Narrative Form', *Forms of Symbolic Action* (American Ethnological Society, 1969), p. 32.
26.   Shoshana Felman, 'Beyond Oedipus', p. 1045 (see note 21).
27.   François Roustang: *Dire Mastery* (Johns Hopkins University Press, Baltimore, 1982), p. 21.
28.   'Oedipus at Colonus', *The Three Theban Plays*, p. 365.
29.   Marie Balmary, *Psycho-analysing Psycho-analysis* (Johns Hopkins University Press, Baltimore, 1982).
30.   George Devereux, 'Why Oedipus killed Laius', in *Oedipus: a Folk Lore Case-Book*, p. 216 (see note 6).
31.   Shoshana Felman, 'Beyond Oedipus', p. 1026 (see note 21).

4

Interim
Part I: *Corpus*, 1984–85

Mary Kelly

Interim is a project, still in progress, in which Mary Kelly explores 'the moment of middle age' as 'a state between' for women. *Corpus* is the first part of the work (four parts are planned). It focuses on the body as definitive of woman – as desirable object or as mother. It was begun in 1983 and first exhibited at the Fruitmarket Gallery, Edinburgh, Kettle's Yard Gallery, Cambridge and Riverside Studios, London in 1985–86.

Installation, The Fruitmarket Gallery, Edinburgh, 1985

Corpus consists of thirty panels of paired images and text, each measuring four feet by three, laminated photo positive, screenprint and acrylic on perspex. The panels are divided into five sections: 'Menacé', 'Appel', 'Supplication', 'Erotisme' and 'Extase'. These titles refer to the 'attitudes passionelles' which the nineteenth-century neuropathologist J. M. Charcot identified as characteristic of the female hysteric in the hallucinatory stage.

Reproduced here are the six panels in the section 'Menacé'.

MENACÉ

The room is crowded yet subdued, almost silent. No music, no dancing. Everyone is talking quietly in couples or small groups. Many are old friends, some I haven't seen for several years. They look different, not just greyer or fatter or more degenerate or less fashionable, just not the same. We are celebrating Lynn's fortieth birthday, "You look great," she says kissing me on both cheeks, "haven't changed at all," then Anna mocks us but affectionately, "well preserved." She smiles. We laugh. I am content. Embalmed by the warmth, the comfort of their compliments, immutable, at least until Ros whispers, "How old are you anyway?" and I remember I am nearly forty-three. I hesitate and Sarah fills the gap with, "See, she can't even say it!" A possible reprieve, Elizabeth comes over and asks me what I'm working on. I tell her it's another long project and hope she won't pursue it. "On what," she insists. I fumble, knowing it will sound dreadful no matter how I say it, "Middle-age, well, that is, I suppose I mean women like us." "I don't feel middle-aged," she snaps, seems offended. I try to explain that it's not so literal, more about the way we represent it to ourselves, almost before the fact. She says she has a phobia about it, tries to change the subject. Sarah interrupts to tell me the leather jacket is lovely but she distinctly remembers that I said I'd never wear one. I confess I finally gave in for professional reasons, that there's so much to think about now besides what to wear, that the older you are the harder it seems to be to get it right and that the uniform makes it a little easier. I look at Maya for confirmation but she disagrees, says there's a certain freedom attached to getting older, not caring so much, being able to get up in the morning and get dressed like a man, confidently, without wasting time primping. I notice she is dressed simply, hair hanging loosely on her shoulders, wearing very little make-up, nearly sixty and absolutely gorgeous. I say I'm not so sure most men are that secure but maybe her confidence comes from knowing she has always been a very attractive woman. She looks surprised, "No one is that confident," she protests, "I must admit I've never missed an opportunity to glance in a mirror as I passed it, or in a shop window or any reflective surface for that matter, hoping to catch a glimpse of myself as others see me." Lynn is lighting the candles, "Watch me," she says, "I'm going to blow them out now". And she does, all forty, without a flicker.

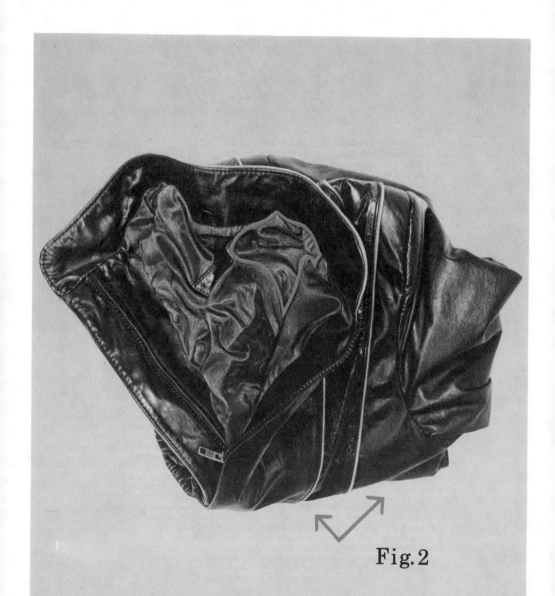

Fig. 2

MENACÉ

The clinic is nearly empty. I am waiting, heart beating, the bell rings, I go in. "Take off your clothes and put this on," he says, "I'll be back in a few minutes." I want to explain first but it's too late, he's gone. I rehearse it. Don't want another child, no can't afford another child, have professional commitments. No, that won't impress him. My first child is almost nine, too old to have another one? He's back, "How old are you?" Do you have any children? When was your last period?" He won't listen, just the facts. Preoccupied with looking, only the evidence. "This won't take long," he says. "Relax." Can't relax, can't talk, can't see. Blind spot. Whose? I ask myself on his behalf. Yours, theirs? No one will talk about it. About what? Pregnancy? No. Menstruation? No, not exactly. Something less specific: secret places, secretions, odd swellings, strange smells, odors, lack of order, disorder, being older? I remember Clara saying that the reason older women often give for having an abortion is not wanting the other children to know. To know what? That she laughs too loudly, eats too much, has sex, desires? It's not becoming to be coming, not at her age anyway. It would be so obvious, obvious in my case that I'm procrastinating, not serious, about my work. "Too soon to tell," he doesn't smile, "We'll have to wait. The lab will send results next week. Ring then." Can't wait. I say I have an important lecture to give, must leave the country by the end of the week, but he isn't listening. Now he isn't even looking. I know he's thinking that's irrelevant, why is this woman so hysterical. I feel like crying. I always feel like crying. This is ridiculous. He hands me the plastic bottle, the white label, the facts, the evidence, "you can get dressed now."

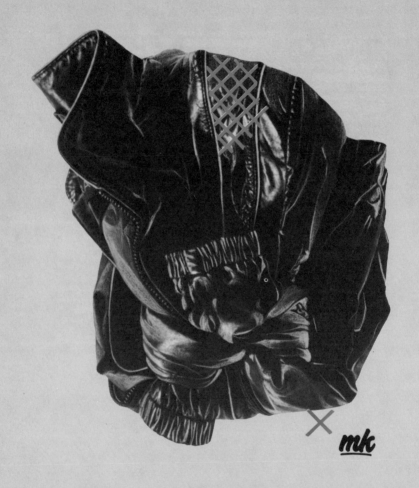

mk

Menacé

The music is loud, too loud to talk. Sound swells and breaks, rolling over me, through me, funky, dissonant, feels good. I want to dance, smile at Ruth soliciting a partner. We push our way into the center of the room and start to move in what I think is perfect unison, except that from a certain position I can see myself in the cloakroom mirror. The image grates. I keep manoeuvering back to it for a re-play, seems so out of synch with how I feel. The clothes perhaps, not tough enough, too sixties. No, the hair, too severe, should fly across my face when I turn. No, its more insidious than that, the expression is wrong, too animated, childish even, absurd at my age. Keep the mouth closed and look cynical to compensate for the double chin. Beware of raising your arms and unleashing untidy ripples of loose flesh that linger thereon. No, the hips, definitely the hips, hardly perceptible but not quite the same, something to do with the feeling of space around the waist. Ruth has gone for a drink and someone is offering me a joint. I feel silly. Everyone I know went back to alcohol years ago. Still, everyone I know is thousands of miles away and everyone here is so goddamn young. Mostly students. I feel like a chaperone. Aren't there any other lecturers for Chrissake. I spot a post-graduate fellow, greying at the temples, looks promising. I corner him. He says he's a fem-inist so I proceed to ramble on about the beginnings of the women's movement saying, "you remember the first meeting at Oxford, don't you?" "No," he says, "I was fourteen in 1968." I am stunned, can't speak, feel deceived. How can he know so much? Why does he look like that? Thirty-five at the very least, but twenty-seven? It's hopeless. I'm reduced to a voyeur. Besides, he's with someone who looks like less than twenty-one. I hate them. He senses it, hands me another drink. For a moment, I imagine that he is Prince Gold Hand bringing the Old Crone a glass of the Water-that-makes-young from the Fourth Well and I croak, "Have you got it, have you got it?" "Yes," he replies and I seize it in my wizened hands, pour it over me and immediately turn into a beautiful maiden. Then, I ask him what he would like as an offering of thanks, but he says he can't think of anything because the Princess is all he desires and she is already standing with her hand in his. At this point, of course, I want to turn them both into frogs and vanish from their sight forever. But instead, I just excuse myself and go to look for Ruth.

5

Re-Presenting the Body: On *Interim*, Part I

Mary Kelly

Corpus concerns the body – how it is shaped socially and psychically in the interim moment of ageing. Importantly, though, it does this in the specific form of an exhibition.[1] As such, the work involves a process of simultaneously visualising and theorising which, in a way, resists interpretation. In the context of this discussion, then, what I would like to do is take up some of the questions that give perspective to an underlying argument, stressing of course that this is not an explanation, but a parallel discourse, something unsettled, hopefully exceeded, by the art itself.

At one level, the conversational mode of the short stories in *Corpus* appears to represent, quite simply, the familiar view of women's experience. Yet, in relation to the image panels, titles and triptych structure of the sections, this has recourse to another order of experience, a political as well as personal history, grounded in the ongoing debates of what is still called, but more tentatively, the women's movement. *Corpus* is the first part of a larger project, *Interim*, which is still in progress. Through *Interim*'s themes (body, money, history, power), many issues which have preoccupied feminists in the past decade are recovered and reworked. First, regarding the project as a whole, the politics of psychoanalysis; that is, following the Foucauldian imperative to place it, historically, among the discourses that define and regulate the realm of sexuality, can it now be said to have become another orthodoxy? Secondly, in Part I, the problem of hysteria – a focal point in theory, but clinically speaking, does it still exist? Thirdly, what is the status, or fate perhaps, of the body and of the image in visual art practice informed by a psychoanalytic overview?

Corpus makes explicit reference to Charcot's now famous photographs of female hysterics by using the titles of 'the five passionate attitudes'

59

(Menacé, Appel, Supplication, Erotisme and Extase) to announce the work's five sections.[2] Citing the attitudes provided a means of linking popular discourses of the body with those of psychoanalysis as well as placing psychoanalysis itself within a historical context by referring to the founding moment of Freud's theory. Charcot's study, which was the first to observe and distinguish the category of non-organic nervous disorders, placed emphasis, almost exclusively, on the *visible* symptom. In the process, madness became a spectacle; the theatre of hysterics, a play dedicated to the production of unreason as a tangible event. Above all, what I found so significant is that it was a theatre in which *women* enacted the stages of the hysteric crisis and that it was the young women in particular who posed in the passionate attitudes. No doubt, there were male hysterics, but it seems that they were not photographed. At least, it is uncertain, since the figures posed in what could be called 'less passionate' attitudes, such as Irony, Repugnance or Terror, are older, 'unattractive' or sexually ambiguous in appearance. The important point here is that Freud, who began the *Studies in Hysteria* while working with Charcot, shifted the analyst's attention from looking to *listening*. With this, he introduced the linguistic moment into the analysis of psychic disorder. In effect, the body was dispersed, made invisible, with the invention of the 'talking cure'.

Corpus takes up some of the implications of that shift, very schematically, as follows. In the first case, what could be called the 'modern' worldview, which Freud represents in contrast to Charcot, language becomes central in a way that makes the visual take on a kind of compensatory value (the

'Attitudes passionelles – extase', plate from J. M. Charcot, *Iconographie de la Salpêtrière* (3 vols) (Paris, 1877–80)

Calvin Klein advertisement, *Vogue* (US), March 1985

unrepresentable, the monstrous, even the sublime). Freud in fact calls Charcot a 'visuel', says he is not a reflective man, not a thinker, that he has the nature of an artist.[3] Thus the visible disorder, expelled from the theatre, reappears in the non-psychiatric discourse of the artist who becomes the prototype for madness. The recovery of unreason is orchestrated through the socially acceptable form of art. More relevant still, at the present time, the body – that repressed object of the medical gaze – returns in the spectacle of contemporary advertising where women's bodies, posed in an infinite variety of passionate attitudes, are all-pervasive. The scale, for instance, of the panels for *Corpus* is based on the dimensions of a small hoarding (or billboard). On that stage, in place of Charcot's figures, emblematic articles of clothing pose, not only as the objects of medical scrutiny, but also as items for commercial exchange or subjects of romantic fantasy. Clearly, there is not *one* body, there are *many*. Moreover, discourses of the body are not synonymous with images of women. But images of women *are* over-determined by anatomical referents and by a certain repetitious form of hysterical posturing. So, once again, this spectacle requires a critical shift, within the space of the picture, from looking to listening.

The second point concerns the psychoanalytic concept of hysteria. In theory and to some extent in clinical practise, hysteria, defined in relation to the conversion symptom (the bodily symptom as the formation of a substitute for the repressed wish) has disappeared. Parveen Adams has pointed out that there are two concepts of symptom and two concepts of hysteria in Freud's writings. The first appears in the 1890s, and is evident in the *Interpretation of Dreams*; the second emerges after 1926 with the work on femininity and the pre-oedipal phase.[4] By that time, both symptom and hysteria are being redefined by the implications of Freud's emphasis on identification and bisexuality. (Dora's cough, for example, is not a substitute but a means of identification with her father which in turn is linked to the repressed desire for Frau K.) At the same time, this emphasis seems to be shifting the whole field of psychoanalysis away from its preoccupation with woman – *her* repressed sexuality, her hysterical symptom, and toward the more encompassing, but also more illusive question of the subject – *its* sexed identity. Here, what interests me is that hysteria continues to have a metaphorical significance. Lacan, for instance, speaks of psychoanalysis as the 'hystericisation of discourse' posing analysis against mastery and hysteria against knowledge. More importantly, for those expelled, not from Charcot's theatre, but from Lacan's *école freudienne* – I am thinking in particular of Luce Irigaray – the hysteric exposes the institution's fundamental misogyny; woman founds the theory of psychoanalysis and sustains it by facilitating the exchange of ideas between male theorists. Thus hysteria, marginalised in one realm, becomes central in another, that is, feminist theory. For Irigaray, the hysteric signifies the exclusion of

Material from the artist's archive for *Interim* and details from Part I: *Corpus*, preliminary artwork, 1984

women from discourse; for Monique Plaza – the revolt against patriarchy; for Michèle Montrelay – the blind spot of psychoanalysis; for Jacqueline Rose – the problem of sexual difference; and for the film collective of *Dora* – the analyst's symptom and therefore the basis for feminism's critique of Freud.

My work is also deeply implicated in this trajectory, impelled to fill in, or perhaps I should say widen, the gaps in the Freudian thesis. I have often thought of dedicating *Interim* to Dora's mother – the woman who never made Freud's acquaintance. He assumed she had housewife's psychosis. Too old for analysis? Too old to be noticed? Precisely in her invisibility, she underlines the dilemma for the older woman of representing her femininity, her sexuality, her desire when she is no longer seen to be desirable. She can neither look forward, as the young girl does, to being a woman, that is, having the fantasised body of maturity; nor can she return to the ideal moment of maternity – ideal in that it allows her to occupy the position of the actively desiring subject without transgressing the socially acceptable definition of the woman as mother. She is looking back at something lost, acknowledging perhaps , that 'being a woman' was only a brief moment in her life.

In an earlier work, *Post-Partum Document*,[5] which explores the implications of the mother–child relationship, I asked what the woman fears losing beyond the pleasure of the infant's body and concluded that it is the

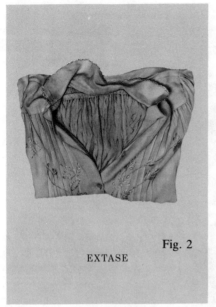

Fig. 2

EXTASE

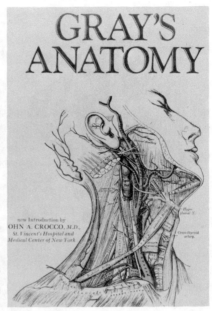

closeness to the mother's body she experiences in being 'like her'. Now, in *Interim*, I am asking how the woman can reconstitute her narcissistic aim and consequently her pleasure, her desire, outside of that maternal relation. In Part I, the stories begin with the decision not to have a child and then continue to explore other forms of identification around which the feminine/masculine terms revolve. Effectively, *Corpus* reiterates the hysteric's question: am I a man or am I a woman? And significantly, with the loss of maternal identity, a different order of fear emerges, one which reveals the importance of the repressed pre-oedipal identification with the father – the desire to be 'like him', but the fear of being the *same*, that is, of being 'like a man'.

At this point, I am prompted to ask, is there no outcome of the Oedipus Complex for the girl which is without neurotic consequences? Does, for instance, as Catherine Millot suggests in 'The Feminine Super-ego', the pre-oedipal identification with the father always entail a regressive transference of the demand for the phallus from him to the pre-oedipal, hence phallic mother?[6] Is it inconceivable that the 'masculinity complex' be considered, in some sense at least, as a resolution of the conflict? It does, after all, necessitate the internalisation of demand and the setting up of a super-ego. This process can lead to inhibition and anxiety, as Millot indicates, but at the same time it makes possible what is generally referred to as a profession, or less mundanely, the kind of sublimated pleasure

Extase

associated with creative work. Notably, it is for this manifestation of 'virility' that women propose to make themselves lovable. As Millot points out, 'the object of desire – and not the object of love – is feminine'.

I find this an intriguing distinction, one which imposes a less obvious, but nevertheless pertinent question. Is the boy's resolution of the oedipal drama really as unproblematic as has been assumed? Could Millot's distinctions regarding the masculinity complex for women be usefully taken up in relation to men? For example, does the woman who fantasises the possession of a penis parallel the man who acts out its absence (transvestism)? Is the woman who masquerades as the feminine type, who disguises the lack of a lack, but makes no demand on her sexual partner, comparable to the man who 'does what he's gotta do' (the male 'display', Lacan calls it) although he senses the fraud and, in fact, has no sexual desire for a woman? Furthermore, taking up what lies on the cusp of the complex – the woman's desire for the child as phallus and the man's desire to give her this 'gift', and what lies outside it – the failure to internalise demand which results in Don Juan's (or Juanita's) continual search for 'something better', all of this begins to give substance to the Lacanian view that there are as many forms of identification as there are demands. For both men and women, demand constructs a rather fragile relation to being and having. No one has the phallus, of course, but women seem reticent to let men (that is, the man they want to love) relinquish it.

This reticence has implications for feminism too. In failing to consider both sides of the oedipal story, perhaps the mother has become too real, too close and consequently blamed for too much. What I am suggesting is that the relation to the mother's body has been privileged in a way that does more than explain a different relation to castration for women; it asserts their difference from men. For instance, it is said that men, if they do experience anxiety over ageing, transpose it into another mode, a metalanguage; while women articulate it in terms of corporeality – pain, feeling of deformation or transformation of features, organs, limbs; or literally embody it, 'beyond words' is the familiar phrase. Michèle Montrelay describes this symptomatically as the woman who never lets up trying to be her sex. Theoretically she elaborates it as a form of 'precocious femininity', that is, an archaic organisation of the drives that bars the woman's access to sublimated pleasure. Although I have some reservations about her thesis as a whole, one of her observations is absolutely central to *Interim*'s discursive schema. 'The adult woman', she says, 'is one who reconstructs her sexuality in a field that goes beyond sex.' This is, of course, crucial for the older woman. It is also here, encapsulated in this statement, that I glimpse the social and political relevance of psychoanalysis for feminism; one which goes beyond the meanings of orthodoxy.

The confessional, the speaking of symptoms or, as Montrelay suggests, 'saying all', bypasses masculine censure because it transgresses a psychic organisation which binds the feminine to passivity and silence. Specifically, the interpretation of sexuality, in the sense pertaining to the analyst's words, does not explain but structures; as Montrelay insists *'it makes sexuality pass into discourse'*.[7] Pleasure is no longer derived from femininity as such, but from the signifier, in other words, by the repression of precocity that it brings about. She gives the example of jokes and of 'writing'. Also, in a political sense, I think this indicates the importance for women of theoretical and creative work, especially work on sexuality itself.

Returning to *Corpus*, my emphasis on the shift from looking to listening is not simply a theoretical point, it is also an artistic strategy. Its aim, first with regard to images of women, is to release the so-called 'female spectator' from her hysterical identification with the male voyeur. What I mean is that, for both men and women, to be pleasurably involved in looking is to be positioned actively as subject of that look; to enter the realm of objects and to desire them. At the same time, the woman, not exclusively, but more emphatically, is caught in a self-reflexive web of identifications – Am I like that? Was I like that? Would I like to be like that? Should I be like that? She is no longer surveying the image but her own reflection in it, 'hoping to catch a glimpse of herself as others see her'. Desire then appears to have no object since satisfaction takes the form of identification itself. Possibly as a defence against the 'masculinity' assumed in looking, she is trying on the 'mask(s) of womanliness' as Joan Riviere described it in her seminal article;[8] yet there never is, never could be a perfect fit.

Alternatively, by placing the 'enigma' of femininity on the surface of the picture rather than behind it, perhaps the process can be reversed. If she identifies, not with the literal figure of the woman, but with her effects, that is, the masquerade, then what she enjoys will be her distance from the alienation or anxiety this usually produces. For the older woman, inevitably, 'the image grates', the mask fails and the options are limited – either madness or laughter. This is why the work does not adopt the tactic of the 'open text'. Instead, it pushes the closure of traditional narrative to the point of parody. The fairytale endings in a sense resemble Montrelay's notion of the joke. Rather than reflect the spectator's fantasy, they repress it, creating an empty space where laughter is possible when the repressed returns in the guise of something else. In this case, something absurd that shatters the autobiographical *trompe-l'oeil* by revealing the function of the brushstroke, the character; it is only a picture, only a story, only a mimicry of the woman's disguise – playing it out on the 'body' of the text.

To represent a motive for one's fear, such as getting older or feeling unattractive, is not anxiety in clinical terms – that would imply the impossibility of rational thought, a 'blockage'. Hence the scripto-visual method I have been describing is a conscious re-presentation invoking an imaginary loss. A representation can only take on unconscious significance when it no longer refers to anything other than its form, not as an attribute of stylistic formalism, but as the precondition for any meaning. Here, significance is contingent upon the affect of the child's first experience of objects as extensions of the mother's body. For me, writing is also simply this – a texture of speaking, listening, touching; a means of visualising exactly that which is assumed to be outside of seeing, unrepresentable, unsaid. Although it is wildly speculative, I would like to think that a work of art could instigate a different kind of pleasure for the woman in seeing herself; one that is linked to the loss of a feminine identity formed in anxious proximity to the maternal body. In this sense, the work refers not so much to the anatomical fact or even to the perceptual entity as it does to the body of fantasy, the dispersed body of desire. Recalling Lacan's description of erotogenic zones as the gaze, the phoneme, the nothing, I am tempted to describe the space of the installation as an instance of the 'gathering' rather than a condition of reading or viewing from a fixed vantage point. Finally, the textual emphasis is more than an effort to create significance out of the *absence* of the woman's image as representational or iconic sign, it is an attempt to alter the implication of her *presence* in the spectacle of practices and histories that determine the postmodern condition of art.

Notes

1. See Mary Kelly, *Interim* (Part I), Catalogue (Fruitmarket Gallery, Edinburgh; Riverside Studios, London; Kettle's Yard Gallery, Cambridge, 1986).
2. J. M. Charcot, *Nouvelle Iconographie Photographique de la Salpêtrière*, volume II (Paris, 1878).
3. Sigmund Freud, 'Charcot', *SE*, III.
4. Parveen Adams, 'Symptoms and Hysteria', *Oxford Literary Review*, vol. 8, nos. 1–2, 1986.
5. Mary Kelly, *Post-Partum Document* (Routledge & Kegan Paul, London, 1983).
6. Catherine Millot, 'The Feminine Super-ego', *m/f*, no. 10 (1985).
7. Michèle Montrelay, 'Inquiry into Femininity', *m/f*, no. 1, 1978.
8. Joan Riviere, 'Womanliness as Masquerade' (1929), reprinted in Victor Burgin, James Donald and Cora Kaplan (eds), *Formations of Fantasy* (Methuen, London and New York, 1986).

6

Per Os(cillation)

Parveen Adams

'It is in the register of the symbolic that femininity comes to acquire its meaning as only its difference from masculinity; and it is not something with a content.' This is Juliet Mitchell in 1982 in an interview with the editors of m/f.[1] It is a position that I, as one of those editors, shared at the time. More recently, reflecting on the implications of Mikkel Borch-Jacobsen's questioning of the relation between object choice and identification in Freud's texts,[2] I began to see that a number of feminine characteristics, passivity in particular, did emerge from Freud's account of the Oedipus complex.

I do not dispute the importance of the symbolic – the 'femininity' and 'masculinity' that Freud is concerned with are positions taken up through different relations to the phallus. But there is another account of femininity tied up with that differentiation. The article which follows extricates this second account and shows that it does not work. Something appears as content and at the same time that content is not explained within the terms of Freud's psychical system.

It is important to be more precise. If something appears as content it is not as a content which is opposed to something that appears as form. To identify a content for Freud's concept of femininity is also to identify its form. This suggests that the relation to the phallus is given as a particular form/content which cannot be derived from the necessity of phallic mediation. If something is missing from Freud's account of form/content it is because nothing of reality has been allowed into it.

'She pictured to herself a scene of sexual gratification *per os* between the two people whose love affair occupied her mind so incessantly.'[3] So writes Freud of the unconscious fantasy underlying Dora's cough, a fantasy he describes as one of fellatio. The two people whose love affair occupied her

68

mind so incessantly are Dora's father and his lover Frau K. Through hysterical identification Dora takes up Frau K.'s sexual position in the fantasy; thereby, the *os* of the fantasy is Dora's mouth. Of course, if as Lacan suggests the fantasy is a fantasy of cunnilingus, the *os* of the fantasy is still Dora's mouth but this time via identification with the father. Dora's symptoms can be related to either fantasy intelligibly.

For Freud there is a certain logic of the relation between identification and object choice, for if Dora identifies with Frau K. (as Freud would have it), she is thereby deemed to have her father as love object. And he would prefer her not to identify with her father, for such an identification would mean that Dora's choice of love object was a woman.

It seems that it is important to specify the underlying fantasy because it concerns Dora's sexual position; that is, she takes up a masculine position if she identifies with her father, a feminine one if she identifies with Frau K. But is this the case? Once Dora identifies with the one, does she not also identify with the other? For fantasy is laid out in scenarios and the subject can take up now one position, now another in the scenario. Freud had pointed out as early as 1905 that a sadist is always also a masochist. And in 1915 the interchangeability of these positions is reiterated and extended to the positions of voyeur and exhibitionist.[4] On the same grounds a further extension can be made, as we will see – Dora must suck and be sucked.

So Dora must take the active place *and* the passive place in the fantasy, the man's place *and* the woman's place. Given the fantasy of a scene of sexual gratification *per os*, it matters little whether we say that she is identifying with a male mouth or with a female mouth. For Dora's object choice cannot be specified through such an identification. Whether or not Dora oscillates *per* her *os*, she oscillates between a masculine and feminine position. I shall argue that it is not possible to determine sexual position through identification.

Yet in Freudian theory identification is crucial at the definitive moment of sexual division, the taking up of a sexual position in the Oedipus complex. This is the moment when the multiple object choices and identifications of bisexuality are channelled into heterosexuality or homosexuality. Freud assumes that the child privileges one of its two parental love objects, that is that the child makes a choice of love object and that this choice is followed by identification with the rival object. This double move on the child's part is crucial to the stabilisation (always a somewhat precarious stability) of sexuality, the assumption of a sexed position. It is claimed that object choice locks identification into place. The trouble is that this identification which is to produce masculinity and femininity bears all the characteristics of oscillation already referred to.

Freud's concept of hysterical identification rests on a triangular situation which bears the Oedipal marks of object choice of one sex and rivalry and identification with the other sex. I shall show that Freud's logic of object choice and identification collapses by looking at the identifications involved in the hysteric's dream of an unfulfilled wish for a supper party, the famous smoked salmon dream, the example with which the concept of hysterical identification is first introduced in 1900, and also at the identifications involved in the example of Dora's fantasy which I have already referred to. For where there is identification with the woman there is also identification with the man. Hysterical identification is characterised, it turns out, by oscillation. Of course, I know that Freud recognised the bisexual identifications of the hysteric. But it is one thing to say that the hysteric identifies with both men and women and quite another to say that where there is identification with one there is also identification with the other.

What I am saying about hysterical identification has serious consequences for Freud's account of the production of femininity and masculinity at the Oedipal moment. For if it turns out that the identification which produces sexual difference within the Oedipus complex is hysterical identification, then the resolution of the Oedipus complex cannot explain the transformation of bisexuality into a fixed sexual position.

It is also possible to consider the adequacy of Freud's explanation of sexual positioning from another angle, by looking at the Freudian concepts of femininity and masculinity. Femininity appears to comprise subordination, passivity, masochism; masculinity appears to comprise superordination, activity, sadism. Notice that there are a number of pairs split up to form the masculine and feminine positions. But these pairs are those very ones which are characterised in Freud's writings as subject to oscillation. How have these interchangeable terms congealed to set up two distinct series? If it is not through the identification of the Oedipal situation which is meant to account for this coagulation, then should we seek another mechanism to account for this? Or does the problem lie in Freud's very conception of sexual positioning as the division of instinctual pairs into distinct groups? That is to say, should the problem be set up otherwise than as the fixing of that which is originally characterised as mobile and fluctuating.

An answer to this begins to emerge when the question of identification, object choice and sexual position is taken up in relation to Freud's theory of masochism as it is set out in 'A Child is Being Beaten' (1919). From the structure of masochism as it is clinically understood today it is very clear that Freud's explanation of the masochistic position is untenable precisely because masochism cannot be defined and determined by fixing on one term of each of a set of pairs of oscillating terms. The subject's sexuality is simply not structured in terms of Freud's pairs. Something of reality, the masochistic scenario of the modern period, is missing from the Freudian theory of masochism. (The earliest reference I have found to this modern masochism of the bedroom in Pico della Mirandola's *Disputationes*

Adversus Astrologiam Divinatricem, 1502.) But if the contemporary clinician works with that reality, none the less the relatively recent appearance of masochism as a sexual perversion seems of no concern to the clinician. The task of theorising it remains.

It looks as though the way Freud determines sexual positions is mistaken. And if the characterisation of the masochistic position requires an additional ingredient of another order, then so perhaps does the explanation of femininity and masculinity.

IDENTIFICATION IN DREAMS

Here is the full text of the hysteric's dream of a supper party as reported by Freud: 'I wanted to give a supper-party, but I had nothing in the house but a little smoked salmon. I thought I would go out and buy something, but remembered then that it was Sunday afternoon and all the shops would be shut. Next I tried to ring up some caterers, but the telephone was out of order. So I had to abandon my wish to give a supper-party.'[5]

The hysteric's associations to this dream refer to three people: herself, her husband the butcher, and a woman friend known to them both. The woman friend liked smoked salmon though she begrudged it to herself; the hysteric herself would like a caviare sandwich every morning but had expressly asked her husband *not* to give it to her. The friend had wanted to be invited to supper. The husband, for his part, had announced that *he* was going to lose weight and to this end would accept no more invitations to supper parties. He himself liked ample women; none the less, he sang the praises of the woman friend who was thin.

Freud makes two successive but not contradictory analyses of this dream. Both rely on a triangular situation between the butcher, his wife, the hysteric and their mutual female friend. That is to say that Freud gives the hysteric's jealousy of her friend as the explanation or motivation of the dream. Freud's first interpretation of the dream is that the wife is unable to give any supper parties because she wished not to help her friend to grow any plumper since her husband admires plump women and is already singing her praises. Freud's second interpretation claims that the butcher's wife has *identified* herself with her friend, has put herself in her friend's place. This identity is expressed through the creation of a symptom, a renounced wish, both in the dream where she has to abandon her wish to have a supper party, and in real life where her friend grudges herself smoked salmon and where she herself, the butcher's wife who would love a caviare sandwich every morning, has expressly asked her husband not to give her one.

This is the moment of Freud's introduction of the concept of hysterical identification. Identification has resulted in a symptom and what the symptom signifies is 'sexual relations'. A hysterical woman identifies in her symptoms most readily with people with whom she has had sexual relations or with people who have had sexual relations with the same people as herself. Freud adds that for purposes of identification, mere thoughts of sexual relations would suffice. So the butcher's wife is simply following the rules of hysterical processes in expressing her jealousy of her friend through identification with her. Freud expresses the thought processes of the dream in detail: my patient put herself in her friend's place in the dream because her friend was taking my patient's place with her husband and because she (my patient) wanted to take her friend's place in her husband's high opinion. Here, in embryo, we have the Oedipal triangle and an emphasis on object choice.

Now, it is perfectly possible to construct another interpretation, standing alongside the first, the patient's identification with her friend, which is its equal in every respect. That interpretation concerns the hysteric's identification with her *husband*, the butcher. And it rests on the same triangular situation and the emphasis on object choice. So why has Freud failed to note the hysteric's identification with her husband, especially when the associations to the dream have been so replete with references to him? I shall return to this question in a moment.

Freud's argument for the hysteric's identification with her friend is as follows: the dreamer's wish is that her friend's wish (for a supper party) remain unfulfilled; instead, she dreams that one of her own wishes is unfulfilled; she has thereby put herself in her friend's place. I am saying that in a perfectly parallel fashion she has also put herself in her husband's place. The identification with the husband is given in the following argument: the dreamer's wish is that her husband's wish (for plump women) remain unfulfilled; instead she dreams that one of her own wishes is unfulfilled; she has thereby put herself in her husband's place.

What elements of the analysis might uphold such an identification? In real life, the hysteric grudges herself a caviare sandwich every morning, her friend deprives herself of smoked salmon *and* the husband has announced *his* intention of depriving himself of supper parties because he is too plump! However the element crucial to my interpretation is that the hysteric has asked her husband *not* to give her a caviare sandwich every morning even though she would like one. This connects the husband to an unfulfilled wish and this is a wish whose fulfilment would otherwise make her plump! So she goes so far as to stop herself being plump in order that her husband's wish for plump women not be fulfilled. If she stops herself from being plump *and* the friend's wish for supper parties remains unfulfilled, then the husband's wish for plump women remains unfulfilled. It all fits together.

None the less, Freud does not appear to have noticed his patient's identification with the husband. We may suppose that is because, precisely, it all fits together. This makes the identification with the husband redundant for Freud's purpose which was to explain the hysteric's dream in terms of sexual relations. The identification with the husband would add nothing to this. But for my purposes the hysteric's identification with both the man and the woman *is* important. For it shows that identification does not identify object choice. Perhaps it leaves open the question whether the point of identification is identification itself.

Now when Freud analyses his own dreams, he does not use the qualifier 'hysterical'. Indeed, in tracking down his own identifications, Freud makes no reference to object choice or sexual explanations. And neither will I. Instead of trying to explain his dreams in terms of the analysis of the smoked salmon dream, I want to show how the smoked salmon dream works in some respects just like Freud's dream of the uncle with the yellow beard, which appears a little earlier in *The Interpretation of Dreams*.[6] Because the dream of the uncle demonstrates that identification is the whole point of the dream.

Here is the dream of the uncle with the yellow beard, itself in two parts, first a thought, then a picture. The thought: my friend R was my uncle – I had a great feeling of affection for him. The picture: I saw before me his face, somewhat changed. It was as though it had been drawn out lengthwise. A yellow beard that surrounded it stood out especially clearly.

Freud feels a resistance to interpreting the dream which he tries to say is nonsense. He gradually realises through his associations that if his friend R was his uncle Joseph he would be saying that R was a simpleton. But the uncle was also a criminal; what comparison was he wanting to make? The preamble to the dream tells us that in 1897 Freud had been recommended for appointment as professor *extraordinarius*. But he had reasons for not having great expectations of this. Then he had been visited one evening by a friend in the same position, this friend having pressed an official at the ministry to clarify his chances and to ask whether it was not his being a Jew that was causing the delay. He was met by prevarications and excuses and of course this strengthened Freud's feeling of resignation.... Now, while trying to understand the dream, Freud remembered another conversation with another colleague, N, who had also been recommended for a professorship but had explained that there had been an attempt to blackmail him and that the ministry might use this against him. Freud, he said, had an unblemished character. Freud concludes that N was the criminal he was seeking. There was reason for R and N not being appointed, but these were not denominational. The facts Freud constructed were that one was a simpleton, and the other a criminal. Freud's hopes could then remain untouched.

Freud insists that he did not consider R really a simpleton, nor N a blackmailer, but the dream had indeed expressed his wish that it might be so. He then proceeds to analyse the feeling of affection in the dream as a cover, precisely, for the thoughts about his colleagues. Thus the feeling of

affection serves the purpose of distortion in the dream. For the time being
this is the end of the analysis of the dream which has been discussed in a
chapter dealing with distortion in dreams. But fifty pages later Freud takes
it up again, this time in a section on infantile material. 'To our surprise,'
Freud says, 'we find the child and the child's impulses still living on in the
dream.'[7] Freud now produces another interpretation of the dream just as
he has done with the smoked salmon dream, which leads once again to the
moment of identification in the dream.

Let us see how Freud arrives at the identification which sets this dream in
motion. Freud again takes up his worry about the contradiction in his
waking and dreaming thoughts about R and N. He insists that he does not
recognise in himself the pathological ambition described in his analysis of
the dream. But ambition there was, and Freud traces it back to two
occasions, one dating from the time of his birth, the other from his
childhood. The first occasion was the prophecy of an old peasant woman at
the time of this birth that he would be a great man. On the second occasion
he was told by a poet that he would probably grow up to be a Cabinet
Minister. This had impressed Freud greatly. Freud now sees that in
mishandling his colleagues R and N because they were Jews and in treating
one as a simpleton and the other as criminal, he was behaving like the
Minister, he had put himself in the Minister's place. 'He had refused to
appoint me Professor Extraordinarius and I had retaliated in the dream by
stepping into his shoes.' These are Freud's own words. The Minister's
shoes are the place of the grown-up, the powerful, the superordinate. I
would like to call this stepping into The Bigger Shoes, for beside them
there will always also be laid out The Smaller Shoes. After all, Freud's
identification with his unfortunate colleagues suffuses the entire account of
the dream; it is the backdrop against which the identification with the
Minister is highlighted.

Certainly, the fulfilment of the dream appears to be the act of identification itself. Retrospectively, it has become clear to Freud that his view of his
colleagues is only the means to a deeper wish, the wish to identify with the
Minister. Freud's wish to think ill of his colleagues then becomes what I
shall call an intermediate wish and in a moment we shall locate what might
correspond to this wish in the smoked salmon dream.

So far, the way in which we have presented that dream has suggested
that it fits with Freud's account of hysterical identification. Freud says that
identification 'expresses a resemblance and is derived from a common
element which remains in the unconscious'.[8] This common element is often
sexual in hysteria. Since the mere thought of sexual relations suffices, the
friend qualifies as the figure to be identified with. The identification
produces a symptom, in this case the renounced wish. This wish meets the
condition that hysterical identification be marked by the similarity of
symptoms, since the friend's symptom is also a renounced wish.

On this account, the hysteric's wish that her friend's wish be unfulfilled is an expression of her jealousy in relation to her friend and to her husband. But there is another possible explanation of the hysteric's wish. For this wish plays the same part in the analysis of the dream as the intermediate wish did in Freud's own dream. That is to say that thinking ill of R and N was only a means of identifying with the Minister, and similarly, in the smoked salmon dream, the wish that the friend's wish be unfulfilled is merely a means to the identification. So surely the hysteric no more *really* wishes her friend to remain thin than Freud *really* wished to pass derogatory judgements on his colleagues.

Of course, the same can be said for the intermediate wish I constructed for the hysteric in relation to her husband – her wish that his wish for plump women remain unfulfilled. Surely she does not *really* wish that – for it applies directly to her husband and herself!

I include both the friend and the husband in the summary of my interpretation of the dream. If the butcher's wife denied herself caviare and a supper party it was because she wished to identify herself with her friend and with her husband. Denying herself caviare marks the identification already present in real life. In order to maintain the identification which has been made on the basis of the renunciation of a wish, the hysteric has little choice but to wish that her friend's wish for supper parties and her husband's wish for plump women be denied. It is clear that she cannot have her friend eating her favourite smoked salmon, for that would lead to the collapse of her identification with her friend. And since the friend would be plump if she ate all the smoked salmon she wanted, then the hysteric's identification with the husband would also collapse. In other words, if the friend eats, the friend's wish is fulfilled and the identification collapses; if she eats she also gets plump and then the husband's wish would be satisfied and so that identification would collapse.

What follows if we accept such a reading in which identification is the aim and the relation of our hysteric to both friend and husband is secondary? Must we not reject Freud's model of hysterical identification in the dream? For that model takes the common element in hysteria to be sexual. The difficulty indeed revolves around how we understand the notion of common element because the common element does not appear to be some unconscious sexual element. In the hysteric's dream it is the renounced wish which is the basis of identification and in Freud's dream it is the derogatory judgement of R and N which is the common element. The common element appears to be something contingent which helps to set up the identification.

But it is possible to go further. If we trace back Freud's dreams to an originating moment of identification in Freud's past we light upon something that might be called a primal fact of identification where Freud replaces another and the common element is nowhere and nothing if it is not set up in and through the identification itself. Imagine a childhood where Freud and his nephew John, his senior by a year, are inseparable friends but often come to blows for all that. Freud constructs a fantasy about a moment that cuts across this childhood: there is a dispute over an object, each claiming to have got there before the other. Blows and might prevail over right. In this fantasy it is Freud who is the stronger and takes possession of the field. John complains to an adult and Freud defends himself, 'I hit him 'cos he hit me'. But Freud wins and is deeply satisfied at his victory. It is an original moment of identification with the superiority of the older boy, an identification through which he replaces John. One replaces the other and that is the point of the identification.

IDENTIFICATION AND OBJECT CHOICE IN DORA

I would now like to turn to the case of Dora and ask if it serves to provide examples of hysterical identification in Freud's sense of the term. What is Dora's relation to the Oedipal triangle? I shall try to give some kind of answer by considering how identification and object choice are to be separated in the account of the case, which shows precisely both bisexual object choice and bisexual identifications.

Does identification with a man, a masculine identification, imply the choice of a woman as object and identification with a woman, a feminine identification, imply the choice of a man as love object? The answer in this case at first appears to be 'no'. Dora's identification with her father does not imply the choice of a female object. But perhaps this is a special case because the hysteric can regress to identification while maintaining the attachment to the object. That is to say that she can identify with the love object. With this exception, which in this case is tantamount to making an exception of Dora's identification with her father, it does seem that the identification with one sex implies that the object chosen is that of the opposite sex. And this holds regardless of whether the identification is with a man or a woman. But of course this bisexuality of identification so typical of the hysteric complicates the question of object choice for there are multiple object choices as there are multiple identifications. There is no basis for pre-supposing who is loved (that Herr K. is still young and attractive hardly constitutes an argument that Dora loves him), but neither can it be deduced from identification who Dora loves (when Dora identifies with a male point of view if *does not* follow that she loves Frau K.).

My point is that the matter is even more complicated. Not only are there identifications with the man and with the woman, but an identification with one *implies* an identification with the other. Let us take as an example one of Freud's interpretations of Dora's cough, the one that takes the cough to mark an identification with Frau K. through a fantasy of fellatio. Here is Freud's argument: Dora had insisted that Frau K. only loved her father because he was a 'man of means'. Freud can demonstrate that this phrase indicates its opposite, 'a man without means', a man who is impotent. Dora indeed confirms this but she knows that there is more than one way of obtaining sexual gratification, that parts of the body other than the genitals can be used for this purpose. But Dora refuses to recognise that the irritation in *her* throat and mouth could have anything to do with this.

However, Freud insists that 'the conclusion was inevitable that with her spasmodic cough, which, as is usual, was referred for its exciting cause to a tickling in her throat, she pictured to herself a scene of sexual gratification *per os* between the two people whose love-affair occupied her mind so incessantly'. From this Freud infers a fantasy of fellatio and hence an identification with Frau K.

This inference has not gone unchallenged. What Freud is accused of is a phallocentric option. As Neil Hertz has put it in his article on 'Dora', from Freud's sentence 'she pictured to herself a scene of sexual gratification *per os*' it is not clear 'who is gratifying whom, *per* whose *os* the pleasure is being procured, or with whom Dora is identifying'.[9] What precisely is left open is the possibility that the fantasy is a fantasy of cunnilingus. And indeed Hertz quotes Lacan's correction of Freud. 'Everyone knows that cunnilingus is the artifice most commonly adopted by "men of means" whose powers begin to abandon them'. Freud is thus accused of the phallocentric option because he has come up with the wrong fantasy.

I think this is a mistaken conclusion which has ignored the fact of the interchangeability of positions within a fantasy, something established in Freud's 1915 paper 'Instincts and their Vicissitudes'. Though Hertz himself refers to an interchangeability of positions, he restricts this to the possibility that the mouth, the *os* of the fantasy, might be a male *or* female mouth – the one yielding the fantasy of cunnilingus, the other yielding the fantasy of fellatio. Hertz wants a decision on this and he does not like Freud's decision that the fantasy is one of fellatio.

But surely the thesis of the interchangeability of positions means in this case that whichever fantasy one may opt for, Dora will take a masculine *and* a feminine position: Dora must suck and be sucked regardless. In fact, there is a close parallel between the image of Dora sucking her thumb with a profound oral gratification and the diagram Freud sets out for scopophilia and exhibitionism in his paper on the 'Instincts and their Vicissitudes'. Dora is both subject and object of sucking in just the same way as oneself looking at a sexual organ = a sexual organ being looked at by oneself. It is this preliminary stage of the scopophilic instinct where there is a looking at one's own sexual organ which seems to me just like Dora sucking at an organ of her own body and thus simultaneously being sucked. In 'Instincts and their Vicissitudes' Freud insists, using the concept of ambivalence, that the active and passive forms of the instinct coexist and that we know this through the mechanism of the instinct's satisfaction. Coexistence, then, does not mean that a choice is available between the two forms but rather that whatever the choice, the opposite form of the instinct is also gratified.

However, Freud himself says nothing of the kind in *Dora*. He takes the persistent thumb sucking of childhood as providing the necessary somatic prerequisite for a fantasy of fellatio even in the absence of direct knowledge of such perverse practices. After all, the thumb was prefigured, as Dora's memories make clear, by her nurse's breast. Freud simply substitutes 'the sexual object of the moment', the penis, for both the nipple and the thumb. And that is why his interpretation involves a fantasy of fellatio. Even if we assume that Freud had dubious 'phallocentric' reasons for talking about fellatio, it still remains the case that converting that fantasy into a fantasy of cunnilingus changes nothing. The upholders of this latter interpretation are making the same mistake as Freud in failing to take the thesis of the interchangeability of positions seriously, perhaps because both sides are caught up in the web of the relations of identifications and objects. Both fail to see that it is only as a consequence of the fact that Dora must suck and be sucked regardless, that she identifies both with the woman *and* with the man. They thereby fail to see that object choice is not primary.

There has been much crowing over Freud's tardiness in seeing the importance of the group of thoughts which indicate that the object of Dora's love is Frau K. It is as though it were a question of right and wrong conclusions: it is right to say Dora loves a woman, Frau K.; it is wrong to say Dora loves the man, Herr K. I do not think the problem is about who Dora loves. Dora identifies Frau K. as a woman, which is not the same thing as saying that Dora identifies with Frau K. or that she chooses her as love object.

Freud, of course, does try to establish that Frau K. is Dora's object of love. I shall consider one of his arguments for this conclusion, an argument which stems from his distinction between knowledge gained from oral sources and knowledge gained from encyclopaedic ones. On the one hand, he assumes the woman to be the oral source of sexual knowledge; on the other, he assumes the encyclopaedia to be a male source of such knowledge. So the argument revolves around Dora's identification with the man's point of view (since her associations betray a knowledge of technical words that could only have been learned from an encyclopaedia), an identification which allows Freud to propose an underlying fantasy of defloration from the male point of view. Frau K. is then taken to be the object of this fantasy of defloration. By now you should expect that Dora will, in her turn, figure as the object of defloration in the fantasy. And indeed, Freud also speaks of Herr K. in relation to the fantasy of defloration where it is Dora herself who is deflowered (an implication Freud draws from her fantasy of childbirth). Dora is both subject and object of the fantasy.

Having indicated that Freud's means of establishing the nature of Dora's relation to Frau K. are insufficient to determine that relation I want to comment on the oral/written distinction itself. It should be clear, though Freud is not explicit on this, that if there is identification with male discourse, then there must also be identification with female discourse. Freud is saying that there are oral and written sources of sexual knowledge for Dora and that these coincide with female and male sources of knowledge. In so far as Dora speaks of female anatomy with encyclopaedic men's words she puts herself in a male place. By the same token, then, Dora's use of sexually ambiguous words that could only have been picked up from women's speech must put her in a female place.

Having said that the identification with male discourse must be matched by an identification with female discourse we should perhaps interrogate Freud's logic in the first place. That logic suggests that reading encyclopaedias is a male activity and that any woman who reads encyclopaedias must be identifying with a male position. Has Freud simply fabricated the oral/written distinction here? Is this sheer male, nineteenth-century prejudice? Or might it be that Dora herself is utilising this distinction to some end, albeit unconsciously? The fabricated oral/written distinction we are dealing with fits well with a familiar mapping of on the one hand, children, so-called primitives, the mad and women; and on the other hand, civilised society and men. That is to say, we could construct two sets of binary opposition such that one set went with the feminine and the other with the masculine.

If Dora is making such an implicit distinction, what then does that distinction mark? I think Freud is right to pick up the distinction and infer identifications with male and female discourse. But we must note that there is something special in this identification with the place of the male and of the female, something different from the identification which has so far been characterised. The identification with the female position does not imply an identification with the male position also and neither does a reverse identification hold. This is unlike the fluidity of the positions in a fantasy where masculine implies feminine and vice versa. We appear to be dealing with something which is not quite hysterical identification.

Utilising the 'cultural' hypothesis I have just outlined leads to the suggestion that there can be a point, a resting place, a temporary arrest of the oscillation of the drive made possible by identification with one term of a culturally given distinction. That is to say that we might speak of masculine and feminine positions but that these, in so far as they imply relatively stable positions, are the product of cultural distinctions. So what exactly is the influence on what constitutes masculine and feminine positions?

We can continue to use the oral/written distinction and we can start by looking at moments in which Freud constitutes himself as feminine, moments that he retrospectively describes from a position that he takes to be fully masculine. Here I am indebted to Hertz who, in the article on Dora referred to earlier, deftly makes the links on the one hand between a knowledge gained from oral sources and Freud's femininity, and on the other between the transcending of these oral sources of knowledge and a scientific, masculine Freud. You will also see how in establishing Freud's femininity Hertz used the pairs I began with, activity/passivity, superordination/subordination.

So how does Hertz establish Freud's femininity? His argument is that Freud needs to make a separation between his knowledge and Dora's knowledge since they both derive from oral sources. And Hertz argues that pursuing this goal has consequences for the treatment of the case. But what is relevant here is that as an analogy to what is happening in the Dora case, Hertz refers to some anecdotes from the beginning of 'The History of the Psychoanalytic Movement' (1914).[10] There Freud tells three stories about three men, Breuer, Charcot and Chrobak, who had all communicated a piece of knowledge, the knowledge that neurosis had a sexual aetiology, without really possessing that knowledge themselves. Hertz, while arguing that Freud is almost flaunting his femininity in these anecdotes, describes Freud's role in them as what he calls Impressionable Junior Colleague.

In the second anecdote, Freud gives an account of overhearing a conversation in French between Charcot and Brouardel. Here Hertz makes a particularly telling analysis. Charcot is saying that it is always a sexual matter, Freud is almost paralysed by amazement but soon forgets the scene, being totally absorbed by the experimental induction of hysterical paralyses. Hertz links these two allusions to paralysis as part of his comment on this scene.

> Freud's distinctly marginal relation to this scene of professional knowingess, almost out of earshot, listening to two men talking – in French, of course – about suggestive matters, *secrets d'alcove*, locates him close to the position of the woman in his analysis of obscene jokes, just as his being paralyzed with amazement aligns him with the (mostly female) victims of hysterical paralysis. In his innocence, in his capacity to receive impressions, he is feminized.[11]

In the third anecdote Chrobak takes Freud aside and tells him that the cause of a female patient's anxiety is her husband's impotence but that all a medical man could do was to shield the domestic misfortune with his own reputation. Hertz comments, and I continue to paraphrase, that Freud is glancing at the structures of complicity that keep the sexual aetiology of the neuroses a well-kept smoking-room secret. While he does not remain in the position of the hysteric taking in knowledge he does not know he has, he none the less remains outside the circle of collegiality. Freud can only put himself into the world of Oedipal rivalry by asserting his intention to be serious about this knowledge, bringing it into the light of conscious reflection and doing so by using a distinction between a casual flirtation and a legal marriage. Hertz points out that then Freud can deploy this knowledge, acquired after the manner in which the hysteric acquires *her* knowledge, as a proper *technique*.

What does this very suggestive analysis actually tell us? We start with the figure of Freud, the feminine, the junior colleague. In the end, he does succeed in overtaking his masculine seniors. That is to say that in the end he is victorious. The feminine is what is *before* taking possession of the field, before the victory. The feminine is the position of the junior colleague being beaten, the younger Freud being beaten by his older nephew, John. But Freud the hysteric, the feminised, the beaten, is transformed into Freud victorious, in possession of the field.

You might well say, so there you are, the feminine can indeed be relinquished and transcended, the masculine can indeed be put in place. But I have left out the *reason* why Freud is victorious: Freud is victorious because he establishes scientific knowledge; he is victorious *qua* masculine scientist. Note that the scientist is masculine by definition, by a culturally produced definition. What stabilises Freud's masculine position is his identification with a discourse which is culturally designated masculine. But as Hertz shows elsewhere in his article, for Freud the man, Dora's analyst, there remains a constant struggle to transcend the oral sources of knowledge which psychoanalytic practice necessarily involves, to avoid the feminine position, for there is no general sense in which he can have put himself beyond and outside it.

MASOCHISM, FEMININITY AND THE OEDIPUS COMPLEX

I now return to the question of what femininity and masculinity are for Freud. I have already indicated how Freud relates these terms to superordination/subordination and to activity/passivity. I now want to consider their relation to sadism and masochism, a relation which is largely mediated through the distinction between activity and passivity in Freud's 1919 paper 'A Child is Being Beaten', which traces the vicissitudes of the instinct which lead to a masochistic position.[12] Here we encounter a familiar problem, the problem of how the multiplicity of the positions available for identification – in a fantasy of a child being beaten, the positions of the beaten, the beater and the onlooker – can be channelled into a relatively stable sexual position that we call masochism.

Now Freud's 1919 paper is particularly interesting because it is clear that in this case the choice of object does not determine identification in any simple way. Where the beating fantasy is found in adults, Freud supposes

'A Child is Being Beaten'

Phase	Girl	Boy
I	*The father is beating the child* (the father loves me alone; I hate the other child; the father hates the other child; the father is beating the other child)	—
II	*I am being beaten by the father*	*I am being beaten by the father*
III	*A child is being beaten* boys are beaten by a male authority figure	*A child is being beaten* boys are being beaten by a woman

Phase		*Sex of the beaten*	*Sex of the beater*	*Place of the subject*	*The drive*
I	G	a child (masc. or fem.)	the father	spectator	sadistic
	B	—	—	—	—
II	G	the subject	the father	the beaten	masochistic
	B	the subject	the father	the beaten	masochistic
III	G	children (masc.)	a male authority figure	spectator	sadistic in form masochistic in content
	B	children (masc.)	a woman		masochistic

an Oedipus complex that has taken the initial form of an incestuous relation to the father for both boy and girl. But while this passive position in relation to the father leads to masochism and femininity in the case of the *boy*, the outcome for the girl is a masochistic content in a sadistic form and is *not* femininity. What then determines this difference in outcome of sexual positions? Is this a moment when Freud produces some account of fixing by explaining this difference?

Let us look at the fantasy in more detail with the help of the tabular summary which I have put together from Freud's paper. The first point is that the conscious fantasies I have referred to so far are to be located at phase III. 'A child is being beaten' is the fantasy as reported by Freud's patients and the details elaborated around that are drawn out in the course of the analysis. Freud provides verbalisations for the two preceding phases as follows: for phase I, 'the father is beating the child' and for phase II,

'I am being beaten by the father'. The sentence for phase I and the elaborations around it are Freud's summary of the first incestuous phase of the fantasy. The sentence for phase II, 'I am being beaten by the father' is an inference that Freud makes, but which is wholly unconscious in the subject.

How do the sexual positions signalled by the final conscious forms of the fantasy relate to the other earlier forms? Very briefly, phase I is the original incestuous fantasy; both the boy and the girl have a fantasy of being loved by the father. This Oedipal fantasy undergoes repression. But since the Oedipal wishes persist in the unconscious, a sense of guilt appears. The phase II form of the fantasy 'I am being beaten by the father' is thus a punishment; but it is also a substitute for the forbidden genital relation. The original fantasy has also undergone regression to an anal-sadistic organisation and in this way it still satisfies sexual love. When the unconscious fantasy of phase II is substituted for by the final conscious fantasy we get 'a child is being beaten'. There has been a further repression.

I have already mentioned that the final fantasy is differently elaborated by the man and by the woman. The lower half of the tabular summary shows that four things can vary: the sex of the beaten, the sex of the beater, the place of the subject and the content of the drive. The variations can take place between phases for one sex or between sexes at any one phase. In phase II there is no such difference between the girl and the boy. However in phase III as you know, there is significant variation. Now it is this variation that leads Freud to conclude that the man is masochistic and feminine but that the girl has given up her femininity, gets masochistic pleasure in the fantasy, but is above all a spectator.

Freud's conclusion is based on this difference in the final versions of the male and female fantasies: that in the female fantasy boys are being beaten by a male authority figure and that in the male fantasy boys are being beaten by a woman. The argument for the female fantasy is as follows: first, that the fact that it is boys who are beaten shows that the girl has given up her feminine role and wants to be a boy; second, that none the less the satisfaction derived from it is masochistic; and finally, that since the girl is not really herself *in* the scene, she is really a spectator *of* the scene. The argument for the male fantasy is that it retains its masochistic form because it is *boys* who continue to be beaten and it retains its genital significance and hence the feminine position for the boy because the figure doing the beating remains of the opposite sex.

Can this argument possibly be right? Is there not a certain arbitrariness in the way Freud assigns certain forms of the fantasy to men and others to women? Certainly since Freud there have been numerous accounts both of masochistic fantasies and of masochistic performances in which the masochist of either sex might occupy any of the three positions of the beating fantasy. The final form of the fantasy is not fixed, either in the sense that there is one form found in women and another in men, or in the sense that the subject occupies only one position in fantasy or in deed. Something about masochism eludes Freud.

We could also ask whether the terms 'passive' and 'feminine' are crucial to an account of masochism. Reading modern accounts of masochism it seems not only that the passivity is at best secondary, but more importantly has nothing to do with femininity.[13] Moreover, it seems that it is not the father who stands behind the figure of the beater; this of course under-mines the derivation of the argument about the child's passivity and femininity.

So the passive, feminine position in the fantasy scenario or indeed in a real scenario is not constitutive of the masochistic position. But if maso-chism is not the fixing of the subject on some terrain laid out by the couples masculinity/femininity, activity/passivity, what is it? As a first step let me introduce the notion of a masochistic scenario. This is a scene of sexual excitement, an enactment of a drama whose plot is agreed and which unfolds in a contractual space: a space of precise timing; of repetition, of suspense, of signification. Partaking in this scenario is a necessary if not sufficient condition of masochism as sexual perversion. It becomes a sufficient condition when this scenario, governed by a particular organisa-tion of pleasure, signifies a certain relation to the Law. It is a sufficient condition, that is, when the subject's role in the masochistic scenario signifies the abolition of the father in the symbolic and hence a subversion of the Law.

What the masochist is doing, and it is quite contrary to Freud, is to defy castration and disavow sexual difference. And this of course is a complete travesty of the Law the Oedipus complex is supposed to institute. It is important to note that the masochist's disavowal does not make him psychotic; his perversion is a stable position grounded in his refusal of the symbolic father and in his contract with the phallic mother. The masochist can subvert the Law because he too knows the paradox of conscience that Freud had recognised, the paradox that the more strictly the Law is adhered to, the greater the guilt. And he submits to the Law all the better to make a fool of it; for he takes his punishment first, in order to experience the forbidden pleasure.

Freud went wrong because rather than rely on masochists and the masochistic scenario, he thought he could develop his account on the basis of a whole set of mixed cases which had beating fantasies as the only common factor. So he develops the account on the basis of cases of hysteria, obsessional neurosis, and so forth. He thereby misses both the specific scenario that is of such importance to masochism and the explana-tion that is specific to masochism. Of course, particular fantasies are not the sole prerogative of any person or group. But it is important to see that a particular fantasy might have a particular signification in some cases; in our present context, those cases precisely that are designated masochist. And in spite of the fact that many kinds of people may have the fantasy, it is none the less crucial to the masochist.

So Freud did not attend to what I will call the reality of the masochistic practices which might have informed his interpretation of the fantasy. Now, contemporary psychoanalytic writings on masochistic practices give an account of the perversion which is fundamentally different from Freud's. But to say that contemporary writings show an understanding of what specifically masochism is today is not the same as saying that contemporary writings give us an explanation of the reality of masochism as a sexual position. That is to say that they do not account for the appearance of this specific perversion in our culture, for this masochism of the bedroom which is such a recent phenomenon. Contemporary analysts seem no more interested in this question than Freud. Of course analysts are not obliged to theorise reality. They are part of it; they practice at the same time and in the same place as their analysands. None the less, as I have argued at length elsewhere, reality is underdetermined by the psychical and that reality remains to be theorised.[14] We do not thereby move outside the realm of the psyche, for reality of course always exists for a subject.

OSCILLATION AND THE OEDIPUS COMPLEX

I will now take up my argument that Freud has no account of the fixing of sexual positions in relation to that femininity and masculinity that are supposed to be constituted by the Oedipus complex. Here if anywhere, some mechanism to explain the fixing of sexual positions should be found. But you will be disappointed if you expect that. For what is at stake in the Oedipal situation in relation to masculinity and femininity is hysterical identification. It should be clear that given my account of hysterical identification, we shall not have any satisfactory explanation of how femininity and masculinity are knotted into positions of relative fixity.

So, Freud's Oedipus complex.

In the most schematic version of the Oedipus complex the boy is supposed to end up relinquishing the mother as love object and identifying with the father and the girl should end up identifying with the mother, though her case is much more complicated. Note that the identification of which Freud is speaking here is regressive identification. In chapter 3 of *The Ego and the Id* Freud suggests that perhaps the sole condition under which the id can give up its objects is identification with those objects.[15] Which is to say that object choice regresses to identification in the Oedipal situation. But this is *not* what we usually find, as Freud admits. The boy's love object was the mother but he does not identify with her; he identifies with the father. It is clear that regressive identification is not what is at stake here. Then what is? My answer is: hysterical identification.

Why do I say that hysterical identification is involved in the Oedipus Complex? Well, two years earlier in *Group Psychology and the Analysis of the Ego* Freud had given an example of the complete mechanism of hysterical identification. The example was of a girl's cough, a cough identifying her with her mother, her rival in the Oedipal situation; the cough thereby signified her father as object choice.[16] Freud was giving examples of hysterical symptom formation and this one is fully Oedipal. In this identification the ego is borrowing the features of the object so as to copy it in its relation to others. But this object is not the love object. Just such an identification appears to determine the femininity of girls and the masculinity of boys.

I have argued that hysterical identification is not a mechanism that fixes or stabilises positions. Hysterical identification is the mechanism which allows the play of bisexuality both at the level of object choice and at the level of identification. This play of bisexuality fits in surprisingly well with Freud's account of the complete Oedipus complex in chapter three of *The Ego and the Id*. The complete complex is composed of the negative as well as the positive Oedipus complex. For example, the boy, in addition to loving the mother and being hostile to the father will show 'an affectionate feminine attitude' to his father and a hostility toward the mother. Now the point is that the positive and negative forms of the Oedipus complex are not alternatives; the complete Oedipus complex is present in everyone. And this complete form of the complex which necessarily produces ambivalence towards the parents is to be attributed perhaps entirely, Freud suggests, to bisexuality and not to identification resulting from rivalry.

The Oedipus complex then, consists of four trends, affection for and hostility to the mother and affection for and hostility to the father. How do these four trends stemming from bisexuality come to result in sexual division? Freud says that the four trends produce both a mother identification and a father identification which are somehow 'united with each other' to produce masculinity or femininity. Notice that for Freud the mother identification and the father identification which he attributes to bisexuality are the product of the coupling of object choice and identification. That is to say that the identification with the mother results from the taking of the father as love object and the identification with the father results from taking the mother as love object. Thus Freud has already taken an implicit step in his explanation of the fixing of sexual difference; he has separated one identification from the other. The two coexist, but one does not imply the other. He has thereby set up two sexual dispositions. But even if we accept that there are two such dispositions in each one of us, how is the choice between them made? To appeal, as Freud does, to the priority of one of the sexual dispositions is clearly no help at all as it merely contradicts the assumption of an initial bisexuality whose transformation into heterosexuality we are trying to explain.

This problem of the fixing of sexual difference was, of course, prefigured the moment we identified hysterical identification as the mechanism involved in the production of masculinity and femininity within the Oedipus complex, because hysterical identification (as I have shown) involves the oscillation, not the fixing, of positions.

I am not saying that humans do not take up positions of relative fixity, live their lives as masculine, feminine, or whatever. But I *am* saying that psychoanalysis contains at least one theory of sexual difference that does not work, which leaves us with an insistent play of bisexuality within the complex of relations that seem to form an everpresent Oedipal situation. How that which we take to be our Oedipal resolutions comes about has to be another story.

You must be exclaiming to yourselves, 'Has she really failed to see that Freud himself has told that other story about fixing, the story which features the phallus?' Indeed this feature of Freud's other story has not escaped my notice. But I do want to emphasise that there are *two* stories and that Freud conflates them. That is to say that he conflates the story concerned with the Law and the phallus with the story about the oscillation of the drive. He is right in thinking that the positions of femininity, masculinity, perversion, can be defined through the subject's relation to the phallus; he is wrong in thinking that these positions can be defined in terms of the oscillatory pairs.

Since we have identified a conflation we must separate the two things in Freud; we must separate the necessity for the subject to live its sexuality in relation to the phallus from the particular form/content of femininity/masculinity. Until now it has seemed that the latter is derived from the former. I have shown that in fact Freud tries to derive his form/content via another story which turns out, moreover, to be an unsatisfactory one. I say form/content because quite properly there is no distinction between these in Freud. The passivity, masochism, subordination of femininity is no more form than it is content (as against the argument of some feminists that there is no content in Freud's concept of femininity). But then it is not possible to relativise the Freudian notion of femininity by reference to its content alone; it is necessary to relativise the Freudian concept of femininity itself. Freud takes the form/content of masculinity/femininity to be inseparable from the necessity of the phallus. My point is a different one: Freud's form/content constitutes one particular relation to the phallus and since it cannot be derived from his argument, perhaps it is to be explained by some reference to reality. Our question must then be, 'Where do masculinities and femininities come from?'

Notes

1. Juliet Mitchell and Jacqueline Rose, 'Feminine Sexuality: Interview – 1982', *m/f* no. 8 (1983), pp. 14–15. (Available from 24 Ellerdale Road, London NW3 6BB, UK.)
2. Mikkel Borch-Jacobsen, *Le Sujet Freudien* (Flammarion, Paris, 1981); translated as *The Freudian Subject* (Macmillan, London, 1989).
3. Sigmund Freud, 'Fragment of an Analysis of a Case of Hysteria' ('Dora') (1905 [1901]), *SE* VII, p. 48; PFL 8, p. 81.
4. S. Freud, *Three Essays on the Theory of Sexuality* (1905), *SE* VII, p. 159; *PFL* 7, p. 73; 'Instincts and their Vicissitudes' (1915), *SE* XIV, pp. 127, 129–30; *PFL* 11.
5. S. Freud, *The Interpretation of Dreams* (1900), *SE* IV–V, p. 147; *PFL* 4, p. 229.
6. *SE* IV–V, p. 137; *PFL* 7, p. 218.
7. *SE* IV–V, pp. 191–2; *PFL* 7, p. 280.
8. *SE* IV–V, p. 150; *PFL* 7, p. 233.
9. Neil Hertz, 'Dora's Secrets, Freud's Techniques', in Charles Bernheimer and Claire Kahane (eds), *In Dora's Case: Freud, Hysteria, Feminism* (Columbia University Press, New York, 1985), p. 228.
10. S. Freud, 'On the History of the Psycho-Analytic Movement' (1914), *SE* XIV; *PFL* 15.
11. Hertz, 'Dora's Secrets. . .', p. 239.
12. S. Freud, 'A Child is Being Beaten' (1919), *SE* XVII; *PFL* 10.
13. See, for example, Theodor Reik, *Masochism in Modern Man* (Grove Press, New York, 1941); Gilles Deleuze, *Masochism: An Interpretation of Coldness and Cruelty* (Georges Braziller, London, 1971); Joyce McDougall, *A Plea for a Measure of Abnormality* (International Universities Press, New York, 1980).
14. Parveen Adams, 'Of Female Bondage', in Teresa Brennan (ed.), *Between Feminism and Psychoanalysis* (Routledge, London, 1989).
15. S. Freud, *The Ego and the Id* (1923), *SE* XIX; *PFL* 11.
16. S. Freud, *Group Psychology and the Analysis of the Ego* (1921), *SE* XVIII, p. 106; *PFL* 12, pp. 135–6.

7

A Question of Survival:
Nations and Psychic States

Homi K. Bhabha

Can there be culture without melancholia? This seems to be the central question posed by contemporary theories of representation which repeatedly associate the making of narrative with the death of the author. What dies with the author is not merely intentionality in interpretation. In its wake arises the figure of the textual sign that resists the 'innate' or autonomous coherence of the corpus and locates meaning on the boundaries of that loss that generates meaning, turning interpretation into an inevitable passage through the intertextual. For Derrida, the process of writing is a form of survival, or living on the borderline[1] of the violence of the letter and its doubles – mark, trace, crypt. For Lacan the scenario of the birth of the ego is staged in the 'fading' of the signifier, as it hangs over the abyss of a dizzy assent in which, he says, we see the very essence of anxiety.[2] Even Lyotard's comic Oedipus, who refuses the melancholic moment of modernity in the postmodern condition, has finally to concede that the terror of 'death' in all its forms traverses the pragmatics of language games and leads him to question the social bond.[3]

If all this sounds rather like a French farce with rapid introductions and hasty withdrawals, my purpose is to translate this scenario of *communicatio interruptus* into quite other narrative worlds. The impulse for this essay emerges from my sense that the 'meaning' of culture that survives *after* poststructuralism reveals the limits, and limitations, of that idea of cultural modernity contained in the concept of an ideal community being both homogeneous and horizontal. This idea is deeply ingrained within the social sciences and is representatively voiced by Hannah Arendt when, in describing the social process of 'normalisation' within mass society, she suggests that 'the victory of equality in the modern world is only the

89

political and legal recognition of the fact that society has conquered the public realm and that distinction and matters of difference have became private matters of the individual'.[4] More recently, writing in the shadow of the *Satanic Verses* controversy, Fay Weldon suggests a solution to the cultural conflict in multiethnic societies on the lines of the American uniculturalist policy 'welding its new peoples, from every race, every nation, every belief into a whole: let the child do what it wants at home; here in the school the one flag is saluted, the one God worshipped, the one nation acknowledged'.[5] Within theories of *communicatio interruptus* there survives a sense of the dispersal of community – *communitas interruptus*. This sense of social liminality is well-expressed in Paul de Man's description of the relation of trope to meaning – 'the nonadequation of symbol to symbolized' – as a process of displacement and fragmentation, 'a wandering, an errance, a kind of permanent exile, if you wish'.[6]

What vision of the coherence of community is possible when the language of cultural symbolisation reveals such a disjunction within the 'sign' of the social? The resistance to totalising the concepts of Nation or Culture is not merely the deft performance of a semiotic sleight-of-hand. To deny the social text its transparency, to question the 'visual' epistemology within which its reality-effects are secured, is to throw open the question of the discursive representation of 'the people' – its strategies of identification and its processes of affiliation. What is identified as the people in the language of the culture? What do the people identify *with* in the rhetoric of the national community? The cutting edge of such questions is revealed in the recent attention to the role of narrative in the construction of the signifying space of national culture. For instance, Benedict Anderson's influential essay *Imagined Communities* suggests that the social narrative of the modern nation is made possible by an apprehension of cultural simultaneity within 'homogeneous empty time'. According to Anderson, the articulation of this historical temporality as a form of cultural subjection – as a medium through which social subjects are collectively identified as the imagined community – 'is a special kind of contemporaneous community which language alone suggests'.[7] The position of the people as enunciatory subjects is developed in Anderson's trope of harmony: Unisonance. It is the production of the national text in a kind of political love for the patria, emblematically seen in the national anthem. Through its utterance it binds the people into a contemporary community 'in which simultaneity is, as it were, transverse cross time, marked not by prefiguring and fulfilment, but by temporal coincidence.'[8] It is a cultural territory of imaginary sound that brings together in the same homogeneous empty time, the selfless citizen and the nation. But is such naturalisation of nationality possible? Musn't we ask with Derrida whether 'the people' will so unanimously, and transparently assemble in the self-presence of its speech? Anderson argues that English-speakers, when they hear the words

'Earth to earth, ashes to ashes, dust to dust', get a *ghostly intimation of simultaneity across homogeneous empty time*, an intimation of *as it were ancestral Englishness*. Despite Anderson's adherence to Auerbach and the narrative of 'national' realism, there is an alienation of the claim to continuity and holism in the ancestry of the English nation which is apparent in the metaphoricity of the language itself. The simultaneity of the Nation – its contemporaneity – can only be articulated in the language of archaism, as a ghostly repetition; a gothic production of past-presentness. In the simulacra of the nation's simultaneity – in the artifice of the people's unisonance – arises, uncannily, the sepulchral 'otherness' of national identity.

Should we then not re-read differently the discursive signs of the *unisonance* of national identity as set out by Anderson – simultaneity, homogeneous empty time, the selfless subject, the disinterested nation? The occasion for this reading of the performativity of patriotism will be Anderson's reference to the burial litany: *Earth to Earth, Ashes to Ashes, Dust to Dust*. If I choose the ritual of burial to talk about this uncanny 'simultaneity' that marks the life of the national people, it is because Anderson so insistently places the birth of patriotism in the event of death; and the *momento mori*, like the burial litany, and the patriotic performance, belongs in part to life and in part to death.

What is striking about this phrase spoken by the living in the place of death and of the dead in the place of life, is the process of repetition through which it stages a 'play' of substitutability between time past and present, between part and whole, between metaphor and metonym. Read from the *intimation of simultaneity*, from an *ancestral Englishness*, it is possible to see a logic of equivalence internally between *Earth and Earth* – and a transformational, metaphoric narrative that progressively reduces Earth to dust. In the continual exchange and identification of the binary division, the cloud is dialectically sublated in the clod and the process of death as divine nature is revealed before us, satisfying the authority of the English Church and the English state. In this illocutionary act of national filiation, the conditions of simultaneity and contemporaneity seem to be met. But what about the people, the survivors who speak the litany, the living who speak in the words of the dead?

This question demands that we repeat the litany of English patriotism from the point of view of those figurative moments in Anderson's original gloss on the burial service which, for him, trace the heroic memory of national tradition. For us, they introduce the notion of repetition as doubling, imitation, mimicry, archaism: a *ghostly* intimation of simultaneity, an *as it were* ancestral Englishness. These adjectives do not merely add a sense of pastness and continuity to the content of the ceremony. Marked in the language of repetition, they make us aware of the disjunctive, non-synchronous linguistic moment which is articulated within the most affective and unisonant discourse of the imagined community.

Read through this archaic doubling, the repetition of *Earth to Earth* raises a referential and epistemological problem in the very naming of the English. The litany is no longer simply the metaphoric story of birth and death but, for us survivors, the metonymic tale of that part of death which is also life, the lives that get taken apart by untimely death; a fable of the *corps morcelé*. For which repetition of earth or ashes or dust names Life and which names Death? The use of the same signifier to name both the places or spaces in the agonism of life and death represents a problem of translation – an uncertainty in this specific utterance, in the naming of the people – which puts under erasure the homogeneous time of simultaneity and the spatial substitution/equivalence of metaphor, but nevertheless *recognises* a difference between life and death and the obligation to mark a boundary (though not a binary or dualistic one).

If you listen to what is articulated in this unauthorised version of the funeral litany, it is not the synchronous voice of national Unisonance, nor is it some simply unrepresentable negativity or difference. It is a complex, cryptic figure of enunciation, where what is spatially differentiated as Life/Death, is temporally re-inscribed in that repetition of signs – *Earth to Earth*. What is temporally differentiated as *Earth–Ashes–Dust*, and its endless roundelay, is then spatially inscribed in the repetition of the same, Earth/earth, Dust/dust. In both cases there is an uncanny performance of substitutability and in that very act an impossibility of simultaneity. The ambivalence of the naming or meaning of life or death is always less than one and double; always in need of an impossible translation. What 'time' fixes, the spatial dimension undoes.

Now you listen to the patriotic utterance with a very different ear from the one that Benedict Anderson appeals to as the heroic memory of the English tongue whose semantic affect is untranslatable but whose full-throated sound is transcendent. For you have now heard the hesitation in the inscription of the people – not the heroic memory but the ghostly ancestry – and you have read the Englishness of language not as she is spoken but, as it were, written between the lines.

What the national 'past' articulates is that space of repetition, the enunciation of ghostly simultaneity; a doubling that is always produced in the present of the nation's discursive performance, *as prior to it*, as an anteriority. Anteriority locates a spatial time of the people that is caught between the fantasmatic trope of archaic tradition – its incessant *repetition* of ancestry – and the need to name the people in the historical present. It is in this sense that appeal to the old English and their ghostly contemporaneity should be understood in the patriotic poem that follows:

> From Guilsboro' to Northampton all the way
>   Under a full red August moon,
> I wandered down. . . Yet the air
>   Seemed throng and teeming, as if hosts

> Of living presences were everywhere;
> And I imagined they were ghosts
> Of the old English [...]
> Now in the warm still night arising, filled
> The broad air with their company,
> And hovering in the fields that once they tilled,
> Brooded on England's destiny.

That was Enoch Powell. It is the function of the excessive symbol-fetishism in such writing that Tom Nairn, in *The Break-up of Britain*, finds most intriguing.[9] Is it simply an archaic surface or is there something more meaningful *behind* it, some ideological *content*? By suggesting, above, that the overheated, baroque language of archaism, of the national past, contains in its articulation of time the semiotic space of anteriority, I have suggested that the accumulative sense of a settled and continuous national tradition is disturbed by a spectral repetition. It is across this unreality, from this sense of national time that cannot be conscious of itself, that the national discourse is both constructed, and becomes a site of disturbance and contestation. Surface and depth are then not the dimensions of meaning that adequately represent the sign of the nation's people. The overwritten obviousness of the national discourse shares that uncanny, obscure transparency that Foucault attributes to the enunciative function: 'Like the over-familiar that constantly eludes one; those familiar transparencies, which, although they conceal nothing in their density, are not entirely clear.'[10] This process echoes in the collective recognition of Englishness as rooted in the 'expressivism' of the English language; but the Englishness of the language itself is paradoxically unrootable, part of the unconscious of its usage, the fantasm of its audibility, finally untranslatable.

In the persistence of the ghost of simultaneity, in the *as-it-wereness* of an English ancestry, we can see the construction of a temporality of writing the nation that changes the very notion of the past as the truth of tradition, and changes too the structure of historical memory. 'Why do nations celebrate their hoariness not their astonishing youth?' asks Benedict Anderson in a more recent essay.[11] Why does this pre-eminent form of the modern cultural community only recall its presence in a putative antiquity? It is the process of remembering-to-forget that gives the national culture its deep psychological hold and its political legitimacy. Stressing Renan's strange syntax of the national memory – *All French citizens are obliged to have forgotten Saint Barthelmy and the massacres of the Midi in the thirteenth century* – Anderson suggests that the textual effect of this forgetting-to-remember produces that sense of national identification, rather like the surprise in looking at old family photographs, that elicits a unisonant – *Ah oui!* But can the troublesome tense of forgetting – to be obliged to have forgotten, to have already forgotten – yield such a naturalised form of national narrative?

Anderson writes that this remembering–forgetting is a defence against the conflict between the 'natural' limits and the political aspirations of the nation: its limited secular stretch (when contrasted with world religions); its limited identity amidst the irreducible plurality of nations; its sense of natural fatality; its fixity in geographical space; its inscription in local vernaculars. The textual symptoms of this conflict are the jump-cut periodisations and fast-forward projections that characterise national histories but these are, according to Anderson, overcome in the serial alignment of homogeneous empty time that 'makes each death not an end but a foreshadowing of each succeeding death, in a long movement towards a resplendent living present'.[12] Need I repeat, in the midst of this resplendent living present, the problematic temporality and textuality of the patriotic speech-act that I demonstrated earlier – *Earth to Earth, Ashes to Ashes, Dust to Dust*?

The archaic time and tense of the national memory – to be obliged to have already forgotten in order to be reminded – will not be so simply normalised; as the repetition of death in the nation's present will not be so easily naturalised. For the temporal pulsation of the remembering–forgetting opens up another 'time of the present' that splits the very movement of homogeneous time, and its representation of the historical. For the archaic forgetting that restores to the memory of the nation its modern community is also the mark of its impossible self-presence. The myth of progress is arrested in the time of its enunciation for as Benjamin has glimpsed it, the Angel of History[13] has his face turned to the debris of the past while his wings are carried into the future. The discursive effect of the splitting of enunciation introduces an anteriority that faces every resplendant moment with the petrification of its presence, its archaic, uncanny double. The Lacanian phallus, for instance, can only play its role veiled, for the demon of Scham always rises when it is unveiled. The temporal production of the past must always come across this afterlife, survive this space of meaning that is double and split. That is why the invention of tradition is not the passage between a soiled present and a glorious future, but always that uncertain space produced in the in-between of the archaic. The gap between the English and their as-it-were ancestry refuses to close or metaphorise, refuses to name without evoking a ghostly simultaneity. In his fine meditation on the symbolic as Babelian performance, Derrida introduces the figure of translation through a fable of colonial violence.[14] The Semites demand a unisonant people, gathered together in the simultaneity of their name, at once an act of colonial violence and the promise of a transparent community. God, however, imposes his ambivalent name, that inscribes the desire for translation, rupturing the rational transparency of any act of meaning or signification, and ending, at the same time, the colonial violence. From this emerges that obligation to read any inscription of the 'originary' or the 'correspondential' – those two tropes that are central to the sense of a culture of community – as a form of supplementarity and retroaction. The originary is always *in* the process of *restoration*, not simply the simultaneity of ancestry or antiquity, but also the distance (and distanciation) of anteriority, the temporality of which is the future anterior – as Derrida describes it, 'to render that which must have been given'.[15] If the very structure of the metaphoricity of language – its act of filiation – emerges from this indebted, retroactive movement of filiation – *that which must have been given* – then its structure echoes that non-homogeneous time of national discourse that I have been trying to establish. That sense of the past, or the origin of ancestry, does not produce a resplendent, continuist national present; in the figure of the archaic, out of the alterity of the nation's historical present, emerges that reference to the future anterior of the nation – that space in which its authority and genealogy is established in relation to that which must have been given. It is remarkable how uncannily similar is this 'time' of *écriture* to Renan's writing of the national memory – the *translation* of tradition – as being obliged to forget the nation's past in order to remember it retroactively in the construction of the national community. The disruptions of national memory are historically diverse and differently written. In an essay so concerned to disrupt the claim that the 'imagined community' is inscribed in an homogeneous empty time, I want to turn now to a language of national diaspora and cultural displacement that weaves the narrative of national belonging around a tragic sense of the loss of both nation and narration. The Palestinians, in the words of Edward Said:

> The Palestinians are a commodity. Producing ourselves much as the masabih, lamps, tapestries, baskets, embroideries, mother-of-pearl trinkets are produced. We turn ourselves into objects not for sale but for scrutiny. People ask us, as if looking into an exhibit case, What is it you Palestinians want? – as if we can put our demands into a neat single phrase.
>
> When did we become a people? When did we stop being one? Or are we in the process of becoming one? We frequently end our letters with the mottoes 'Palestinian love' or 'Palestinian kisses'. . .
>
> The present tense is subject to echoes from the past, verbs of sight give way to verbs of sound and smell, and one sense interweaves with another. . . Our characteristic mode then is not a narrative in which scenes take place seriatim, but rather broken narratives, fragmentary compositions, and self-consciously staged testimonials, in which the narrative voice keeps stumbling over itself, its obligations and its limitations.
>
> There is no completely coherent discourse adequate to us. . .

Miscellaneous, the spaces here and there in our midst include but do not comprehend the past; they represent building without overall purpose, around an uncharted and only partially surveyed territory. Without a centre. Atonal.[16]

What phantoms of memory engage this writing of history? How does this atonality of the voice of exile, migration, diaspora disrupt the powerful oratory of the unisonant? How do we read the representation of a people who, in their response to domination and dissemination, must invent a sense of themselves, must create the shadow of the past to throw upon a future that is fragile and unfulfillable?

It is Fanon who, in speaking of the temporality of a people in a struggle, gives us some sense of the complex intentionality of the committed intellectual. He writes:

It is not enough to try to get back to the people in that past out of which they have already emerged; rather we must join them in the fluctuating movement which they are just giving shape to, and which, as soon as it has started will be the signal for everything to be called into question. Let there be no mistake about it; it is to this zone of occult instability that we must come.[17]

It is to this zone of occult instability that we have come to seize the time of the people, in that form of historical memory, the time of the now, which Walter Benjamin has described so powerfully as 'the tradition of the oppressed [which] teaches us that the state of emergency in which we live is not the exception but the rule'.[18] In contrast to the problematic unisonance of the patriotic people, the desolate silences of the wandering people require a history of that 'oral void' that emerges when the Palestinians abandon the metaphor of a *heimlich* national culture. For the Palestinians who send Palestinian love and kisses also ask, 'are there really such things. . . or are they neither politically significant nor particular to a nation or a people?'[19]

With these questions of those dispossessed of a national home we are pushed not merely to the edge of the discourse of a national culture, but to the limits of a metaphor of the modernity of Western Man at the point at which he encounters the Other. In the tryst of man and his doubles, Foucault writes, 'the whole of modern thought is imbued with the necessity of thinking the unthought – of reflecting the contents of the in-itself in the form of the For-itself... it is reflection, the act of consciousness, the elucidation of what is silent, language restored to what is mute, the illumination of the element of darkness that cuts man off from himself, the reanimation of the inert'.[20] It is in the overcoming of this unthought, this humanising silence, this silence of the human sciences – either in dialectical thinking or through forms of cultural relativism – that there emerges a normalised epistemological 'distance' through which the subject of culture produces knowledges of social contradiction or cultural and temporal difference. Whether it be in the reflectionism of what Bernard Williams appropriately calls the relativism of distance – where judgement is of ethical outlooks rather than practices, therefore taking a holistic and realistic view of the Other;[21] whether it be in the neo-pragmatic view of Richard Rorty for whom there is only the 'long conversation' with the Other, only the dialogue, only *us*, no transcultural rationality;[22] *then*, in each of these cases, as truth returns to Man, history to myth, a representational sign translates the Other as the Same. Silence speaks in the luminous metaphors of Culture, the letter made Spirit (of Law, Language, History), the Word made Flesh (Consciousness, Community).

With the Palestinian it is Otherwise. The opaque silence of the atonal, overwritten space of the Palestinian – Abandon the metanarrative! – petrifies the present, barring access to any such reflective, representationalist distance of knowledge, or time of return. The questions of the Other, 'What do you Palestinians want?', cannot simply be answered in the images of identity or the narrative of historicism, because they are also asked in the language of Desire: *He is saying this to me but what does he want?* And that question cannot be replied to directly because it leads us past the place of meaning or truth and leads us to the enunciative level, to the moment that determines unique and limited existence of the utterance – the broken, fragmentary composition of the Palestinian: the atonal void. It is from such a scenario of social and psychic antagonism that the history of this testimony should be read. The silence or void dangerously decomposes the narrative of the national culture, but equally dangerously it spatialises the sites and practices of struggle and antagonism. This unsettles the horizon of cultural identification, and we are forced to ask again, as I have been urging, the commonest questions of our culture, in a way that makes us wandering strangers to ourselves: When did we become a people? When did we stop becoming one? Is there Palestinian love? In an apt spatial metaphor, Said reveals this dangerous boundary of the time and truth of 'otherness' when the occult instability of the nomadic, wandering people comes to be signified in the circulation of the monadic silence or void whose history of representation I have tried to tell. 'There is no completely coherent discourse adequate to us. . . Miscellaneous, the spaces here and there in our midst include but do not comprehend the past', building without purpose, territory without centre. What kind of boundary – of the politics of the people or culture of the social – forms when the past is ambivalently encrypted in the time of modernity? When aggressivity spatialises the play of both power and the psyche? When the language of culture is a kind of decomposition?

Said makes his answer through the alternating dereliction and fetishism of Palestinian culture; the circulation of the Palestinian people as commodities; a confusion of time in the incomplete translation of verbs of sight into sound and smell; the dissolution of history as fragmentary composition; the de-composition of narrative voice. Through this dissemination there circulates that monadic silence, that void that splits the history of the Present, and reveals its structure as an ambivalent, spatial antagonism for which there is no completely coherent discourse. The miscellany of Said's random histori-cal spaces, here and there, *include* but do not *comprehend* the past and such an iconic inclusion of time is in fact an arrest of its motion – like the freeze-frame that Lacan identifies as the image of paranoia, like the strangely familiar archaism that I have associated with the enunciation of anteriority, like an old, *unheimlich* family photograph. We are in a territory where the knowledge of culture comes to be written across that shared boundary between paranoia and melancholia; a language and a boundary that is always deeply ambivalent between spaces and times: for paranoia a timeless Outside; for melancholia, an incorporated, encrypted space inside. We are on the grounds of a Manichean split that Fanon inscribes in the colonial world:

> A world divided into compartments, a motionless, Manichean world, a world of statues: the statue of a general who carried out the conquest; the statue of the engineer who built the bridge. . . The first thing the native learns is to stay in his place and not to go beyond certain limits. When the native is confronted with the colonial order of things, he finds he is in a state of permanent tension. . . We have seen that the native never ceases to dream of putting himself in the place of the settler – *not of becoming the settler but of substituting himself for the settler.*
>
> The native's guilt is never a guilt which he accepts; it is rather a kind of curse, a sword of Damocles. The symbols of social order – the police, the bugle-calls in the barracks, military parades and waving flags – are at one and the same time inhibitory and stimulating: for they do not simply convey the message 'Don't dare to budge'; rather they cry out 'Get ready to attack'. The impulse to take the settler's place implies a tonicity of the muscles the whole time. . . The settler is an exhibitionist . . . he keeps alive in the native an anger which he deprives of outlet; the native is trapped in the tight links of the chains of colonialism . . . but inwardly in a state of pseudopetrification.[23]

Fanon's cinematic staging of the relation of coloniser to colonised discloses the political dialectic of that relationship in the language of psychoanalysis. By attempting to represent the politics of colonialism through the psychic logic of a fantasmatic 'acting-out', Fanon discloses the peculiar power of the political unconscious to find resources of subversion and subalterneity in situations where more positivistic or functionalist theories of power are limited by their totalising perspectives. Such theories of political power are limited in the way in which they conceive of the directionality and the positionality involved in the enactment of social antagonism or contradiction.

Their political rationalism suggests that political reality – or should we call it 'realism'? – can only be grasped in the play of polarities, Subject/Object, Self/Other, Oppressor/Victim, Power/Powerless. And it also suggests that such polarities are grounded on a holistic view of social transformation where the structure of contradiction is informed by an immanent and essentialist difference between the subject positions that constitute the binary structure. Fanon's psychoanalytic point of view deconstructs this binary structure and the danger inherent in it of a mere inversion of the positions of power and powerlessness. His subversion of holistic and dialectical modes of thought consists in demonstrating that the directions of social authority and psychic authorisation are ambivalent between the incommensurable inscriptions of social reality ('Don't dare to budge!') and psychic reality ('Get ready to attack!'). The relation of these two registers of reality is neither binary nor can they be holistic because, as Fanon points out, the symbols of social order are '*at one and the same time inhibitory and stimulating*'. This ambivalent 'time' of enunciation, when the *presence* of the symbol, its spatial similitude, is disturbed by the arbitrary and iterative temporality of the sign, becomes the discursive modality of social meaning. At that point of the ambivalent intersection of sign and symbol, which is also the moment of the representation of the social event as psychic *mise-en-scène*, the political subject is neither transcendental or teleo-logical, nor interpellated in miasma of ideological misrecognition. The political subject is split in the sense that the 'pseudopetrification' of *both* coloniser and colonised – their taking up of antagonistic positions – is an enactment of political authority that is based on 'subjects in process'; that is, subjects whose negotiation of the political process depends strategically on the secondariness or belatedness through which they are constructed in the relay of otherness or the unconscious. The exhibitionism of the settler is dependent on the native's muscular tonicity in order to represent itself; the native's angry body that 'contains' the split between despair and attack is constituted as a subaltern subjectivity through the complex psychic staging of the settler's exhibitionism.

Freeze-Frame: the statuesque, exhibitionistic Master; the tense, muscled native. *Split-screen*: the native in the master's place in the dream of the native in the Other's space. *Double-take*: the symbols of order turn into the fantasmatic structures of insurrection: 'Don't dare to budge'/'Get ready to attack!' And in this stasis, this frozen silence, the blur of the tense body of the native is in that place of the colonial carceral where the effects of power can never be homogeneous. If the native is disciplined in the panoptic eye of the statue, then, as Fanon records, in that same place she is inscribed in a different time of desire: 'I dream that I span a river in one stride ... followed by a flood of motor-cars that never catch up with me'.[24] This boundary of agonism and authority that divides the colonial city and splits the colonial body – both white and black – is not the scenario of the master-slave because manichean division is a symptom of what Fanon calls dual narcissism. There is the crucial absence of a form of negation as sublation, which would enable the mutual recognition between master and slave to be constitutive of the moment of objectification or transcendence within Hegelian dialectic.

In the colonial condition, the dictates of the Law and the authority of the superego – embodying moral values, taking a coherent place in the world – become forms of cultural knowledge constituted of guilt and doubt. The colonial subject constitutes its identity and authority, not in relation to the 'content' of the Law or its transgression of its edicts. His existence is defined in a perpetual performativity that intervenes in that syntax or grammar of the superego, in order to disarticulate it. 'The native's guilt', Fanon writes, 'is never a guilt which he accepts; it is rather a kind of curse, a sword of Damocles . . . he is overpowered but not tamed'. The installation of the phallic Damoclean sword as the agency that installs a social ideal evokes an ambivalent social identification embodied in the muscular tension of the borderline native. His 'disincorporation' in paranoia and in melancholia are attempts to break the marginality of the social and political limits of space; to redraw the boundaries in a psychic, fantasmatic space. The Damoclean sword installs an ambivalence in the symbolic order, where it is itself the immobile Sign of authority whose meaning is continually contested by the fantasmatic, fragmented, motility of the signifiers of revolt. The Law is entombed as loss at the point of its ideal authority. But as the dominating force of symbolic ordering it also 'mummifies' the authority of the native social order. The colonial sword is constituted in an indeterminate doubling; the native superego is itself displaced in the colonial contention. Here in this 'encrypted', chiasmatic order signifying a double loss we encounter what may be a representative symbolic space for a certain kind of cultural survival that I want to explore – a *melancholia in revolt*.

It is the shadow that guilt casts on the object of identification that is the origin of melancholia, according to Freud. Fanon's 'guilt' is intriguingly different. Patterns of avoidance amongst the oppressed are those of the death reflex that, at the same time, never cease to drive the oppressed to resist the authority of the oppressor, to usurp his place and to transform the very basis of authority. The sword of Damocles is double-edged. How do we get from the melancholia of repeated loss to the melancholia of revolt? In what sense can melancholia provide a semiotic for the narrative of social marginality? Melancholia, Freud writes, is the reaction to the 'loss of a loved person, or to the loss of some abstraction . . . such as one's country, liberty, an ideal and so on'.[25] I use the word 'semiotic' to refer both to the construction of the sign through difference and 'absence' and to the subject as installed repeatedly and metonymically in the field of the Other. The work of melancholia – like the labour of the narrative – is predicated on a splitting and a sliding of the sign of the lost object, so the melancholic 'knows whom he has lost but not what he has lost in him'.[26] The image persists in a dead fixity; identification becomes erratic, fragmented, inchoate and 'incorporate'. The double-loss of the coloniser's sword of Damocles would be an apt illustration.

If we take Freud at his word – melancholics display an insistent communicativeness which finds satisfaction in self-exposure'[27] – then the narrative of melancholia preserves the icon of the Ideal – Nation – but by virtue of identifying with it from a position of loss and absence, exile and migration; the signifying act that gives it meaning cannot be contained or incorporated within the sign. Remember the fragmentary, broken Palestinian narratives that consistently overran the containment of the historical 'present', and decentred the miscellaneous spaces that did not comprehend the past. Consider also the psychic and fantasmatic space that Fanon constructs in the fable of colonial social relations that he expounds in discussing the Algerian who steals his native neighbour's dates:

> Under the colonial regime anything may be done for a loaf of bread or a miserable sheep... For a colonized man ... living does not mean embodying moral values or taking his place in the coherent world. To live means to keep on existing. Every date is a victory; not the result of work but the triumph of life. Thus to steal dates ... is not the negation of the property of others, nor the transgression of the Law ... You are forced to come up against yourself. Here we discover the kernel of that hatred against the self which is characteristic of racial conflicts in segregated societies.[28]

The Algerian dates represent an acting out of a violence that articulates a hatred against the self, of which the colonial 'pseudopetrification' of the subject is at once the cause and the symptom. Such a Damoclean 'guilt' or curse neither simply exceeds the letter of the Law nor transgresses the 'spirit' of the superego, but produces a form of contestation that exists *Abseits*, or beside the point of Order. Its 'irrationality' displaces the ethical rationale of colonial domination. The narrative structure of such an encrypted inscription of melancholia will become clearer if we adapt Derrida's account of it.[29] The ultimate referent – the Country, Nation, Honour – is never present to itself within the narrative 'in person'. The space of narration is asymptotic, which shows that the 'original' reference or Ideal is itself touched by fiction and constructed in a deferred narrative, as a form of repetition. The specificity of this melancholic repetition as a narrative form is also present in Freud's account. The encrypted referent initiates a narrative address that is carried out bit by bit, as Freud writes, at the great expense of time and energy. The double-loss of the ideal, be it the Nation, Culture or the sword of Damocles, generates a narrative of repetition, of metonymic part objects. They are, at the same time, symbolic presences and liminal signifiers of the ambivalence and antagonism within the space of cultural representation: think of the commodification and splitting of the Palestinian identity; think also of the overdetermined space that the Algerian date occupies. What is particularly important for understanding historical and cultural 'loss' in this context is the inversion of meaning that constitutes melancholic address and its identification with its object. The melancholic discourse, Freud says, is a plaint in the old fashioned sense. Its insistent self-exposure and the repetition of loss must not be taken at face value for its apparent victimage and passivity. Its narrative metonymy, the repetition of the piecemeal, the bit by bit, its insistent self exposure, comes also from a *mental constellation of revolt*. The melancholic 'are not ashamed and do not hide themselves, since everything derogatory they say about themselves *is at bottom said about somebody else*.'[30] This inversion of meaning and address in the melancholic discourse, when it 'incorporates' the loss or lack in its own body – displaying its own weeping wounds – is also an act of 'disincorporating' the authority of the Master. Fanon again says something similar when he suggests that the native wears his psychic wounds on the surface of his skin like an open sore – an eyesore to the coloniser.

In these Fanonian spaces – as in the fragmented territories of the Palestinian – we find a boundary where the voice of mastery splits in its enunciation between order and opposition, producing a *differend*, an undecidability, between the directives of governmentality and the fantasmatic drives. Here the symbols of Order – answering the Palestinian plea for *amor patria*, love and kisses, or obeying the bugle call – are profoundly ambivalent and produce, as Fanon says, a kind of lack of guilt, a form of obedience that can lead to a form of political desire that is far removed from the inversion of oppression or reactive resistance or any such duality of deliverance. The limits and gaps of one's history can lead – through the intensification of atonal voids and obstacles – to an intensification of a desire 'not of becoming the settler but of *substituting* himself for the settler' – that is for the native to be in the place of freedom, not mastery, that is also the place of its difference. *The Black man is not. Any more than the White Man*, Fanon has written.[31] From that marked void or caesura that splits any naively liberatory or sovereign sentence of freedom there emerges a political vision of equality. It is a vision articulated at the 'edge' of the *not* that will not allow any national or cultural 'unisonance' in the imagined community of the future.

Notes

1. Jacques Derrida, 'Living On', in Harold Bloom *et al.* (eds), *Deconstruction and Criticism* (Routledge & Kegan Paul, London, 1979).
2. Jacques Lacan, 'Some Reflections on the Ego', *International Journal of Psycho-analysis*, vol. 34, 1953, p. 15.
3. Jean-François Lyotard and Jean-Loup Thébaud, *Just Gaming* (Manchester University Press, Manchester, 1985), p. 99.
4. Hannah Arendt, *The Human Condition* (Chicago University Press, Chicago, 1959), p. 41.
5. Fay Weldon, *Sacred Cows* (Chatto Counterblasts, London, 1989), p. 32.
6. Paul de Man, 'The Task of the Translator', in *The Resistance to Theory* (Manchester University Press, Manchester, 1986), p. 91.
7. Benedict Anderson, *Imagined Communities: Reflections on the Origin and Spread of Nationalism* (Verso, London, 1983), p. 132.
8. Ibid., p. 30.
9. Tom Nairn, *The Break-up of Britain* (Verso, London, 1977), p. 258.
10. Michel Foucault, *The Archaeology of Knowledge* (Tavistock, London, 1974), p. 111.
11. Benedict Anderson, 'Narrating the Nation', *The Times Literary Supplement*.
12. Ibid.
13. Walter Benjamin, *Illuminations* (Cape, London, 1970), p. 259.
14. Jacques Derrida, 'Des Tours de Babel', in J. F. Graham (ed.), *Difference and Translation* (Cornell University Press, Ithaca and London, 1985), pp. 169–70.
15. Ibid., p. 176.
16. Edward Said, *After the Last Sky* (Faber, London, 1986), pp. 38, 129.
17. Frantz Fanon, *The Wretched of the Earth* (Penguin, Harmondsworth, 1969), p. 183.
18. Benjamin, *Illuminations*, p. 259.
19. Said, *After the Last Sky*, p. 34.
20. Michel Foucault, *The Order of Things* (Tavistock, London, 1974), pp. 327–8.
21. Bernard Williams, *Ethics and the Limits of Philosophy* (Fontana, London, 1985), p. 162ff.
22. Richard Rorty, *Philosophy and the Mirror of Nature* (Princeton University Press, Princeton, 1979), pp. 14–15.
23. Fanon, *The Wretched of the Earth*, pp. 41–3.
24. Ibid., p. 40.
25. Sigmund Freud, 'Mourning and Melancholia' (1917 [1915]), *SE* XIV, p. 243.
26. Ibid., p. 245.
27. Ibid., p. 247.
28. Fanon, *The Wretched of the Earth*, p. 249.
29. See Jacques Derrida, '*Fors*: The Anglish Words of Nicholas Abraham and Maria Torok', Foreword to N. Abraham and M. Torok, *The Wolfman's Magic Word* (Minnesota University Press, Minneapolis, 1986).
30. Freud, 'Mourning and Melancholia', p. 248; my emphasis.
31. Frantz Fanon, *Black Skin, White Mask* (Pluto, London, 1986).

8

Underworld USA: Psychoanalysis and Film Theory in the 1980s

Elizabeth Cowie

This chapter is an attempt to review the role of psychoanalysis in film theory, and in particular, the way it has been used to propose a meta-psychology of cinema. The use of the term metapsychology follows Freud's description of his papers on 'Instincts and Their Vicissitudes', 'Repression' and 'The Unconscious', published in 1915, as metapsychological; that is, concerned with producing general theoretical concepts for the understanding of human psychology. In a similar way, a metapsychology of cinema will be concerned with the phenomenon of cinema in general for the individual psyche. It asks, how is the spectator a subject, in the psycho-analytic sense, for cinema? How does cinema work on us and for us as psychical subjects, that is, as subjects of desire?

The assumption that the cinema spectator is positioned by and for the film has become a fairly general tenet of film theory. However, the nature of that positioning and its implications have not been fully explored or explained. The stake of these debates, as they were first elaborated in the French film journal *Cahiers du Cinéma* and in the British journal *Screen* – which has perhaps been lost sight of – was the attempt to locate the ideological role of cinema. Cinema was identified as imaginary, following Althusser's use of the term to describe man's lived relation to the world. Althusser was here adopting and adapting the psychoanalytic meaning given the term by Jacques Lacan: a miscognition by the subject of itself as a unified subject who acts on the world. The cinema, too, was seen as imaginary in that it was held to offer the spectator the same illusion of omniscience, and this became identified as the ideological function of cinema.

One consistent theme which has emerged in these debates has been the issue of a moment of the fixing – and hence also a moment of the before of fixing – of the subject in discourse. In conjunction with this there has been an emphasis on the moment of unfixing taken as a radical mechanism of disjunction, of the exposure of the construction, whether of social relations or of the psychical subject. Along with this there was a privileging of a certain kind of cinema, namely a cinema of deconstruction, which fore-grounds its own conditions of production, and which refuses to ensnare the spectator in an imaginary lure of identification and pleasure – a Brechtian, deconstructionist cinema. But this can never be to put the subject outside discursive constructions, outside the signifying chain; the 'meaning' of the unfixedness can only be located, along with the subject, in the discourse and this is always in some sense fixed. There is no ideal outside of fixing, although there is an ideal of that outside, and indeed one which can be seen continually at work in film theory and practice. The nature of this subject of the deconstructionist cinema has, moreover, never been specified except in contrast to and as 'other' of this mainstream cinema. It is this which I hope to address in order to suggest why psychoanalysis remains an important theoretical approach for considering cinema, although its role as in some sense a theory of ideology, that is, of the ideological construction of the subject psychically, must be reconsidered. Indeed I hope to show that the very conceptual terms which have brought this metapsychology to something of an impasse – namely, the cinema as fetishistic, as imaginary, and even as, contradictorily, symbolic in the sense of re-establishing in its narratives patriarchal symbolic relations of men and women in terms of women's 'castration' – could suggest a rather different metapsychology of cinema. Such a metapsychology, once separated from a requirement to be also a theory of ideology, of the imaginary and misrecognised relation to the subject the real relations within the social, may then contribute to an understanding of film as a cultural object and hence to that domain termed the study of 'ideological forms'.

It is in this context of that I will consider Samuel Fuller's *Underworld USA* (1960), a film that deviates from the norms and conventions of the classical Hollywood film.[1] V. F. Perkins has commented that 'Fuller has, one suspects, little sympathy for anyone who lives vicariously in the cinema. A verbal equivalent for his camera's attitude would be "Don't just sit there. Do something".'[2] Peter Wollen's response to Fuller takes this further: 'it seems to me that Fuller is the film director whose methodology closest approaches Brecht's theatre'.[3] I want to relate the film's 'demand for action' to the debates about ideology and deconstruction just outlined.

Underworld USA poses a dilemma. On the one hand, it seems to call for action on the part of the spectator. On the other hand, no clear or simple line of action is proposed. This reaches its extreme with the death of its hero, Tolly, raising the contradictory question of why Tolly died. For the

film's ending involves not only not giving a happy ending, it also refuses to
give a satisfactorily unhappy, tragic, ending. It withholds a resolution in
which the narrative drive is completed, in which the demands set in play by
the film are fulfilled, placed; it refuses, therefore, to offer an imaginary
resolution, whether in terms of a plenitude in a happy ending, or simply a
re-placing of a demand, frustrated in an unhappy ending, but nevertheless
'spoken', and not given up. At the same time the ending of *Underworld
USA* is not really open, the narrative is not an anti-narrative, deconstruct-
ing the pleasures of the story. We are always 'inside' the story, caring about
our characters, and the ending does not expose this as false in any sense. It
does not cruelly tear away the veil of the cinematic illusion, excising our
pleasure in a deconstruction. More devastatingly, it holds us to its story,
forcing us on to the bitter end, to a death which is scandalously 'meaning-
less'. Tolly does not die nobly, a romantic though tragic hero, nor does he
die – more didactically – to teach us a moral truth.

In Brecht, the alienation effect depended on an identification with the
characters on the part of the audience. This was juxtaposed with moments
when the audience would be forced out of such identification and made to
see the characters as types, and thus to understand the determinations –
social and economic – on and for those characters. In Brecht's writing
identification is often presented as a capture by the narrative, as opposed
to alienation which returns the spectator to her or his full subjectivity
outside the narrative. Brecht is critical of such identification as an aesthetic
strategy on its own. He seeks instead to use the discrepancy, or opposition,
between identification and alienation in order to open a way in which to
confront the spectator.

The 'Brechtianness' of *Underworld USA* lies in this play between
identification and alienation rather than a set of Brechtian techniques of
distanciation. (Its non-classical style may also qualify *Underworld USA* to
be called Brechtian in this latter sense.) My question is how our position as
spectator-subjects is constructed by the film and how this can be understood psychoanalytically as involving a relation to the symbolic. Thus
psychoanalysis will no longer be called upon to play a part in a general
theory of ideology where ideology is a unified and mono-causal field (even
where this is seen as a structure of elements all of which are held to work
for a single cause).

PSYCHOANALYSIS, IDEOLOGY, FILM

The introduction of psychoanalytic concepts into the study of cinema had
at least three different aspects. The first was a revised theory of ideology
which incorporated psychoanalytic concepts into the Marxist theory of
ideology. The epistemological assumptions of Althusser's theory have

been shown to be untenable by Paul Hirst in his critique – there can be no necessary unity to the ideological, for example. Althusser's invocation of psychoanalysis has not been similarly addressed, even though Hirst raises the question of why ideology should necessarily be imaginary. The imaginary, Althusser argued, provided the form of the subject's lived relation to society. Through this relation the subject was brought to accept as its own, to recognise itself in, the representations of the social order. The subject is thus 'interpellated'. That social practices address and so interpellate us as subjects for their discourse is clear, and we can speak of the subject of medicine and the subject of law – whether man, woman, or dog as Hirst so often put it. That this requires an imaginary relation is less clear; it is certainly not necessary for dogs. One implication of ideology as an imaginary relation has been to sustain at some level the presumption of ideology as a misrepresentation, as if the miscognition of the subject of the mirror phase involved the identification with a false image – of a false unified subjectivity – whereas the miscognition is in fact that the image is unified. As a result Lacan's concept of the imaginary cannot support a theory of ideology as misrepresentation and hence as mask, covering up and hiding a truth and reality lying elsewhere, behind the (mis)representation.[4]

The second aspect was a critique of the theory of the subject which centrally draws upon psychoanalysis. This is summarised in the editorial to *Screen*, volume 16, number 2, which also included Metz's 'The Imaginary Signifier', on the metapsychology of cinema. The editorial invokes writers in literary and cinema semiotics such as Barthes, Kristeva, and the editorial boards of *Cahiers du Cinèma* and *Cinéthique*. Such theorists

> have long insisted on the limitations of the tradition of structuralist semiotics and aesthetics deriving from the work of Saussure, Jakobson and Hjemslev, [and] argued that this tradition was condemned to empiricist or phenomenological description or formalism so long as it took as given a subject, empirical or transcendental, in possession of the codes, giving it access to meaning, and proposed that the problem of the relation between subject and signifier could only be resolved by resort to historical materialism but a historical materialism that has integrated the scientific revolution inaugurated by Freud and psychoanalysis (p. 5).

That integration so optimistically looked for in the mid-1970s has not occurred, in part because of the role psychoanalysis was also called upon to play in Althusser's theory of ideology. The importance of the critique of the transcendental subject remains, however, and psychoanalysis is central to this critique.[5]

The third aspect has been the role of psychoanalysis as an explanatory system, as a metadiscourse whose concepts can be brought to bear on the cinematic textual system. On the one hand, this has been undertaken in relation to the cinematic signifier in general, in Christian Metz's essay on cinema as the imaginary signifier, and hence as ideological. On the other hand, psychoanalytic concepts have been used to uncover the unconscious not of the author, but of the ideological inscription of the text. This was the approach of the editors of *Cahiers du Cinèma* in their analyses of *Young Mr Lincoln* and *Morocco*. They wanted to 'account for the repressive operation which, in each scene, determines the realisation of a key signification' in order 'to understand the scriptural operation (overdetermination and repression) which has set it up'.[6] They are drawing on psychoanalytic concepts – of repression, castration, unconscious desire, fetishism – in order to read the text 'symptomatically', in a kind of de-coding, which of course is only part of their role in analysis itself. Ben Brewster has pointed out that this approach is made possible, despite the absence of any equivalent to the unconscious of the patient in analysis and which, in analysis, provides the resistance to interpretation which also confirms that interpretation, because the elements in the film act as signifiers and each

> acquires its signifier precisely as do other cinematic and non-cinematic codes – by its motivation in parallel with the detective-story code and the Fordian code, inversely with respect to the 'early life of the hero' generic code.[7]

What is revealed is not the neurosis of a subject, the psychoanalytic patient or the 'author' of the film-text, but the production of meaning in the film-text itself. In John Ford's film, *Cahiers du Cinèma* argue, the ideological enounced (*enoncé*) of the generic sub-code 'the early life of a great man' is subverted by the Fordian writing (*écriture*), so that it fails to ground the later achievements of Lincoln in the earlier events shown in this film, thus failing to naturalise his later actions as pre-figured in his earlier life.

Psychoanalysis here does not have the role of a metapsychology of cinema. Rather, it is a method of interpretation or, as Ben Brewster put it, a form of decipherment. It is used not to reveal the film's ideology, but the failure of the film's ideology in so far as it shows the operation of the Fordian sub-code, for example the role of the mother, as subverting what the *Cahiers* authors see as the ideological project of the film.[8]

The discussion of psychoanalysis and cinema is further complicated by the existence of several over-lapping approaches to theorising a metapsychology of cinema. These include most notably the work of Jean-Louis Baudry and Christian Metz, as well as the more specific writings of Raymond Bellour, Mary Ann Doane, Stephen Heath and Laura Mulvey.[9] All these involve more or less explicitly a metapsychological approach: the theorising of a fixing of the spectator as subject for the film – always in fact a male subject – and of cinema as voyeuristic and fetishistic. As Constance Penley explains:

The metaphorical construction of the cinema as an apparatus was a response to the need to account for several aspects of film ranging from the uniquely powerful impression of reality provided by the cinema and the specific mode of positioning of the subject as a film spectator, to the very desire intrinsic to cinema-going itself... Broadly speaking, the cinematic apparatus achieves its specific effects because of the way it manages to re-enact or mimic the scene of the unconscious – the psychical apparatus – and duplicate its mechanisms by way of illusion.[10]

For these approaches cinema is a machine, Constance Penley argues, and a bachelor machine at that, for its chief distinction is that it is male.[11]

Psychoanalysis is taken as a theory of the construction of the subject as a psychical subject, a subject of the unconscious. The theory of the subject was to be used to understand the construction of the spectator-subject in cinema.

The problem is to understand the terms of the construction of the subject and the modalities of the replacement of this construction in specific signifying practices, where 'replacement' means not merely the repetition of the place of that construction but also, more difficultly, the supplacement – the overplacing; supplementation or, in certain circumstances, supplantation (critical interruption [i.e. Brecht]) – of that construction in the place of its repetition.

The film spectator is already a subject, but cinema is a process or a machine which *re-makes* the subject for its images.

Our hypothesis, therefore, is that a crucial – determining – part of the functioning of ideological systems is the establishment of a series of machines (institutions) which *move* – placing of desire – the subject ('sender' and 'receiver') in an appropriation of the symbolic into the imaginary (the definition of miscognition).[12]

Mainstream cinema is here clearly put in place as a machine of the imaginary. In his writings Stephen Heath has also emphasised the role of the mechanism of fetishism for representation, drawing on Roland Barthes' comments in 'Diderot, Brecht, Eisenstein' and arguing that 'the structure of representation is a structure of fetishism' in which

the subject is produced in a position of separation from which he is confirmed in an imaginary coherence (the representation is the guarantee of his self-coherence) the condition of which is the ignorance of the structure of his production, his setting in position ... this structure focuses a centre, the subject it represents, which derives its unity, its untroubled centrality, from the split it operates between knowledge and belief, between knowledge which disperses the stability of the subject, opens a production of desire in which the subject has everything to lose, and belief in which the subject positions himself in his structural plenitude.[13]

Thus the knowledge of lack, of castration – in the woman – is disavowed, overturned, and the lack repaired in the fetish substitution, as that which makes whole again. The realism of classical cinema, for example, covers over the nature of film as illusion and in a *Screen* editorial in 1974 Ben Brewster and Colin MacCabe argued for a struggle in the cinema 'against the fetishistic position of the spectator – fixed in his position securely by the reality of the image'.[14] The cinema as imaginary is thus aligned with fetishism.

Two kinds of cinema are implied by such a position. One is a cinema which re-makes the subject as imaginary, a full, centred subject of the miscognition of the mirror-phase; the cinema as imaginary. The other is a cinema in which the spectator-subject is posed as split, aware of the work of representation – Brechtian. Cinema is then divided into the good and the bad in what is perhaps a uniquely Anglo-Saxon ethic. Good cinema is didactic, refuses identification to the spectator, it presents itself as a construction through self-reflexive devices – it is worthy, educational, but also more often than not it is found to be boring. Bad cinema is pleasurable – centring narrative, fantasy and identification. Narrative cinema is a vice, like sex for the monk, which we cannot quite give up. I want to overturn this dichotomy and suggest that narrative structures, scenarios of fantasy and positions of identification may all be involved in producing an unfixing of the spectator. Before that I shall review the arguments that the cinema, narrative cinema, is imaginary, in order to argue that a different use of psychoanalysis is possible, and necessary.

CINEMA AS IMAGINARY

Christian Metz, in an article published in French in a special issue of *Communications* in 1975 and simultaneously in English as 'The Imaginary Signifier' in *Screen*, vol. 16 no. 2 (1975),[15] argued that cinema's very condition of existence is that it is imaginary.

> More than the other arts, or in a more unique way, the cinema involves us in the imaginary: it drums up all perception, but to switch it immediately over into its own absence, which is nonetheless the only signifier present (p. 45).

Metz is dangerously close here to arguing that cinema is mere perceptual delusion, and *thus* is imaginary. Yet the imaginary is not an ontological fact, to be located in the coincidence of certain phenomena of absence-presence as Metz suggests. Rather, it depends on the relation of desire set in play, that is, the desire to make present what is absent, to fill the lack, the gap. As Derrida has shown, it is the condition of existence of *any* signifying system that it makes present what is absent (as Metz in part acknowledges), that it signifies absence in a presence-ness. Metz's formulation in relation to cinema makes it appear that the stake is the 'unreality' of the signifier; that we respond as spectators to the projected image as if the people and objects which are shown were 'really there'. The imaginary is not, however, a relation of illusion, or even of delusion. It is a subjective relation to desire, not a material phenomenon of perception.

The second element in Metz's argument is that the 'spectator identifies with himself as pure act of perception' (p. 49). For Metz the cinema cannot reduplicate the mirror phase in the spectator since he or she has already passed through it, and the cinema screen does not offer the spectator its *own* body with which to identify as an object. The ego, Metz says, is already formed: 'But since it exists, the questions arises of precisely *where it is* during the projection of the film'. Metz therefore asks 'But *with what*, then, does the spectator identify during the projection of the film? For he certainly has to identify ...' (p. 47). Metz rejects identification with characters in a film as merely secondary identification, for such identifications are intermittent and, more importantly, Metz sees these as contingent upon a prior identification, one which enables the spectator to *be* a subject for cinema at all. This identification, Metz says, is an identification by the subject as all-perceiving, an identification 'with himself as pure act of perception (as wakefulness, alertness): as condition of the possibility of the perceived and hence as a kind of transcendental subject, which comes before every *there is*' (p. 49).

Again, this is not unique to the cinema. Indeed, it is the condition for any signifying system that the subject be the (imagined) site of unity of meaning for and of the message – the fiction of the unity of the subject is not abandoned with entry to the symbolic, but made relative in relation to lack. The cinema posits the spectator as a spectator and thus predicates its place as 'I'. It is not a function of the cinematic signifier alone, but of human subjectivity as such. This function is already in place, constituted in the mirror phase whereby the subject identifies with its own image *and* as one who looks. In so far as it does identify with its own look, it does so from the place in which the Other sees.

The specific role of this mechanism in cinema can be clearly seen when cinema and theatre are compared. Cinema is not different (or 'better than') the theatre merely because it can show us more, or show things that a staged play cannot (landscape, cavalry charges, burning hotels, etc.). Rather, the difference lies in the *way* in which it shows us its events, objects and people. The theatre, too, requires an all-perceiving (and hearing) subject, yet in the theatre – in the main – the subject's position of address is both fixed and multiple, whereas in cinema it is variable and unique. In a theatre there may be three hundred or five hundred or however many different places of view, as many as there are seats. But in each place the point-of-view is fixed, bar minor head movements, and opera glasses notwithstanding. In the cinema all the spectators see from the same position – everyone sees Garbo's face as a profile but this point-of-view will be continually changing: now close-up, now in long-shot, now from this character's position now from another's. In other words, the spectator's look is aligned with and made identical to another look, the camera's, which has gone before it and already 'organised' the scene. The spectator thus identifies with the look of the camera and becomes the punctual source of that look which brings into existence the film itself, as if it were by one one's own look that the film unfolds before one in the cinema.

This process has been traced back to the very nature of the cinematic apparatus and the optics on which it is based, namely, the monocular perspective perfected in Renaissance painting. The *camera obscura* was developed as an aid to achieving 'correct' perspective and this, along with the 'vanishing point' used in such painting, inscribes, Metz says, 'an empty emplacement for the spectator-subject, an all-powerful position which is that of God himself, or more broadly, of some ultimate signified' (p. 49). The spectator, it is said, identifies with the camera as an omniscient, omnipotent look. Metz then argues:

> And it is true that as he identifies with himself as look, the spectator can do no other than identify with the camera too, which has looked before him at what he is now looking at and whose stationing (= framing) determines the vanishing point (p. 49).

In these few words Metz has locked the whole thing together. The misrecognition of the mirror phase is now allied directly to the cinematic signifier in the identification with the camera – hence the *same* illusion of control and mastery, which ensures for Metz that such cinema is indeed imaginary.

Some of Metz's arguments need to be unpacked here. He has rejected cinematic identification as a replaying of the mirror-phase since this has already 'happened' for the subject. Instead he asserts that the spectator simply identifies with himself or herself as 'pure act of perception'. I take this to mean that the spectator takes up a position of omniscient perception – which is exactly the position of the mirror-phase. Moreover, by rejecting the mirror-phase as such as the process in play in cinema, Metz also rejects the corollary of that process, namely the self-alienation of the subject in the very moment of its precipitation as subject. Jacqueline Rose takes issue with Metz in relation to this:

> The fact that the subject's own body is not on the screen does not necessarily distinguish its experience from that of the mirror stage: the subject never specularises its own body as such, and the phenomenon of

transitivism demonstrates that the subject's mirror identification can be with another child.

And the mirror-phase is not a *moment* but a relation to subjectivity which is continually replayed once it is inaugurated.

Returning to the mirror-phase as the structure for cinematic identification allows the re-introduction of the subject as an alienated subject, and not as simply a unified, an imaginary, coherence. To identify with one's image thus also always implies an identification with the place of looking – 'I am the image I am looking at' – which also contains the supplementary position of 'I am looked at by an other'. The structure of specularity thus undermines the imaginary as a field of subjectivity. Jacqueline Rose goes on to argue that:

> The relationship of the scopic drive to the object of desire is not one simply of distance but of externalisation, which means that the observing subject can become object of the look, and hence elided as subject of its own representation.[16]

In identifying with the other (the mirror image) we are also separated from it as other. It is this which allows us to both be and *not be* the camera. We take the camera's look as our own, yet we are not at all disturbed when it suddenly pans, although we have not turned our own heads. This does not require the transcendental identification with the camera which Metz claims.

Identification with the camera is therefore, I suggest, closer to what Freud called 'empathy'. This is arrived at on a path which 'leads from identification by way of imitation to empathy, that is, to the comprehension of the mechanism by means of which we are enabled to take an attitude at all towards another mental life',[17] Thus identification – the mechanism which constitutes the subject as such – also allows the subject to take up the position of another subject, or look. Certainly this will include all that is entailed in that constitution of the subject, namely the misrecognition of itself as omniscient. But also, and as a corollary, it includes the sense of the lack in being thus inaugurated. The imaginary, then, is characterised not by a full, unified subject, but by a subject already divided, and already initiated into the structure of lack. It is not signification or representation as such that is imaginary, but the relationship constructed for and in the spectator. It is therefore also open to question how far all signification, all representation, more or less involves a play, a putting in jeopardy, of all that it presumes, the centred subject.

The cinema may indeed be imaginary, but this is not guaranteed by the apparatus, nor can this any longer imply a simple plenitude. This has consequences for the way in which cinema as ideology and cinema as imaginary become identified.

CINEMA AS FETISHISTIC

The second premise, that cinema is fetishistic – and voyeuristic – also needs examining. For Metz fetishism and voyeurism are additional structures which he sees as important but not determining of cinema as imaginary. For Stephen Heath, however, fetishism is central to the functioning of cinema as imaginary. He relates this to Brecht's practice:

> Fetishism describes, as we have seen, a structure of representation and exchange and the ceaseless confirmation of the subject in that perspective, a perspective which is that of a spectator in a theatre or a movie-theatre – in an art of representation. It is this fixed position of separation-representation-speculation (the specularity of reflection and its system of exchange) that Brecht's distanciation seeks to undermine.[18]

It is central, therefore, to the subject-position of the spectator in cinema in general. This contrasts with the positions taken by Bellour, Mulvey and Doane.[19] Although they differ from each other, they all take fetishism more specifically as a defence, a particular mechanism in play for the spectator in cinema, for the male spectator, but not necessarily constitutive of the cinematic-relation as such. In addition, Heath sees fetishism as a relation to the represented as structure, not as a set of contents.

A problem immediately arises here, one which is recognised by these writers. Clinically, fetishism is a male perversion. The structure described by this term seems to be a masculine structure in so far as fetishism is the attempt to deal with the reality of castration by producing a substitute for the penis missing on the woman's, the mother's, body. Of course, the problem of castration for the woman is not organised in this way, though psychoanalytic theory remains divergent in its views as to how the woman, the little girl, *does* deal with castration. This is only part of a larger problem presented by the use of psychoanalytic theory, for psychoanalysis, at least in the work of Freud, and in the re-reading of Freud by Jacques Lacan, places sexual difference as a central mechanism, and problem, for the human subject. This is represented and resolved through the phallus as signifier of difference, and through the accession to the symbolic via an acceptance of the Name-of-the-Father of the Law prohibiting incest, of cultural and social relations as described by Lévi-Strauss: a law of the fathers, patriarchal. Psychoanalysis seems, therefore, to be a theory of the dominant culture and it now becomes a means to demonstrate the ways in which cinema, too, is patriarchal, and a means to the theorising of cinema's oppressive representation of women. For example, Raymond Bellour has said that the only means to pleasure for the woman in Hollywood cinema is by a masochistic identification with the male character.[20] As a result the metapsychology of cinema is now only a partial theorising, specifying only a male spectator position and describing only a certain part of cinema

– patriarchal cinema – since it is also assumed that not all film is patriarchal. Though the alternative remains unspecified. Thus, on the one hand, the theorisation of cinema as ideology and as patriarchal is complete. On the other hand, this very theorisation presents a set of problems which begin to dismantle it. Apart from giving a very limited account of female pleasure in cinema, it addresses only a particular kind of cinema – fetishistic cinema. Further, the approach is based on the assumption that through psycho-analysis we can understand the construction of the subject in patriarchy, and hence be in a position to change it. This implies either the overthrow of the unconscious of our time – Juliet Mitchell's thesis in *Psychoanalysis and Feminism*, but one which it is difficult to imagine in practice – or else it implies the discovery of an alternative understanding from within psycho-analytic theory of the construction of sexual difference; that is, a displace-ment of the phallus as the privileged signifier. In either case, it is assumed that ideology and the subjectivity described by psychoanalysis are the same thing, that to be a subject in language is to be a subject of ideology. Thus Stephen Heath writes of the 'individual as subject-support for ideological formations in the symbolic', a question, that is, 'of the subject of language' but where he adds the rider to this that language 'is at once constitutive and not reducible to the ideological'.[21] This is attractive, but also difficult to think. It begs the question, too, of what is the other and the outside of this ideological. This is in fact the impasse of Althusser's appropriation of psychoanalysis for a theory of ideology: it remains in effect a theory of miscognition which assumes a true knowledge available to the subject, a non-ideological knowledge.

Yet, at the same time, it is clear that the issue, the stake of representa-tion, is the way in which it *does* fix us as subjects for its discourse. The concept of fetishism provides only a partial understanding of this mechan-ism, but then introduces the issue of sexual difference for representation in a way which has not been fully resolved.[22] Furthermore it is this fixing itself which produces the subject – as shown in Lacan's schema of identification, with the retrospective action of the signifier in and for the subject. This is the work of the symbolic, of signification and language. Slavoj Žižek has shown how such a fixing is also involved in ideology:

Ideological space is made of non-bound, non-tied elements, 'floating signifiers', the very identity of which is 'open', overdetermined by their articulation in a chain with other elements, i.e. the 'literal' signification of which depends on their metaphorical surplus-signification ... The 'quilting' performs the totalisation by means of which this free floating of ideological elements is halted, fixed, i.e. by means of which they become parts of the structured network of meaning: if we 'quilt' the floating signifiers through 'Communism', for example, 'class-struggle' confers a precise and fixed signification to all other elements, to democracy

(so-called 'real democracy' as opposed to 'bourgeois formal democracy'
as a legal form of exploitation), to feminism (the exploitation of women
as resulting from the class-conditioned division of labour), to ecologism
(the destruction of natural resources as a logical consequence of profit-
oriented capitalist production), to the peace-movement (the principle
danger for peace is adventuristic imperialism), etc, etc. What is at stake
in the ideological struggle is precisely which of the 'nodal points', of
points de capiton, will totalise, include in its series of equivalences, these
free-floating elements.[23]

The term '*points de capiton*' is the way in which Lacan describes the fixing
of the subject in the chain of desire, of signification, and Žižek seeks in this
essay to show, not that ideology is the same as the construction of the
subject, but that in both, the fixing of meaning is never quite complete,
there is always a left-over, a residue – the *objet petit a* – and thus a lack,
and it is through the structures of fantasy and of disavowal via the fetish
substitute, that the subject, and ideology, domesticate or 'gentrify' in
Žižek is words, the lack. By this Žižek is able to show that the trick of
ideology is not the mask which hides something, but the fetish which masks
the lack, the 'non-sense' which the symbolic 'quilting' has sought to
overcome, but which always fails. In this approach ideology is no longer a
'bad thing' but a necessary aspect of the social; but nor is fetishism or
fantasy the 'bad' processes which we should now struggle against. This
strategy would itself be a fantasy, for in attempting to get rid of that which
is seen as obscene, excessive, intrusive, it designates a 'something' as the
'bad thing'.

Žižek's discussion is a complex and brilliant contribution which goes
beyond what I can attempt here. The key point for my argument, however,
is that this 'fixing' of the subject is not simply the same as ideology – if
ideology is understood only as a false consciousness, or miscognition of the
real relations of subjectivity. Problems must arise, in fact, if the 'fixed'
subjectivity is simply taken as the incorrect position, implying that the
'unfixed' is politically correct, and this is even more the case if this 'fixed'
subjectivity is held to be equivalent to the imaginary relation. For what
then is the 'unfixed'? Is it the symbolic, or something before the imaginary?
Julia Kristeva has taken up the issue of a 'something between' extensively
in her work, using the concept of the semiotic chora to locate in the
imaginary, or rather somewhere near it, a resistance to the positioning
implied by the symbolic. Kristeva, however, has emphasised that this does
not simply undermine the symbolic, and that it is not necessarily simply a
'good thing'. Attempts to appropriate the concept for a political project of
opposition to mainstream or dominant forms have been discounted by
Kristeva herself. Indeed it is inherently antithetical to the concept,
Jacqueline Rose has argued.

Kristeva has, however, been attractive to feminism because of the way she exposes the complacent identities of psychosexual life. But as soon as we try to draw out of that exposure an image of femininity which escapes the straitjacket of symbolic forms, we fall straight into that essentialism and primacy of the semiotic which is one of the most problematic aspects of her work. And as soon as we try to make of it the basis for a political identity, we turn the concept inside out, since it was as a critique of identity that it was originally advanced. No politics without identity, but no identity which takes itself at its word.[24]

Once psychoanalysis is no longer harnessed to describing the bad object ideology, however, the problem of finding the 'other' place to ideology is removed. Instead, I would argue, it is necessary to examine the specific work of a particular film and the way it places, or rather 'moves' the spectator across and between imaginary and symbolic relations of subjectivity, of desire. It is this movement or play which I hope to show at work for the spectator in *Underworld USA*.

THE SYMBOLIC IN CINEMA

What is implied by symbolic relations of subjectivity in cinema? The symbolic is posed in Lacan's work in two apparently opposed ways. On the one hand, it designates the accession to the domain of the social, in terms of the rule of Law, the Name-of-the-Father, of social relations and the rules governing them, most specifically, the incest taboo – that prohibition which, in securing the circulation and exchange of women, establishes kinship relations and inaugurates culture. This, as noted earlier, implies a fixing of the subject. On the other hand, the introduction of the symbolic, and the intervention of the father as third term in the dyadic, imaginary relation of mother and child, is represented as a rupture.

The appearance of the father within the dual mother-child relationship, sets in play the symbolic: introduces a rupture in the imaginary; sets up a lack; breaks the plenitude of the mirror; sets in motion desire; and introduces the law (the prohibition of incest) based on exclusion and difference. The introduction of the symbolic allows a language to function as the grasping of opposition and difference.[25]

Stephen Heath has also described the movement between the imaginary and the symbolic as a disruption involving:

(a) an imaginary relation with the object wanting, [which] produces figures of the accomplishment of desire in the narrative as memory-spectacle, the representation of unity and the unity of representation;
(b) a symbolic production of the object as lost, past in the ceaseless gap

of the present, in the circulation flow of the film, 'death at work' ('la
mort au travail' – Straub, borrowing a phrase from Cocteau); (a) is the
negation of the subject of the enunciation in the symbolic, (b) is the loss
of the subject of the enounced, re-traced in the tensions of desire.[26]

The symbolic cannot be equated simply with language, or the social, but
must refer to those relations, those structures, which require the subject to
submit his or her desire to a law, an order, which is constructed outside of
them – the order of the Other. (Kristeva writes that 'the symbolic – and
therefore syntax and all linguistic categories – is a social effect of the
relation to the other'.[27] The Name-of-the-Father constitutes the figure of
law as a symbolic function and which is therefore never the real father as
object of real familial relations or of narcissistic identification.

The domain of the symbolic is not symbolisation as such (though it
includes it) but the symbolisation of one's relation to desire as a relation of
lack, of lackingness, castration. A film presents a setting in play of desire, it
moves (as Heath emphasises) the spectator. This cannot be produced
simply by a narrative resolution for the characters in the film which
involves an acceptance of the Law – for example as described by Bellour in
his analysis of Hitchcock's *North by Northwest* and the role of Thornhill as
an Oedipal journey.[28] The film involves a fantasy, of the overthrow of
the
bad father and of the taking of the woman away from this bad father, all of
which is sanctioned and enabled by the good father. This does not,
however, involve the giving up of any object, of the mother. Moreover, it
is necessary to show how the film constitutes this symbolic narrative
resolution as a symbolic relation for the spectator outside the film. And
what will be determining here, I would suggest, is not just a representation,
or a recognition of lack, not just the loss of the object of love and object of
the demand for love, but the acceptance that it can never be, has never
been, obtained. The acceptance, therefore, not of a *frustrated* wish or
demand – which would be imaginary – of the object of desire *withheld* –
but with the acceptance of castration, symbolically, as the impossibility of
the fulfilment of the demand, of the desire that is, for the mother or
rather, for the *phallic* mother. It is therefore the experience that one's own
lack is already the lack of the Other itself. The Other has not got it, either.
Without this lack in the Other, the Other would be a closed structure and
the subject forever caught in a demand which is frustrated. Such a total
alienation is avoided not by filling out one's lack but by identifying oneself,
one's own lack, with the lack in the Other. But more, the Other, who also
does not have it, is itself blocked, desiring, and there is the question
therefore of the desire of the Other who lacks. For if the Other is lacking, it
must also desire and hence arises the question, what is the desire of the
Other, which appears as the question: 'What do you want' *(Che Vuoi?)*
None of this, of course, emerges as a directly represented content in the

film. It is not signified as such but rather it is what falls out of the narrative, a something else and something more which cannot quite be placed in the film, and instead it is the spectator in whom it is placed. It is produced as a result of a dialectical relation between identification and structures of 'making strange' in Brecht's sense, and works to 'move' the spectator for more than the duration of the film, inasmuch as the process involves an outside of the film, a third term, as the spectator's only resort in relation to the irresolvable paradoxes presented in it. This is not a shift from a place as an imaginary subject of identification within the film to a place as a subject of the symbolic outside the film, and hence as fully present to oneself as a subject, it is not a question of a dualism: inside/outside, in which the film as imaginary is the inside, while the symbolic is the outside as a kind of 'status quo' which can be returned to (and hence implying the subject of the symbolic as a subject fully present to itself). Rather, it is the production of a movement in the spectator herself or himself as a negotiation of the narrative paradox, and which is also an acceptance of the radical otherness, of the impossibility of the object of desire. This implies a transgression and a transcendence of the conventional boundary between the diegetic world of the film and outside reality since there is no simple duality of the spectator as subject of the film and subject 'in reality'. Slavoj Žižek has suggested

> The circular movement between the symbolic and the imaginary identi-fication never comes out without a certain left-over. After every 'quilting' of the signifier's chain which retroactively fixes its meaning, there always remains a certain gap, an opening which is rendered in the third form of the graph by the famous '*Che vuoi?*' – 'You're telling me that, but what do you want with it, what are you aiming at?' The question indicates the insistence of a gap between utterance and its enunciation – between what is said and what is desired as a result of what is said, what is it that is wanted of me through it?

This is also, I have suggested, the question which emerges in *Underworld USA* and it is this process which I seek to explore in the following discussion of the film.

UNDERWORLD USA

In *Underworld USA* the narrative paradox the spectator is presented with is the issue of why Tolly dies. Altogether many answers can be supplied, none, nor even all together, are sufficient. Something is unaccounted for. And the very filmic strategies which might be called Brechtian exacerbate this paradox, for they affirm the expectation that – didactically – Tolly should die for something, that we should understand something from his

death. The following notes on the film attempt to show the way in which
this narrative paradox is constructed and played out in relation to Fuller's
filmic strategies.

I

Fuller scripted, produced and directed *Underworld USA* for Columbia
Studios; it was released in 1960. An ostensibly conventional Hollywood
film in the 'B' feature mould, it is formally aberrant in that it contains only
some 570 shots compared with a norm of 800 to 900 shots for a film at this
time. Not only are exceptionally long takes used, but also non-classical
editing structures, with frequent jump-cuts and even a jump-dissolve.
There are almost no conventional point-of-view shot structures. Instead,
there is frequent use of big close-ups, often with characters looking away
from each other – for example, in the park bench scene where Tolly and
Cuddles sit beside each other but not looking at each other, or later when
they are talking together on the bed at Sandy's, each facing the opposite
direction away from the other.

II

Fuller is a director who risks obviousness. For example, Sandy's dolls:
these are first seen in her room at the back of the 'Elite Bar' she owns,
they are then motivated as the sign of her own infertility – Tolly's father

1 Sandy tends the young Tolly's wound while he holds one of
her dolls

2 One of the dolls in Sandy's bedroom in a shot which can be read as Cuddles's point-of-view as she awakens after being rescued from Gus by Tolly

3 Sandy declares that she wants to have children with Tolly, to be married, to 'be like other people'

has told him that she can't have children – and thus also motivate her relation to Tolly as her surrogate child. But their excess both in the sheer number of dolls, and in the number of shots in which they appear, is jarring. The young Tolly holds one while Sandy tends the wound on his head from a broken bottle another kid used to try to get the watch and other things Tolly had just stolen from a drunk in the street. Later, after he's come out of jail where he got the names of the other men involved in his father's murder from Vic Farrar, Tolly picks up another doll, a musical baby in nappies which he winds up to play as he speaks of getting the punks who killed his father; when Cuddles awakes in Sandy's house the camera shows her point of view as she gazes around the room, the dolls appearing distorted and alarming; the dolls are the absent family, ironically contrasted with Tolly's project of revenge. Finally, there is a photograph of a baby in centre-frame on the wall behind Tolly and Cuddles on a bed when Cuddles declares her love for Tolly and her wish to have a child with him and to 'kick our way of making a living', but is brutally rejected by Tolly (though he changes his mind later). The dolls are emblematic, but not as a singular sign. (There are also numerous other references to family and children in the film involving different ideas of family relationships and family responsibilities.)

Another, more singular, emblem, is the fist which is shown in a series of images: first, as Tolly grips the bedsheets in the orphanage he is sent to after his father's murder; second, grasping the safe lock as he pursues his profession of petty thief; and finally clenched, in death, at the end of the film. This last image is fixed and transfigured by a slow zoom into a freeze-frame shot with grainy image suggestive of a newspaper photo, the camera

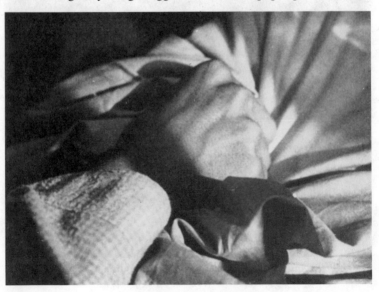

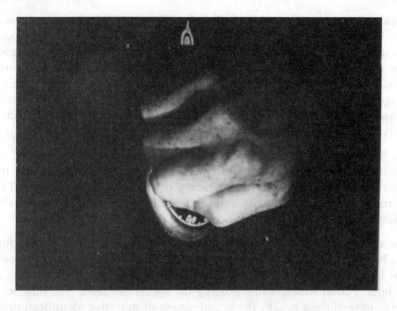

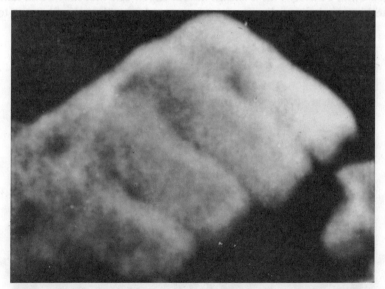

4,5,6 Tolly as a boy at reform school, his hand gripping the bedclothes. The adult Tolly plying his skills as a safe-breaker, his fist grips the dial of the lock mechanism. The final image of the film, which fills the screen, is Tolly's fist, clenched in death, its grainy quality reminiscent of a newspaper photograph, it seems to stand as an emblem for the film.

tracking in to a big-close up of Tolly's fist. These can be seen as gestural in
Brecht's sense: namely, as a, here repeated, gesture in which a whole social
situation can be read, which implies a social context in order to be read.
The fist metonymically refers to Tolly, and metaphorically to his resistance as well as subordination to social forces outside of him. In the final
image it becomes, as well, what Barthes calls a 'pregnant moment',
following Lessing's description in the *Laocoon*. That is, an instant which is
marked as in some way separable from the whole

> a hieroglyph in which can be read at a single glance (at one grasp if we
> think in terms of theatre and cinema) the present, the past and the
> future; that is, the historical meaning of the represented action. This
> crucial instant, totally concrete and totally abstract, is what Lessing
> subsequently calls (in the *Laocoon*) the *pregnant moment*.[29]

The shots do not function to advance the story as such, although the first
can be read as signifying Tolly's state of mind, of alienation, unhappiness
and resistance. Rather, they work at the level of the cinematic process as
an intervention which, while holding the spectator 'inside' the film, as it
were, nevertheless breaks the seamlessness of narrative identification by
the emphasis on the social context of its meaning.

Another example, which is very clearly a set-piece, is the suicide of
Police Chief Fowler. This is shown in four shots. The first shows him taking
something we later realise is a gun from a cabinet; then the film cuts to a

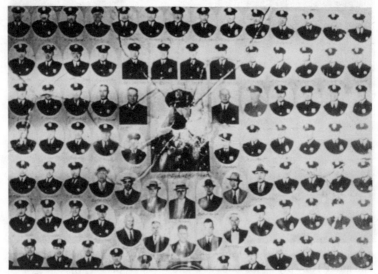

7 The photograph of the policemen of the station precinct, with the
Police Chief's larger picture in the centre, shot through as he commits
suicide.

close-up on his face; then a cut, returning to the end of the previous shot –
Driscoll realises what Fowler is about to do and leaps to stop him; finally,
cut to the fourth shot of a close-up of a photograph of the men at the police
precinct which is hanging on the wall behind Fowler. There is the sound of
a gun shot, and the image of the glass breaking in the photo-frame.
Fowler's image – at the centre of the photo – has been 'shot' by the same
bullet, we must assume, which has killed him. It is a highly stylised image,
and extremely condensed in signification. And ironically it functions in the
same way in which fetishism in cinema is described – the narrative flow is
halted to give a moment of contemplation, and the image is cut out from
the narrative action, from the events before and after, fixed and held for
the gaze.[30]

III

Unlike Brecht, however, Fuller effects a close identification with Tolly as
an individual from the very beginning, presenting him as a young boy
through a series of shots from his point of view, rolling a drunk then, when
he hears a policeman approach, showing his fear and flight. As spectators
we are 'with' our character – and have sympathy for him, too, as a kid out
alone on New Year's Eve night. He is presented as a figure of identification
as well in the sense that his desire is our desire, as developed in the
sequences with Cuddles. These involve Tolly's move from a disparaging

8 Having obtained the names of the other men involved in the murder
of his father, Tolly smiles as he reneges on his promise to forgive the
Catholic Farrar.

9, 10 With Smith in prison as a result of Cuddles's testimony, and
Gunther burned by Gela and Gus as a result of Tolly's misinformation
suggesting Gunther was doublecrossing the organisation, Tolly sets up
Gela for a fatal visit from Gus, having first viciously beaten Gela as he
explains the trap and the reason for his vengeance.

rejection of marriage with Cuddles, via Sandy's scathing outburst when she declares he's 'a midget' compared with Cuddles because she is willing to risk her life by standing as a witness for a murder, just for love of him, to an acceptance of the value of Cuddles' love for him and a commitment to marriage with her.

As the film's protagonist, however, identification with Tolly is complex. On the one hand he is a loser, repeatedly caught for robberies, but on the other hand he is extremely successful in getting his father's murderers – in rescuing Cuddles and as a result setting a lure for Gela, then arranging their deaths, just as any hero should. At the same time Tolly's motive, revenge for his father's death, does not seem to promote identification. Although it is an enunciated desire on Tolly's part, it remains an abstract aim until brought into play in a narrative situation, for example the suspense in relation to whether Vic Farrar will betray the names of the other men involved in Tolly's father's death, or the pleasure at the way in which Tolly deceives Gunther, Gela and Smith, as well as Connors, does. Finally, while the film carefully tells us that Tolly never carries a gun, some of his actions appear sadistic: his brutal treatment of Vic, for example, from whom he extracts a death-bed confession (Vic is Catholic) in return for a promise of forgiveness but on which he reneges, or the way he beats up Gela before delivering him to his death at the hands of Gus.

IV

Fuller is said to have quoted approvingly Goethe's statement that 'Nothing is more terrible than active ignorance'. Fuller's didacticism can be clearly seen in Driscoll's speech to his officers, and in the words of Chief Fowler's daughter when she repeats to her father that he had always said that a crooked cop was the lowest of all. Commenting on his reputation as an 'action' director, Fuller said

> None of my films is, for me at least, an action film, even though there is action in all of them. That's why I put action in my films, so that the action can carry the message and so the public doesn't get the idea that I'm trying to deliver a sermon or a lecture. For me, the greatest art form in the world is education.[31]

But for Fuller this means not education in knowledge as such, but in what people are afraid to know and see. Of *Shock Corridor* he said

> I'm not ashamed to show what's wrong. I'm still basically a journalist. Most people think that it's up to the newspapers to discuss these problems. But I say on the contrary, that they must be put in dramatic form. (p. 115)

Fuller's example for this is the story of one of the asylum inmates in *Shock Corridor*, a soldier brainwashed to turn communist in Korea. No one had

been able to persuade him to return home to the USA until another soldier
visited him

> to talk to him about his family to reveal to him something he had never
> known before and to make him cry... What made him return was this
> revelation of a love he had never known ... Over there, he felt that he
> missed America. Then the second tragic element appears. No one in the
> US wants anything to do with him. (p. 116)

Of another film (never finished) called *Tigero*, Fuller said:

> The story, in a sentence, is about two people very much in love. In the
> face of death, the husband *could* sacrifice his life to save his wife, but lets
> her die because although he loves her a lot, he loves himself more –
> that's all. (p. 107)

Fuller's stories go for the jugular – metaphorically speaking, pushing the
spectator up against what she or he would prefer to leave unseen, unsaid,
unknown. This, not only because such narratives are themselves different
or unusual, but rather because Fuller offers in them no authorial voice, no
objective narrator within the fictional world through which the spectator
can 'handle' the story. Captured directly to the drive of desire – 'two
people very much in love', we are then brought up against not only its loss
but this as an unacceptable loss. If *both* died that would be acceptable, but
for one to live – the man – at the cost of the other is to leave us, in an
intolerable way, with the continuing fact of loss. If there is irony in such
narratives it is perhaps the irony of the choice 'your money or your life'.[32]

Tolly's death in *Underworld USA* seems to me to be a similar wry slap in
the face by life, where life is understood not as the misfortunes of fate, or
of nature, but as the shortcomings of the human, of society. Why does
Tolly die? He had everything to live for, so what is the narrative function of
his death? For of course he does not die, the story kills him. A number of
aesthetic and cultural motivations can be suggested for Tolly's death but I
will argue that these are finally insufficient and that this very insufficiency
makes apparent a 'difference' in *Underworld USA*.

First of all, current conventions of verisimilitude – as defined by Genette
and as manifested in the requirements of, for example, the Production
Code (or Hays Code) in Hollywood, would demand that crime should be
shown not to pay. Tolly thus dies because he's bad, a criminal. (An earlier
scenario was rejected by the Production Code Authority for exactly this
reason, though, as Fuller retorted, crime does pay.) However, Tolly is not
that 'bad'. His is a basically good character caught up by life's circumstances in the 'wrong' business, rather than an essentially 'bad' character
who redeems himself momentarily and whose death is therefore a repara-
tion to society. By 1960, moreover, it would have been possible to allow
Tolly to live given his intention of going straight with Cuddles. Fuller had

got away with something similar in his much earlier *Pick Up On South Street* (1952) which has its two lovers, a prostitute and a pickpocket, not only survive but also remaining unregenerate, 'the girl still a prostitute, going to live with a man who will continue as a pick-pocket, neither having gained anything from the whole business except falling in love with each other' (p. 104). The film closes on their defiance: the government man forecasts 'You're worthless. In a week I'll find you picking the pockets of a drunk or a corpse'. The woman replies, with all the scorn she can muster, 'You wanna bet?' and laughs; the man laughs too, as Fuller says, 'at the cop and the government man' (p. 104).

Second, Tolly's death is nevertheless consistent with a modern convention of narrative realism; namely, the unmotivated or undermotivated action or event. In so far as there is no reason – that is, no narrative or fictional requirement – for Tolly to die (unlike little Jenny Mencken) it is realistic in the sense that life is the unexpected, the unpredictable. To some extent, as Genette has suggested, it is an anti-narrative convention, since it overturns the generic requirements and expectations of narrative, of logical relations of cause and effect motivating events. It is a convention of realism established most clearly by the Italian neo-realists and seen in particular in Rossellini's *Germany Year Zero* (1947). In addition, it is realistic in terms of the Hollywood convention which places happy endings as fantasy, as unreal, and hence which, by contrast and tautologically, defines unhappy endings as realistic.

Third, the film produces a formal narrative closure with Tolly's death, effecting the literalisation of the truism 'like father like son' in the symmetry, repetition and rhyming of Tolly's death, keeled over in a dark, wet alleyway, with that of his father twenty years earlier. But the very strength of this visual, formal, closure exposes the way the closure is limited to this level alone. It poses its insufficiency for other levels in the narrative. In particular, although Tolly's death reiterates his father's, it is also different. How can we understand its difference, and how should we understand the 'truth' of the unmotivated realism of his death? For, like Rossellini, Fuller clearly assumes that reality has a meaning, a truth. Is there a moral truth, such as that the desire for revenge destroys the avenger?

Tolly dies as a result of killing Connors, the head of the crime organisation. He is not one of the targets in his revenge for his father's murder, but an obstacle to his future happiness with Cuddles. Here the film presents a painful irony: Tolly is invincible in his pursuit of vengeance, but fatally vulnerable when he seeks to assure his own future – a future not based on vengeance but in opposition to it. It is as if Tolly's change of heart – to becoming the decent man he always could be, who desires a socially-adjusted future of wife and family, going straight – makes him vulnerable, like Jenny Mencken or Chief Fowler, in a way that as a thief he

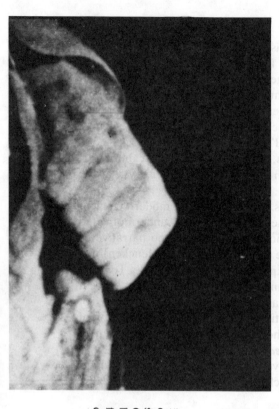

11–17 The killing of Tolly's father at the beginning of the film, in a dark alley (*the first in the sequence*) is echoed in Tolly's own death slumped by garbage cans in another dark alley at the end of the film. Cuddles runs up and holds Tolly, but Sandy urges her to leave – she may be in danger from Connors's men who have followed Tolly – in order to finish the job for Tolly. She reluctantly leaves, and the film cuts in to a close shot of Tolly's chest and fist, which dissolves into a big close-up of just his fist.

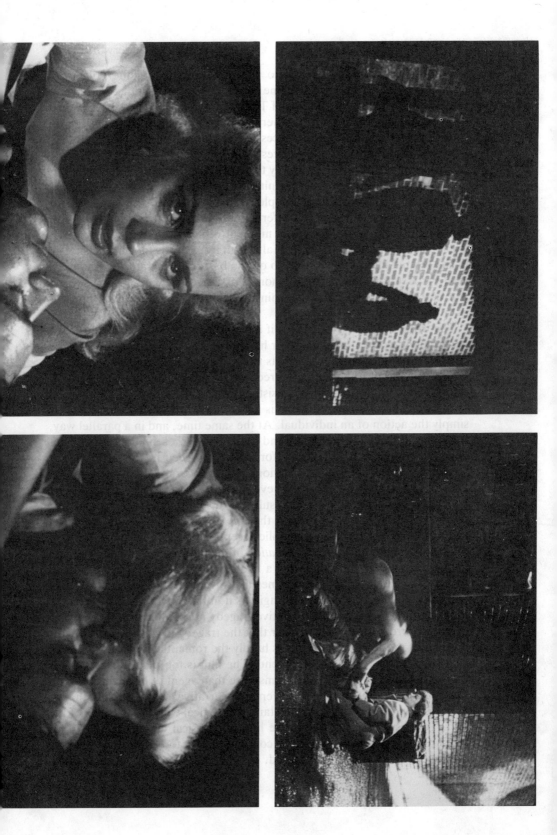

simple the action of an individual. At the same time, and in a parallel way

was not. Moreover the film in no way reassures us that the police *can* protect the honest citizen. And one wonders whether Cuddles will live to sing on Smith, one of the killers of Tolly's father whom Cuddles will stand witness against in relation to another murder – for though Driscoll's speech to his officers emphasised the necessity for the struggle against 'men like Connors' the film in no way assures us of success.

Thus irony arises as a fourth way to understand Tolly's death. Yet this is not irony in the sense of one meaning being commented upon and placed by another superior or more complete meaning. It has been argued that, in so far as it introduces a self-referentiality into a text and in so far as it exposes the text as spoken in its moment of speaking another meaning, irony can be a radical device. But although irony tends to split the subject of the textual enounced, it does so on the basis of a narrator before and a reader/spectator after, each of whom is assumed to be a knowing subject who can decode the different meanings – a unity who can speak of 'himself' as split, other.

The irony of *Underworld USA*, if it is ironic, is that of the pessimist: life never allows you your desire, your happiness. But the film presents rather more of a paradox, for it constructs two radically irreconcilable meanings. On the one hand, there is the correctness of Tolly's attempt to secure his future with Cuddles, which is consistent with the actions of all Hollywood heroes; on the other hand, there is its inevitable failure inasmuch as it is simply the action of an individual. At the same time, and in a parallel way, the forces of society, the police and the law, are presented as correct but never as effective. It is Tolly's efforts which succeed in getting Gunther, Smith and Gela, as well as Connors. The police and District Attorney Driscoll, while shown as correct, never do anything. Tolly is wrong, but he does the 'right things'. As a result the irony shifts from that of the pessimist, which is in any case only the erection of frustration into a general truth. It is a resistance to a symbolic acceptance of lack by substitution in the fatalistic acceptance of the *negation* of the imaginary demand. The film implies at one and the same time a fatalism *and* the message that human action can change things. It becomes irresolvably paradoxical.

Finally, then, Tolly's death is tragic. Is it in this way that we can resolve the narrative? The issues of narrative tragedy are too large to be properly explored here. However, it is clear that the tragedy of *Underworld USA* is not that of the Romantics. Tolly is hardly the romantic hero whose flawed character brings about his tragic end. The film is too materialist; Tolly is more acted upon by external circumstance than agent of his own downfall. The spectator is thus denied this avenue of narrative closure as well, that is, as a position from which to understand and to deal with the paradox of the film. Tolly is perhaps closer to the hero of classical Greek tragedy in his quest for a revenge which runs counter to the forces of social order. However, as I have already noted, it is not his quest for revenge which brings about Tolly's downfall, but his attempts to secure his future with Cuddles outside of crime.

The film seems to be saying that Tolly's death is somehow unnecessary, while not showing how it could have been prevented. There is no comfortable – imaginary – narrative closure, not even that of tragic melodrama, the 'if only' response.[33] However, the film itself does not bring us as spectators to accept this loss, this frustration. Rather, the spectator is forced to resolve his or her frustration by an acknowledgement that wishes – for Tolly to have his future – are not always fulfilled. The film demands that we acknowledge a limitation on our wishes. In this sense it puts the spectator in a relation to his or her desire which is that of the symbolic relation. The final shots of the film seem to confirm this: Cuddles is holding the dead Tolly in her arms, while Sandy urges her to leave.

'If they find you here they'll kill you too!

The film cuts to a close-up of Cuddles and Tolly.

'I don't care about Smith.'

But Sandy urges her:

'You've got to finish the job for Tolly, or he died for nothing.'

Cuddles sobs while Sandy repeats:

'Come on.'

And the two women leave Tolly, walking out of screen frame. The film thus explicitly substitutes the law for desire, although this is still not straightforward. The job Cuddles will be finishing for Tolly is his revenge for his father's murder, whereas what Tolly died for was the chance of a future with Cuddles. However, the revenge on Smith that he achieves is under the law, whereas he set up Gunther and Gela to be killed by their own associates, and hence outside the law. Moreover, it is Cuddles who is thus constructed as an agent in relation to the symbolic order; that is, acting in terms of an imperative from the Other. Although Sandy's words imply that this 'Other' is Tolly, and hardly the Law, the filmic narration implies a universal Law in its transformation of the final shot of Tolly's fist into a newspaper-type photograph.

The film requires us as spectators to change register, to move from an involvement through identification with the characters and the narrative, to a realisation of the place of human action as regulated by law. But yet where the 'law' itself is shown to be flawed, insufficient, in effect – castrated. The film can thus be seen, retrospectively, as the *problem* of the law in its insufficiency. Tolly rejects the law at the beginning of the film, he is a thief and he refuses the help of the law – Driscoll – in finding the men

who murdered his father; 'I'm no fink' he says. He comes to accept the law
through his relation to Cuddles at the point where he agrees to marry
Cuddles, to go straight and 'kick our way of doing things', to become 'like
other people'. As a result Tolly moves from acting in the present to seeking
to ensure his future, and Cuddles. In this the law should support them, but
it is shown to fail them, without thereby negating the necessity of their
choice. It is, after all, only from the point of view of the imaginary that the
law is omnipotent.

We are confronted at the end of the film, then, with the lack in the
Other, and *Underworld USA* offers no simple fantasy with which to
'gentrify' this lack. This is the 'left-over' from the circle of interpellation,
the movement between imaginary and symbolic identification. But this
proposed beyond of imaginary and symbolic has nothing to do with some
kind of irreducible dispersion and plurality of the signifying process, that
is, with the fact that the metonymic sliding always subverts every fixation of
meaning, every 'quilting' of the floating signifiers, which has at times
produced an idealism of 'plurality'. For what emerges here is not the
subversion of meaning, but the fact of non-meaning, meaninglessness.
Paradoxically, the constitution of the symbolic for the subject also produces the real beyond the symbolic (for Lacan, the lack in the Other and
the real of the drive), as distinct from the real lying behind the imaginary.
There is of course no truth, indeed no content at all in this. Instead it
throws the subject back into the symbolic, but which is now exposed in its
arbitrariness, for it does, after all, fail to guarantee meaning, since it
throws back the question, finally, '*Che vuoi?*'

The film does offer a form of fantasy to cover this lack at the end in a
clearly fetishistic image of Tolly's fist; fetishistic as part object, and in its
separation and transformation in the newsphoto-style imaging of it. No
doubt it symbolises struggle, but struggle by whom, for what? *Che vuoi?*
The film, just like any representation, involves a setting in play of desire
with multiple points of entry, of subject-position, but *Underworld USA*
also shifts the spectator-subject's relation to desire. Desire in narrative is
not an object as such, but an effect of representation, and it comes into
existence for the film, and the spectator, in the representation of lack and
in the production – in fantasy – of its becoming present. Fantasy, as the
support of the symbolic, covering over its lack, is necessary, rather than
'bad'; it does not oppose the reality-principle but rather supports it by
ensuring the continuance of meaningfulness. *Underworld USA* does not
subvert this by its failure to supply such a concluding fantasy but rather
presents the space and necessity of such a fantasy, even at the risk of
proposing the law as the thing which makes Tolly's death worthwhile, even
though the film has shown it to be flawed. The film produces the demand
for fantasy in its requirement that we confront the lack in the symbolic.
The film says the equivalent of 'my country right or wrong', thus instigating

the need to affirm 'my country, *because* it is right'. This is no less ideological than it is necessary.

METAPSYCHOLOGY

For this discussion, psychoanalysis has ceased to be a metapsychology of cinema, that is, a general theory of the spectator's psychical relation to the film. Instead, psychoanalysis as a theory of human subjectivity has been used to try to describe a particular instance of the construction of a subject-spectator for film in *Underworld USA*; this is, of course, an effect of the cinematic codes at work in the film, but these have not been seen as determined by cinematically-specific psychical mechanisms. In one sense, however, psychoanalysis *is* thus a metapsychology for cinema, in so far as it is a theory of human subjectivity and hence can describe the construction of subject positions in relation to film. But the role of psychoanalysis as a metapsychology has undergone important changes. Its theory of the subject is of a subject which is divided – the division of conscious and unconscious which was Freud's first discovery in psychoanalysis, the division of ego/super-ego/id, and the divisions involved in the very emergence of the super-ego – those various identifications internalised by the ego. Lacan's work has only clarified and extended Freud's theories in this respect. As a result, while indeed psychoanalysis is a theory of subjectivity, it is of a subjectivity always split and divided. These divisions do not necessarily, if at all, produce a harmonious whole, an integrated unit; they involve conflict and negotiation. Psychoanalysis describes the dynamic determinants at work on and for the subject. Thus, it can hardly be applied as metapsychology, since it can only speak of the means to the fixing of subjectivity, but which as such is never fixed. It can, however, contribute to the understanding of the construction – the 'fixing' of subject-position – in discourse, in film, in the movement of the film-as-text.

Notes

1.   *Underworld USA*, USA 1960. Distributed by Columbia (A Globe Enterprises Production). Directed, produced and written by Samuel Fuller. Photographed by Hal Mohr. Art Director: Robert Peterson. Set decorator: Bill Calvert. Music by Harry Sukman. Edited by Jerome Thomas. Assistant director: Floyd Joyer. 98 minutes. With: Cliff Robertson: *Tolly Devlin*, Dolores Dorn: *Cuddles*, Beatrice Kay: *Sandy*, Larry Gates: *Driscoll*, Richard Rust: *Gus*, Robert Emhardt: *Connors*, Paul Dubov: *Gela*, Gerald Milton: *Gunther*, Allan Gruener: *Smith*, David Kent: *Tolly as a boy*, Neyle Morrow: *Barney*, Henry Norell: *prison doctor*, Sally Mills: *Connie*, Tina Rome: *a woman*, Robert P Lieb: *police officer*, Peter Brocco: *Vic Farrar*.

My interest in this film developed when analysing it with students at the University of Kent in 1983 as part of a course involving the close study of a single film. I am grateful for the discussions with those students and with my colleague and co-teacher on the course Ben Brewster, from which many of the ideas here have emerged, as well as for the detailed shot-breakdown collectively produced which I have drawn upon extensively for this analysis.

2.   David Will and Peter Wollen (eds), *Samuel Fuller* (Film Festival, Edinburgh, 1969).

3.   From an article written by Peter Wollen under the name of Lee Russell and quoted by Sam Rhodie in his article on *The House of Bamboo* in *Samuel Fuller*, ibid., p. 37.

4.   For Hirst's discussion see *On Law and Ideology* (Macmillan, London, 1979), especially ch. 3, 'Althusser and the Theory of Ideology'. Slavoj Žižek takes up this issue in *The Sublime Object of Ideology* (Verso, London, 1989), ch. 1, and reintroduces the notion of ideology as mask but in a way which inverts the usual relation (the published translation is slightly different):

> There is a kind of positive ontological dimension of the misrecognition at work here: of course, the ideological discourse is distorting the reality, but this reality cannot sustain itself without this distortion; of course there is reality hidden behind the ideological mask, but if we take off the mask, we lose at the same time the reality behind the mask, far from being able, finally to grasp the naked reality in itself. It's then the paradox of being which can reproduce itself only insofar as it is misrecognised, overlooked: the moment we see it 'as it really is', this being dissolves itself into nothingness or, more precisely, it changes into another kind of reality. That's why we must avoid the simple metaphorics of demasking, of throwing away the veils which are supposed to hide the naked reality: in doing this, we may lose reality itself. We can see why Lacan, in his seminar on *The Ethics of Psychoanalysis*, distances himself from the liberating gesture of saying finally that 'the emperor has no clothes'. The point is, as Lacan puts it, that the emperor is naked only beneath his clothes, so if there is an unmasking feature of psychoanalysis, it is more close to the well-known joke of Alphonse Allais quoted by Lacan: somebody points at a woman and utters a horrified cry 'Look at her, what a shame, under her clothes, she is totally naked'.

5.   These problems were recognised within *Screen*; see for example Rosalind Coward, 'Class, "Culture", and the Social Formation', *Screen*, vol. 18, no. 1 (1977).

6.   'John Ford's *Young Mr Lincoln* – A collective text by the editors of *Cahiers du Cinèma*', translated in *Screen*, vol. 13, no. 3 (1972), p. 14.

7.   Ben Brewster 'Notes on the Text "John Ford's *Young Mr Lincoln*" by the editors of *Cahiers du Cinèma*', *Screen*, vol. 14, no. 3 (1973), p. 38.

8.   An earlier editorial in *Cahiers du Cinèma* by J.-L. Comolli and J. Narboni distinguished categories of films according to the way in which the films related to ideology, whether they were directly critical of the dominant ideology or were wholly in the service of that ideology, or, as was claimed for the films of John Ford (and, for example, Rossellini and Dreyer), the films appeared at first sight to belong within the dominant ideology but turn out to be so only in ambiguous manner. 'An internal criticism is taking place which cracks the film apart at the seams. If one reads the film obliquely, looking for symptoms; if one looks beyond its apparent formal coherence, one can see

that it is riddled with cracks: it is splitting under an internal tension which is simply not there in an ideologically innocuous film' 'Cinema/Ideology/Criticism', translated in *Screen*, vol. 12, no. 1 (1971), pp. 32–3.

9.   Christian Metz, 'The Imaginary Signifier', *Psychoanalysis and Cinema*, Celia Britton Annwyl Williams, Ben Brewster and Alfred Guzzetti (trans), (Macmillan, London, 1982). Jean-Louis Baudry 'Ideological Effects of the Basic Cinematographic Apparatus', trans Alan Williams, *Film Quarterly*, vol. 27, no. 2 (Winter 1974–5); 'The Apparatus: Metapsychological Approaches to the Impression of Reality in the Cinema', Jean Andres and Bertrand Augus (trans), *Camera Obscura*, no. 1 (1976). Mary-Ann Doane, see for example, '*Gilda*: Epistemology as Striptease', *Camera Obscura*, no. 11 (1983), and her book *The Desire to Desire* (Indiana University Press, Bloomington, 1987). Stephen Heath, see for example, 'Difference', *Screen*, vol. 19, no. 3 (1978). Laura Mulvey, 'Visual Pleasure and Narrative Cinema', *Screen*, vol. 16, no. 3 (1975), and *Visual and Other Pleasures* (Macmillan, London, 1989).

10.   Constance Penley, 'Feminism, Film Theory and the Bachelor Machines', *m/f* no. 10 (1985), p. 10.

11.   Constance Penley writes (ibid. p. 39) that 'Characteristically, the bachelor machine is a closed, self-sufficient system. Its common themes include frictionless, sometimes perpetual motion, an ideal time and the magical possibility of its reversal (the Time Machine is a bachelor machine), electrification, voyeurism, and masturbatory eroticism, the dream of the mechanical reproduction of art, and artificial birth of reanimation.' The term was used by Marcel Duchamp to designate the lower part of his 'Large Glass: The Bride Stripped bare by Her Bachelors, Even' and was borrowed by Michel Carrouges in his book *Machines Célibataires* (Paris, La Chêne 1975 (1954)) where he described such texts as Mary Shelley's *Frankenstein* or Fritz Lang and Thea von Harbou's *Metropolis* as 'Bachelor Machines'. Constance Penley observes that cinema, too, by this definition, is a 'bachelor machine', which, quoting Michel de Certeau, 'does not agree to write the woman as well ... The machine's chief distinction is its being male' (in Claire and Szeeman (eds), *Les Machines Célibataires*, p. 94, a catalogue of an exhibition of 'Bachelor Machines', Venice Alfieri 1975).
         I am indebted here to Constance Penley for her article's very clear articulation of the role of psychoanalysis for these theories.

12.   Ben Brewster, Colin MacCabe and Stephen Heath, 'Reply to Julia Lesage', *Screen*, vol. 16, no. 2, (1975), p. 87.

13.   Stephen Heath, 'Lessons from Brecht', *Screen*, vol. 15, no. 2 (1984), pp. 106–7.

14.   Editorial, *Screen*, vol. 15, no. 1 (1974), p. 19.

15.   The article later appeared in a collection of Metz's writings entitled *Psychoanalysis and Cinema*, Celia Britton, trans. Annwyl Williams, Ben Brewster and Alfred Guzzetti (Macmillan, London, 1982). Page references, which are given in the text, are to this edition.

16.   Jacqueline Rose, *Sexuality in the Field of Vision* (Verso, London, 1986), p. 158.

17.   Sigmund Freud, 'Group Psychology', *SE*, XVIII, fn. 2, p. 110.

18.   Heath, 'Lessons from Brecht', p. 108 (see note 13).

19.   See Mulvey, 'Visual Pleasure...'; Raymond Bellour, 'Hitchcock the Enunciator', *Camera Obscura*, no. 2 (1977) and the interview with him in *Camera Obscura*, nos 3/4 (1979); Doane, '*Gilda*', *The Desire to Desire*, and also 'Film and the Masquerade: Theorising the Female Spectator', *Screen*, vol. 23,

nos 3/4 (1982), 'Caught and Rebecca: The Inscription of Femininity as Absence', Enclitic, vol. 5, no. 2/vol. 6 no. 1 (double issue) (1981).

20. In the interview with Camera Obscura, p. 97.
21. Heath, 'Lessons from Brecht', p. 115.
22. This issue is taken up in more detail in my book, To Represent Woman: The Representation of Sexual Difference in the Visual Media (Macmillan, London, 1990).
23. Slavoj Žižek, 'Identity, Identification and its Beyond', in Ernesto Laclau (ed.), New Reflections on the Revolution of our Time (Verso, London, forthcoming); also The Sublime Object . . ., ch. 3.
24. Rose, 'Julia Kristeva – Take Two', in Sexuality. . ., p. 157.
25. Colin MacCabe in his introduction to Metz's 'The Imaginary Signifier', Screen, vol. 16, no. 2 (1975), p. 11.
26. S. Heath, 'Anata mo', Screen, vol. 14, no. 4, (1976/7), p. 64.
27. Julia Kristeva, Revolution in Poetic Language, Margaret Waller (trans). (Columbia University Press, New York, 1984), p. 29.
28. R. Bellour, 'Le blocage symbolique', Communications, no. 23 (1975).
29. Roland Barthes, 'Diderot, Brecht, Eisenstein', Screen, vol. 15, no. 2 (1974), p. 36.
30. See, for example, Laura Mulvey's description of Dietrich in Morocco, in 'Visual Pleasure . . .'.
31. From a 1963 interview with Jean-Louis Noames, in Samuel Fuller; further page references to this interview are given in the text.
32. Lacan uses this phrase as an example of the alienation of the subject. At the moment when it appears – that is, when it is produced by the signifier – it fades, since it is only the effect of that signifier: 'Your money or your life! If I choose the money, I lose both. If I choose life, I have life without money, namely a life deprived of something.' 'The Subject and the Other: Alienation', in The Four Fundamental Concepts of Psychoanalysis, trans Alan Sheridan (Penguin, Harmondsworth, 1979), p. 212.
33. 'The words "if only" mark both the fact of loss, that it is too late, yet simultaneously the possibility that things might have been different, that the fantasy could have been fulfilled, the object of desire attained. . .' Steve Neale, 'Melodrama and Tears', Screen, vol. 27, no. 6 (1986), p. 22.

9

Psychoanalysis and Political Literary Theories

Robert Young

Psychoanalysis, which could be described as a theory of unhappy relationships, has itself a long history of unhappy relationships. In the first place
there is the story of the tense relationships within psychoanalysis between
analysts, the psychoanalytic politics that has been charted by Paul Roazen,
François Roustang, Sherry Turkle and others.[1] In the second place,
psychoanalysis has a history of relationships with other disciplines; but
while it has always exercised a fascination for other forms of thought in the
human sciences, liaisons have tended to be short and not always sweet.
You could say that psychoanalysis, though now at the grand old age of
90-odd, still finds it hard to settle down. I want to look at three of those
relationships in the sphere of cultural analysis – with literary criticism, with
Marxism, and with feminism. For even if it has not yet settled down
psychoanalysis has, in the last twenty years, undergone a sort of sea-change
and entered into a new kind of relationship that has almost reversed its
former identity: that is with politics.

In fact, of course, politics is really an old flame from the 1920s and 1930s.
But since the failure of that intimacy psychoanalysis has generally been
regarded as the very antithesis to the political and both Marxism and
feminism, with some notable exceptions, have been hostile towards it.
Notwithstanding its own tangled history, psychoanalysis, it has often been
claimed, neglects history. In literary criticism, by contrast, it was the very
lack of politics, the concentration on the cosy pleasures of subjectivity,
without having to be bothered by all those social and historical factors, that
provided the main attraction of psychoanalysis as a way of reading
literature.

But today, although the psychoanalytic establishment in Britain at least remains much the same as ever, the use of psychoanalysis as a theory has changed dramatically. It is now employed in a whole range of specifically political cultural theories, particularly those associated with Marxism, feminism, and critiques of colonialism. Indeed nowadays the politicisation of psychoanalysis, in direct contradiction with its former identity, means that you cannot discuss it at all without, say, raising questions of gender and sexuality. This means that a 'pure' psychoanalytic literary criticism is no longer possible.

But what is the status of psychoanalysis in these theories? And why has this change come about? How did psychoanalysis get politicised again? Perhaps it is easier to begin by asking when it came about, and here, looking at the history of psychoanalytic criticism, of Marxism, and of feminism, it is obvious that the shift came with Lacan. Lacan's rereading of Freud effectively changed the whole terrain of the use of psychoanalysis in contemporary cultural theory.

Lacan changed psychoanalysis because he shifted it from a seemingly self-referential body of technical knowledge into a metaphorics of language. Less charitably, you could say that Lacan produced the most effective repression of sex of all by semioticising it, turning it into a sign system and denying sex's ontological status in favour of that of linguistics. Be that as it may, Lacan showed how the structures of sexuality could be mapped onto linguistic ones: thus the Oedipus complex, for instance, is translated into the story of the subject's accession into language and law.

The metamorphosis of psychoanalysis into a semiotic metalanguage meant that psychoanalysis could be correlated with any other form of social knowledge through the analytic method known as structuralism. Since structuralism was a method of investigation that used the model of language for the analysis of a whole range of cultural forms and disciplines in the human sciences, the use of the linguistic model within psychoanalytic theory meant that for the first time psychoanalysis could be grafted onto other kinds of analysis, and even become a model for them. Anywhere that structuralism had gone, psychoanalysis could follow.

At the same time, of course, such a transference opened up psychoanalysis the other way, and made it possible to bring other forms of knowledge to bear on it, allowing a new access to the pressure of the social and the political.

So Lacan's structuralism enabled an articulation of psychoanalysis, a theory of subjectivity, with theories of culture and the social, such as Marxism or feminism. They met in language and ideology, and in Coward and Ellis.[2] To everyone's convenience, suddenly it seemed as if Marxism and feminism could acquire a theory of the subject, and psychoanalysis a theory of the social.

The problems with such a coupling, however, was that psychoanalysis was already a theory of the articulation of the subject with the social: if desire, for instance, is the desire of the Other, this means that desire is a social phenomenon. Furthermore, as the concept of desire itself suggests, psychoanalytic theory amounts to the argument that the structure of the relation of the psyche to the social is one of incommensurability – which does not mean that they do not interact, only that they do so unhappily. When social analysis has tried to link itself with psychoanalysis, it seems often not to have noticed this aspect of psychoanalytic theory, with the result that those marriages between forms of social explanation and psychoanalysis, far from being able to exploit psychoanalytic theory, merely repeat the narrative of incompatibility that it theorises.

Let me illustrate this by returning, once again, to the story of Oedipus – which I want to suggest comprises an allegory of the whole problem of the articulation of the individual with society that psychoanalysis theorises, as well as of the articulation of psychoanalysis with politics. During the course of the play, Oedipus goes through a double process of interpretation. He begins by considering that the truth of things corresponds to the way in which he sees the world: his own interpretation of the experience of his life shows him to be entirely innocent – he has done nothing wrong and has avoided fulfilling the dreadful prophecies. But then Teiresias accuses him, as René Girard puts it, of being 'a man who, at all times, is what he thinks he is not, and is not what he thinks he is'.[3]

All the play then consists of, in a way, is a process of a massive re-interpretation by Oedipus of his own life in which he has to separate his own experience from what emerges as the social truth about it – that is that he has indeed killed his father and married his mother. The play shows that far from constituting his own meaning he has been caught as a function in a larger impersonal process utterly indifferent to, and unrelated to, his own account of his experience.

Oedipus undergoes the rather painful discovery that, in Lévi-Strauss' formulation, 'to reach reality we must first repudiate experience'.[4] In other words, he finds that there is a gap between experience and meaning. What has happened to Oedipus is that his subjective point of view has been put alongside an objective, or social one. He has to learn to live in the discourse or locus of the other. Not only is he the subject of his interpretation, and of his curse, but as he discovers, he is also their object.

When Oedipus abandons his own account of things in favour of that of others, he is effectively decentred from the position of the human subject as a single, determinate being, as an agent who is the source of his own actions, responsibilities, experience and self-identity. 'My words', Oedipus comments, 'are uttered as a stranger to the act'. The paradox of his story is that he becomes a stranger to his own tale and to himself.

Oedipus' reversal illustrates the two possible polarities for any form of interpretation. The result will depend on where you started. There are basically two positions from which you can begin any interpretation, or indeed any philosophy in general, and that is, in Coleridge's description, the *I am* or the *It is* – the first or third person, Kant or Spinoza. Now interpretation, especially literary interpretation, has tended to emphasise the *I am*, that is the perspective of the individual on society and the world, rather than the *It is*, in which the individual is seen from the perspective of the social.

But if there is one shift that is common to many current but different forms of theory it has been that this perspective has been reversed, that is that we now tend to consider the individual from the perspective of the social rather than the social from the perspective of the individual. Structuralism, for instance, constitutes a method of analysis which considers the meaning or significance of any individual element not in terms of any intrinsic identity that it may possess in isolation but in terms of its relation to the system of which it forms a part. It represents a shift in our time from seeing experience from the perspective of the first person to that of the third, and even, I would suggest, from that of the first world to that of the third.

Oedipus Rex, then, could be said to be the story of the move from the *I am* to the *It is*, or an allegory of what happens with structuralism. The play is an attempt to think experience in the manner of the late as well as the early Oedipus, and to think through the problem of the relation between them. If experience can be interpreted from the perspectives both of the first and the third persons, *Oedipus* shows the extent to which these two accounts are often in tension with each other. The living through of this incompatibility between the individual and the social is the subject of the play and of psychoanalysis.

Both Marxism and feminism, then, in incorporating psychoanalysis, have tried to use it as a way of articulating the individual with the social, or subjectivity with society. But they then tend to get caught up in acting out the conflict between the psychic and the social, rather than, as psychoanalysis itself does, producing a theory of that incompatibility. The lesson of psychoanalysis is that they have to be lived simultaneously as two irreconcilable positions – which is why we have an unconscious. We are not just the product of a marriage – we are also the scarred children of interminable proceedings for divorce.

PSYCHOANALYTIC CRITICISM

If Marxism and feminism have both a history of tense relationships with psychoanalysis, the same could be said in a different way for literary criticism. Psychoanalytic criticism began of course with Freud himself, but in spite of continued attempts to develop it in an autonomous critical form, it has always remained something of an embarrassment. It is a relief therefore to be able to announce that psychoanalytic criticism, as an autonomous critical method, no longer exists. As I have argued in greater detail elsewhere, you cannot just be a pure psychoanalytic critic' anymore.[5]

At first it seemed as though the return to Freud would merely produce a new version of psychoanalytic criticism. The declaration of a new Lacanianised form was made by Shoshana Felman in her introduction to the influential Yale French Studies *Literature and Psychoanalysis*.[6] Proclaiming that the relation between literature and psychoanalysis had to be 'reinvented', Felman called attention to the whole problem of the very concept of a 'psychoanalytic criticism' in so far as it implies bringing a body of knowledge, psychoanalysis, to bear on a body of unselfconscious experience, literature, the first of which is then utilised in order to interpret and understand the second. Effectively, this means that one discourse is being read in terms of another, a work of translation, of 'psychic reductionism'.

This is of course essentially the structure of a whole range of criticisms, such as Marxist criticism, which bring a body of knowledge to bear upon a text. However, Felman questioned the usefulness of this enterprise; for one thing it is unlikely to produce anything that the body of knowledge did not know in the first place, and in the second, it consigns to oblivion the specificity of the object being examined, such as the fact that literature is constituted in language. The renewed emphasis that Lacan placed upon the function of language in psychoanalysis led to the sense that perhaps literature contained more knowledge for psychoanalysis than had been allowed for – think of the extent to which psychoanalysis uses literature not only to test its hypotheses but also to construct its conceptual framework and even to name itself – the Oedipus complex, narcissism, masochism, sadism, etc. (Perhaps it would be unwise to speculate too much on what such a list suggests about literature.) This means that if the knowledge of psychoanalysis is at least partly grounded in literature, then it cannot also provide a grounding for literature.

Felman therefore spoke of there no longer being an *application* of psychoanalysis to literature, but of a mutual *implication*, or interimplication. Literature and psychoanalysis, she argued, are enfolded within each other, traversed by each other, both outside and inside each other. This seemed to augur well, but what was not perhaps realised at the time was that Felman's redefinition implied the end of a psychoanalytic criticism as such.

The problem is that, as the title *Literature and Psychoanalysis* suggests – as soon as you reject the notion of psychoanalysis as a masterful body of knowledge being brought to bear upon literature then the notion of a 'psychoanalytic criticism' as such must be rejected also, for it precisely implies the use of psychoanalysis as a method or form of knowledge that is being brought to bear upon literature, in the same way as, say, with Marxist or structuralist criticism.

Felman's re-invention of the relationship between literature and psychoanalysis, then, had the effect of ending psychoanalytic criticism. But if the 'new psychoanalytic criticism' never really materialised it was also because it had meanwhile become something else. The reason here was that, as I have been suggesting, subjectivity itself became a matter for intense political debate, and therefore any use of psychoanalysis could not but raise political issues. In particular, the feminist rereading of the Lacanian rereading of Freud pushed to the fore the question of sexuality and of gender. The idea of writing a psychoanalytic criticism without engaging with these issues became absurd.

The function of psychoanalysis in criticism and cultural theory therefore changed radically. Instead of being autonomous and apolitical it was used instrumentally for specific political ends. The analysis of the forms of subjectivity was no longer a refuge, but a way of understanding, and changing, dominant ideological formations. Paradoxically, perhaps, the very moment when literary criticism decided that it could not be grounded on psychoanalysis because in some sense psychoanalysis itself was grounded on literature, the moment when it stopped considering it as a science and realised that Freud's writings offered an exceptionally rich text for new forms of literary analysis derived from psychoanalysis itself, this was the same moment that Marxism began to relent in its hostility towards it.

MARXISM

The basis of Marxism's traditional objections to psychoanalysis are summed up in Horkheimer's story about the beggar who one night dreamt that he was a millionaire. As he awoke, he had the good fortune to meet a psychoanalyst and so he told him his dream. The psychoanalyst explained that the millionnaire was a symbol for his father. 'Curious', remarked the beggar, not entirely convinced.[7]

This story illustrates quite neatly, I think, the real problem in the relations between Marxism and psychoanalysis. They both provide mutually exclusive causal explanations – that is, economics and class versus sexuality and the unconscious. And in spite of what might seem like a possible *rapprochement* when Marx begins *Capital* with an analysis of fetishism, and Freud writes an essay with the suggestive title 'The Economic Problem of Masochism', the two explanations of economics and sexuality tend to stay resolutely apart.

The common Marxist accusation has of course always been that psychoanalysis is the last refuge of bourgeois individualism and its philosophies of consciousness. This is certainly the position that can be found in the 1930s in a writer like Christopher St John Sprigg – better known by his less aristocratic nom-de-plume Christopher Caudwell.[8] For Lukács too psychoanalysis was simply a symptom of capitalism: in his essay 'The Ideology of Modernism' he berated modernism for its morbid subjectivism, and for portraying 'man as a solitary being, incapable of meaningful relationships'.[9] Pathology, according to Lukács, is the surest refuge of modernist writers, and 'it is the ideological complement of their historical position'. He continues:

> This obsession with the pathological is not only to be found in literature. Freudian psychoanalysis is its most obvious expression. The treatment of the subject is only superficially different from that in modern literature. As everybody knows, Freud's starting point was 'everyday life'. In order to explain 'slips' and day-dreams, however, he had to have recourse to psychopathology... Freud believed he had found the key to the understanding of the normal personality in the psychology of the abnormal ... It is only when we compare Freud's psychology with that of Pavlov, who takes the Hippocratic view that mental abnormality is a deviation from a norm, that we see it in its true light.[10]

Lukács's claim that 'as everybody knows, Freud's starting point was the slips of the tongue and daydreams of "everyday life"', suggests that his own reading of Freud was somewhat limited, though the same idea seems to form the basis of Timpanaro's critique.[11] But of course detailed knowledge about psychoanalysis was not in itself necessary for Lukács, since he was at this point simply following Communist Party orthodoxy that had rejected Freud in favour of Pavlov.

Yet in spite of this general hostility it is quite obvious that psychoanalysis has exercised a continual fascination for Marxism. In fact in the early days in the Soviet Union psychoanalysis was the subject of intense debate. One of the few sustained Marxist critiques of psychoanalysis, Voloshinov's *Freudianism: A Critical Essay*, published the same year as Pavlov's *Conditioned Reflexes* in 1927, contained a long chapter 'devoted to a refutation of arguments by four Soviet scientists in favour of incorporating at least certain aspects of psychoanalysis into Marxism' – a chapter which is, symptomatically, omitted in the English translation.[12] Ironically, it was the visit to the Soviet Union two years later of the Marxist psychoanalyst Wilhelm Reich that seems to have been partly responsible for the clampdown on psychoanalysis, when Reich proclaimed that unless there was a sexual revolution too Communism would degenerate into a bureaucratic state.

Reich is only one example of what Fredric Jameson has called 'the experience of a whole series of abortive Freudo-Marxisms'.[13] The continual fascination with psychoanalysis is sometimes explained because it is claimed that it offers the theory of subjectivity which Marxism lacks. This is the way in which the fusion of existentialism with Marxism used to be justified. The philosophy of Sartre did offer a way of integrating a theory of subjectivity or consciousness with a theory of the social; however, this was effectively achieved at the expense of psychoanalysis, specifically the theory of the unconscious. Symptomatically, it was at the moment that his commitment to Marxism began to wane that he began to turn to psychoanalysis.

The basic problem with the whole project of trying to combine psychoanalysis with Marxism, as Ernesto Laclau has pointed out, is that the very idea of adding a theory of subjectivity to Marxism is misconceived, because Marxism is constituted in the first place by a negation of subjectivity.[14] This perhaps accounts for the attraction of the anti-humanist description of subjectivity through which the most recent *rapprochement* of Marxism and psychoanalysis took place in the work of Althusser and Lacan. Althusser, a member of the Communist Party who was himself analysed by Lacan, for the first time brought psychoanalysis into the mainstream of Marxist theory. Not only did he declare that psychoanalysis was a science, comparable to Marxism, he also went on to claim that psychoanalytic theory was implicitly based on historical materialism because it constituted an analysis of 'the familial ideology'.[15]

The integration between the two was somewhat precariously achieved through Althusser's reformulation of the concept of ideology. One long-standing ground of dispute between Marxism and psychoanalysis has been the conflict over their concepts of history. Althusser's description of ideology as being eternal in the same way as the Freudian unconscious – that is, that they have no history – provided a new basis for the pact between them. Furthermore, Althusser's use of Lacan's concept of the imaginary, his stress on the representational form of ideology, and his description of the interpellated subject in terms of Freud's account of the stages of sexuality, meant that psychoanalysis was effectively proposed as the mode through which to understand the place of the subject in ideology. (This in spite of the fact that the theory of ideology was designed to provide an account of the reproduction of class relations.)

The question of gender becomes somewhat overdetermined in Althusser's account. Take his example of being hailed through a closed door:

> We all have friends who, when they knock on our door and we ask, through the door, the question 'Who's there?', answer (since 'it's obvious') 'It's me'. And we recognize that 'it is him', or 'her'. We open the door, and 'it's true, it really was she who was there'.[16]

It's difficult not to believe that Althusser is here reversing Lacan's famous example of the girl and boy in the train drawing up along side the two doors labelled 'Ladies' and 'Gentlemen'. Althusser insists here on the question of gender difference in the construction of individuals as subjects.

This really complicated things. The place of the subject was left so empty in Althusser's account that it needed further definition. The problem for

Althusser, or rather Althusserianism, however, was that if it borrowed a theory of subjectivity from Freud for its account of ideology, that account placed a primacy on gender rather than on class. And that, indeed, was what happened.

What went wrong for the theory of the subject was that although Althusser's theory of interpellation seemed to offer a place for feminism also, the old difficulty of the predominance of class or gender refused to go away. The predicament, as always, is that as long as Marxism holds onto the primacy of class it must always subsume other categories such as those of gender or race. This position is graphically evident when, in *The Political Unconscious*, Fredric Jameson talks of:

> The reaffirmation of the existence of marginalised or oppositional cultures in our own time, and the reaudition of the oppositional voices of black or ethnic cultures, women's and gay literature, 'naive' or marginalised folk art, and the like.

He then adds:

> Only an ultimate rewriting of these utterances in terms of their essentially polemic and subversive strategies restores them to their proper place in the dialogical system of the social classes.[17]

Since feminists have argued so persuasively that constructions of subjectivity cannot be thought without consideration of the question of gender, this has meant a tendency for male Marxists to back away from the once highly popular 'problem of the subject' – a tendency, perhaps, validated by Althusser's general anti-humanist stance. Even when Marxism did begin to import the psychoanalytic theory of the subject, decentred and conflictual, it did not much like what it found, and became loath to lose the old unified revolutionary subject of history that it had relied upon up to that point.

Althusser's theory of ideology did produce some extremely important work, particularly in the area of film and related forms of cultural analysis. In literary criticism, the story is rather less happy, largely as a result of the fact that psychoanalysis was used with a good deal less precision. Althusser's disciple, Pierre Macherey, attempted to produce an Althusserian theory of literary criticism, but failed to develop a theory of the interpellation of the subject by a literary text, beyond an analysis of the function of literature within the educational ISA.[18] In as much as Macherey did attempt an analysis of the representational form of ideology he attempted to extend Althusser's claim, via Lenin's theories of reflection, that art occupies a special place between ideology and knowledge and so can 'make us see'. The briefest comparison between Lenin's form of analysis and that of Freud was in turn enthusiastically endorsed and extended by Terry Eagleton in *Criticism and Ideology*.[19] But the literary text as dream was about the oldest trick in the psychoanalytic critical book. It remained nothing more than an updated analogy, still dependent on a theory of reflection, and merely provoked a seemingly endless hunt for 'gaps' in literary texts which could be arbitrarily proclaimed their unconscious moment of ideological conflict.

The only other concerted effort to use Althusser's theory of ideology in Marxist literary criticism has been that of Fredric Jameson in *The Political Unconscious*. This is an extremely interesting book, the complexity of which I do not have space to discuss here. There is, however, one basic problem in Jameson's use of psychoanalysis that is of relevance in this context. Jameson, correctly in my view, criticises certain Marxist theorists in terms of their continued reliance on categories of the individual subject: even 'the notion of "class consciousness", as it is central in a certain Marxist tradition, rests on an unrigorous and figurative assimilation of the consciousness of the individual subject to the dynamic of groups'.[20] Althusser's description of history as a 'process without a subject' is precisely designed to counter this tendency to be found not only in Lukács, of course, but also in the Frankfurt School.

Nevertheless, Jameson himself tends to slide towards the use of Lacan's account of the psyche as a model for the state as a whole. Here, perhaps implicit in Althusser's own account, the Imaginary ideological representations of the individual become the psyche, the Symbolic becomes the social structure, and the Real 'History itself'. This schema then becomes a descriptive model for society. Similarly, though he criticises the perfunctory introduction of a Freudian scheme into a discussion of cultural or political history in the work of Adorno and Horkheimer, or the use of psychological categories for the description of social categories in Christopher Lasch's *The Culture of Narcissism*, Jameson's own use of Lacan's account of schizophrenia to describe the fragmented subject of the 'new cultural norm' of postmodernism quickly becomes a description of the 'randomly heterogeneous ... fragmentary and aleatory' structure of society itself.[21]

In spite of the problems, Althusser's intervention has meant that psychoanalysis has been allowed a more credible place within Marxist theory. But in effect this has meant a tendency to revert to the forms of the state-as-psyche global repression theories of the Frankfurt school. What's wrong with the use of the model of the psyche for the state? The answer is because it is an untheorised transference: the psychoanalytic model is precisely about the incommensurability of the psyche's relation to the social, and therefore it makes no sense to apply that model to the social as such. If the social is like a psyche, then what's the social for the social?

In fact the model of the psyche as the state is simply a contemporary version of the time-worn metaphor of the state as a body, familiar from Hobbes, Menenius's speech in *Coriolanus*, Edmund Burke and many others. To the degree that the mutual solidarity of the parts of the body, generally presented as an organism, was useful for a Burkean vision of one nation, the image of the state as a body was not an appropriate metaphor for Marxism in so far as Marx's argument was always that capitalism is less of a community (a homogeneous body) than a system of mutual antagonisms. Freud's account of the psyche as a system of conflictual forces by contrast offers itself as a perfect metaphor for the class struggles of the social. But, as I have said, such a model paradoxically has then to exclude the social itself.

The missing paternal realm of the social when the psychoanalytic model of the psyche is translated into the state is perhaps why such forms of analysis tend to paranoid descriptions of global capitalism, the culture industry, etc., which offer no possibilities of resistance, and in which it seems that nothing can be done beyond indulging in a nostalgia for the unfragmented totality of the lost bourgeois subject. This is the inheritance of the pessimism of the late Freud evident in the work of the Frankfurt School. When we think of the general conservative tendency of images of the state as a body then perhaps it is possible to see why the image of the state as a psyche tends to take on the same political colour.

Althusser's work, then, facilitated the (re)introduction of psychoanalysis but since Althusser there has been no fundamental reassessment of Marxism's relation to it. Marxism has always tended to restrict its use of psychoanalysis to the occasional importation of one or two concepts in order to construct a model; it has never allowed it to affect the terms of its own theory substantially. Psychoanalysis always remains marginal to it, but it has rarely attempted to rethink the Cartesian inside/outside dichotomy on which this division is based and which psychoanalysis challenges. A reworking of that dualism would also have to include a rethinking of the exclusive claims of the forms of rational logic on which it is predicated. The question, I suppose, is whether Marxism can continue such neglect or whether the force of other forms of politics, notably feminism, will eventually make this impossible. Even here, it is notable that when Marxism does use psychoanalysis, it always sticks to the patriarchal versions. But if Marxism did re-examine its relation to psychoanalysis, particularly feminist psychoanalysis, would it end up in the dreaded position of being 'post-Marxist'?

FEMINISM

As is well known, American and British feminism in its modern phase since 1968 began in an aggressively anti-psychoanalytic mode, with Freud regarded as one of the worst of patriarchs. As the introduction to the Penguin *Rights of Woman* puts it, 'The twentieth century has also seen the popularization of a formidable anti-feminist ideology – Freudianism.'[22] Marxist feminism, too, has often taken up a similar position, adding complicity in the oppression of women to the more habitual objections of

Marxism to psychoanalysis. So Lilian S. Robinson, in a refinement of Lukács' comment, argues that Freud's 'ideas are simultaneously a product or symptom of a cultural evil and a force to justify and perpetuate it'.[23]

But then came French Freud, Lacan, anti-biologism, and anti-essentialism, which changed the politics of psychoanalysis. In Britain it enabled Juliet Mitchell to suggest that psychoanalysis was not 'a recommendation *for* a patriarchal society but an analysis *of* one',[24] and could therefore be of central importance in the analysis of the ways in which gender is constructed, a first step towards ending that patriarchal ideology and its oppression of women. In particular she stressed, as she was to do again in her introduction to *Feminine Sexuality*,[25] that in spite of the evident ambivalence in his accounts of feminine sexuality, Freud had opposed the Jones/Horney position of an essential femininity.

Marxism is a constant point of reference in Mitchell's book and in introducing the name of Lacan she allied the enterprise of feminism with the contemporary Marxism of Althusser. As we have seen, Althusser's theory of ideology was open to reinscription with a gendered subjectivity. Mitchell pointedly ends her book by setting feminism alongside Marxism: 'as the end of "eternal" class conflict is visible within the contradictions of capitalism, so too, it would seem, is the swan-song of the "immortal" nature of patriarchal culture to be heard'.[26] But this happy coupling of Marxism's eye with psychoanalytic feminism's ear was not to last.

Psychoanalysis was not to turn out to be an effective marriage broker between Marxism and feminism. In fact alliances between the two have tended to be predicated upon the exclusion of psychoanalysis. In *Women's Oppression Today*, for example, Michèle Barrett admits the problem of Marxism's neglect of feminism, and adds that 'it is certainly true that many aspects of sexual relations are simply irreducible to questions of class'. But Barrett remains 'unconvinced' by Mitchell's attempt to recover Freud for 'a materialist feminist theory of gender and sexuality', arguing that she 'offers an unduly charitable reading of his position' and that her interpretation 'involves some stretching of what Freud actually said'.[27] She then adds two further reservations about the compatibility of psychoanalysis and a Marxist feminism: the first is its universalism, the second is its implication that women's oppression is exclusively ideological in character rather than an effect of the material structures of women's oppression under capitalism (production, family, the state).

There are three objections to psychoanalysis here. The problem with the first two is that they could apply equally well to Marxism itself. If Freud has to be 'stretched' in order to draw out a critique of patriarchy from his work, Marx certainly has to be pulled almost out of all recognition. If Barrett is herself proposing, as a Marxist feminist, some modification of that historical form of Marxism, it is hard to see why Mitchell should not be allowed to do the same for Freud. In the second place, psychoanalysis's universalism, emphasising 'the mythic "law"-like agencies at work in psychosexual development' and adaptable in this form to any cultural variation, may be universal, but hardly any more universal than Marxism's reading of all history according to the universal operation of the dialectic: with all human history, as Jameson tells us, sharing 'the unity of a single great collective story . . . a single vast unfinished plot'.[28] The advantage of psychoanalysis's universalism could be that, as Jacqueline Rose argues, it is able to offer an account of the historical unspecificity of the oppression of women which does indeed take different specific historical forms but which is by no means exclusive to capitalism.[29] Barrett's last objection is perfectly valid in its own terms. But one might want to argue with the claim that psychoanalysis implies that women's oppression is *exclusively* ideological.

The objection that ideological oppression claims an autonomy at the expense of specific material structures of oppression in fact reproduces the founding opposition between psychic and social structures that represents the competing claims of psychoanalysis and Marxism with which we began. It still seems to be a question of balancing the contesting antithetical claims of the two. On the one hand, psychoanalysis is presented as a theory of the social construction of gendered subjectivity, offering forms of analysis that can expose this process working in a whole range of cultural and social forms, in short the sphere of ideology, that space in which material effects are given representations and worked on at the level of fantasy. But on the other hand, such understanding does not in itself necessarily include analyses of historical and institutional factors or offer prescriptions for material change. In this sense, feminism could be said to have settled down into the same polarities as Marxist criticism: ideology critique *versus* social analysis and prescriptions for change.

The argument still continues to be governed by the unresolved tension between the psychic and the social. As Cora Kaplan puts it:

> While socialist feminists have been deeply concerned with the social construction of femininity and sexual difference, they have been uneasy about integrating social and political determinations with an analysis of the psychic ordering of gender . . . Thus semiotic or psychoanalytic perspectives have yet to be integrated with social, economic and political analysis.[30]

The problem here seems to be that the polarisation of psychic and social explanations continues to be seen as an antithetical subjective and objective dualism that needs to be synthesised. The reason that they have not yet been integrated may well be because they are indeed incompatible: here I would like to recall my argument that psychoanalysis is itself a theory of the incompatability of the psychic and the social. This suggests that a different kind of thinking and different kind of logic would be necessary to think them both together at the same time. The problem would then be to what extent such thinking would still be Marxist, or even perhaps feminist.

Some feminists have in fact already made the claim that 'because psychoanalysis has assured the link between psychosexuality and the socio-historical realm, psychoanalysis is now linked to major political and cultural questions'.[31] Marxist feminists, however, such as Angela Weir and Elizabeth Wilson point to the continuing 'absence of a theory of the relationship between them' and suggest that psychoanalysis still needs to be grounded in a materialist theory of ideology.[32] Nevertheless, as Weir and Wilson have to acknowledge, it is not quite so easy for Marxist feminism to reject psychoanalysis altogether on the classic Marxist grounds of idealism. It is less readily dismissed as a theory of subjectivity because the political intervention of feminism has precisely been to redefine or reclaim this ground as a valid political space. If some Marxism has, unsuccessfully in my view, tried to turn the state into a psyche, then feminism has much more effectively shown that the psyche and the body are a form of the state.

One of the forms of the oppression of women is that the personal, the domestic, sexuality, the family, and so forth are denied political, or even 'serious' status of any kind. So what feminism has done is to politicise psychoanalysis, not by adding the 'real' world of the social to it, but by showing the extent to which its own space is already political. Thus politics enters a realm which was of course always highly politicised but the political nature of which had previously had been repressed. But to what extent has sexual politics been registered in Marxist theory, as they say, 'proper'?

Has its rejection of psychoanalysis on Marxist grounds in fact helped Marxist feminism to shift Marxism itself? Here the answer often seems to be no. If we take Perry Anderson, for example, one of the most influential of British Marxists, we find in his recent consideration of contemporary theory a confident rejection of Lacanian psychoanalysis in the space of a couple of pages. Does this lead him to consider women's oppression from a more materialist perspective? Anderson comes to a consideration of feminism only in a postscript at the end of his book. Though he acknowledges the challenge of feminism to the traditional scope of Marxism he adds a comment on what he calls

> the paradoxes of the relationship between socialism and feminism. For if the structures of sexual domination stretch back longer, and go deeper, culturally than those of class exploitation, they also typically generate less collective resistance, politically. The division betwen the sexes is a fact of nature: it cannot be abolished, as can the division between classes, a fact of history.[33]

It does not seem that the argument for the difference between sex and gender has yet made much impact upon Anderson's Marxism.

Unlike Marxism, there is no problem for feminism in what Anderson calls the 'precarious recourse' to a psychoanalysis that is as much grounded on literature as it is 'scientific'. Literature is not as peripheral to feminism as it is to Marxism. For literature, particularly the novel, historically has afforded one of the few permitted spaces of articulation for women that has been constructed by them and written for them, as Virginia Woolf suggests when she turns Orlando into a woman with the beginnings of the novel in the eighteenth century.

In the same way, while for Marxism psychoanalysis has always been a worry at its margins, for feminism psychoanalysis has been much more crucial – and the different forms of feminism could be said to divide up according to their attitudes towards it. Psychoanalysis has been critical for its redefinitions, critiques and explorations of questions of sexuality and identity.

Psychoanalysis has also been at the forefront of debates about the problems for feminism in the use of theory at all, and here the pressure of the political on psychoanalysis has had important effects. While for a long time psychoanalysis was brought to bear upon cultural phenomena as a form of explanation, with feminism this relation has for some time now been reversed: in particular, in France the pressure of feminism has led to a series of attempts to rewrite psychoanalysis outside the patriarchal mode – it is no longer just a question of the influence of psychoanalysis on feminism. This process, which could still be taken further, has only recently begun in Britain and the States, where there has been in the past something of a tendency to defend Freud and Lacan at all costs.

In French Feminism, in writers such as Irigaray, Cixous, and Kristeva, we find 'a way of thinking that appears to be at once feminist and psychoanalytic, and also highly literary'.[34] The literary has been one of the main ways through which Freud has been rewritten. Conversely, one of the problems with thinking about feminist literary theory is that the psychoanalytic forms of it have succeeded in breaking out of such academic categories altogether. This could perhaps be compared to Derrida's work, and indeed one of the problems of writing about feminism and psychoanalysis, particularly in France, is that its relation to deconstruction makes matters complex. It was Derrida, after all, who not only produced one of the earliest critiques of Lacan's phallocentrism, but who has also made one of the most sustained and influential attempts to write against patriarchal discourse. The problem for Derridean feminism, however, is that as soon as it moves thus far into deconstruction, then it becomes merely one part of a more general project, and we have the same problem as with Marxist feminism of its being subsumed in a 'greater' cause.

The problem with the use of psychoanalysis for feminism seems to be that it either leads to essentialism, which many do not want, or if it does not, and the feminine is proposed as a purely relational category, then it means that 'woman' has no absolute identity as such and risks being subsumed by other related forms of politics. Unless you are prepared to claim that the point about deconstructive feminism is that it avoids this by holding essentialism and relationalism together simultaneously, then it seems that it becomes a question of essentialism versus post-feminism.

For Kristeva, as for Lacan, to define woman is to essentialise her: 'woman' as such does not exist. So Toril Moi in her account of Kristeva emphasises that she does not so much have a theory of femininity as one of positionality: 'if femininity has any definition at all in Kristevan terms, it is simply as "that which is marginalised by the patriarchal order" '.[35] The displacement of femininity into a more general 'theory of marginality, subversion, and dissidence' means that, whether it likes it or not, the theoretical position of this form of feminism can be appropriated for use by any other marginalised group. In fact feminist criticism is already distinguished by the way in which it has more recently marked out a space for its own, as it were marginalised, groups, particularly lesbian and black women writers. But if feminism has become a theory of the marginal itself, this does mean that its theory becomes available for appropriation by any other marginalised group – not just, say, by gay or black men, but even by a category such as the avant-garde. The question, therefore, is whether feminism wants to provide a theory that goes beyond itself? Beyond, as they say, feminism?

Although this may explain some of the male interest in feminist theory, it has to be said the appropriation of feminist theory by marginalised men has not really yet occurred. Take colonial discourse analysis, for example, where the use of individual psychoanalytic concepts still seems somewhat fetishistic: metonyms that can easily be exchanged for another from somewhere else within psychoanalytic theory or even from elsewhere. While certain structures of sexuality are provocatively mapped onto those of race, gender itself is eliminated in favour of an undifferentiated 'colonial subject'. And once again, the psychoanalysis that is used is that which many would consider to be the patriarchal version.

IDENTITY

In conclusion I would like to return to the story of Oedipus. When I spoke of Oedipus before I left out any consideration of the more directly political dimension to his story, which happens also to be the story of why psychoanalysis is rejected by some forms of Marxism and feminism.

Oedipus, after all, begins the play as the King. In his first identity, in which he has avoided the curse, and solved the riddle of the Sphinx, he wields effective political power. The story, from one perspective, is about his loss of that power, until the moment when from being a King he wanders out into the wilderness in total abjection. If, as Freud suggests, Oedipus' process of self-discovery is analogous to the unfolding of a psychoanalysis, then it also suggests that that process will produce a loss of political power.

This problem has been lived out in the uses that Marxism and feminism have made of the psychoanalytic theory of the subject. As people have been saying recently, deconstruct identity and you deconstruct the agent of history and of politics. We have therefore witnessed calls to bring back the subject on the grounds of political necessity. So Weir and Wilson, for instance, argue that 'The concept of the "fractured self" ... questions the very possibility of a coherent identity, and this process of the deconstruction of the self could also be seen to question the very possibility of women uniting politically around their existence as "women".'[36] In other words, we cannot afford, politically, to go through Oedipus' process of self-understanding: so – bring back the bourgeois subject.

This question of identity remains one of the major problems in the relation of psychoanalysis to the political. But the call for the old unified subject seems to me to raise as many problems as it offers to solve. In the first place, it requires a kind of imperialism of identity, so that we are only allowed one, and our politics then has to have a single meaning too. So, Weir and Wilson tell black women that the question of race must ultimately give way to the more important issue of class. In the second place, the demand for a single identity assumes that we can choose to have a single coherent, unproblematised identity as a matter of will. In the third place, the argument for the necessity of the unified subject for politics relies on a fairly crude theory of intentionality, which imagines that you need a totally unified subject to be able to have any form of will or agency at all. Finally, it presupposes politics as an entirely intentional activity. The point about the challenge of psychoanalysis is that it questions all that.

Notes

1.   Paul Roazen, *Freud and His Followers* (Allen Lane, London, 1976); François Roustang, *Dire Mastery: Discipleship from Freud to Lacan*, Ned Lukacher (trans) (Johns Hopkins, Baltimore, 1982); Sherry Turkle, *Psychoanalytic Politics: Jacques Lacan and Freud's French Revolution* (Burnett Books, London, 1979).
2.   Rosalind Coward and John Ellis, *Language and Materialism: Developments in Semiology and the Theory of the Subject* (Routledge & Kegan Paul, London, 1977).
3.   René Girard, 'Tiresias and the Critic', in Richard Macksey and Eugenio Donato (eds), *The Structuralist Controversy: The Languages of Criticism and the Sciences of Man* (Johns Hopkins, Baltimore, 1970), p. 17.
4.   Claude Lévi-Strauss, *Tristes Tropiques*, John and Necke Mander (trans) (Cape, London, 1973), p. 71.

5.   'Psychoanalytic Criticism: Has It Got Beyond a Joke?', *Paragraph*, no. 4 (1984), pp. 87–114.
6.   Shoshana Felman, 'To Open the Question', in S. Felman (ed.), *Literature and Psychoanalysis: The Question of Reading: Otherwise, Yale French Studies*, nos 55/56 (1977), pp. 5–10.
7.   Russell Jacoby, *Social Amnesia: A Critique of Conformist Psychology from Adler to Laing* (Harvester Press, Hassocks), p. 73.
8.   See Christopher Caudwell, *Illusion and Reality: A Study of the Sources of Poetry* (Macmillan, London, 1937); *Studies in a Dying Culture* (The Bodley Head, London, 1938).
9.   Georg Lukács, 'The Ideology of Modernism', in *The Meaning of Contemporary Realism*, John and Necke Mander (trans) (Merlin Press, London, 1963), p. 24.
10. Ibid., p. 30.
11. Sebastiano Timpanaro, *The Freudian Slip* (New Left Books, London, 1976).
12. V. N. Voloshinov, *Freudianism: A Marxist Critique*, I. R. Titunik (trans) (Academic Press, New York, 1976).
13. Fredric Jameson, 'Imaginary and Symbolic in Lacan: Marxism, Psychoanalytic Criticism and the Problem of the Subject', in Felman, *Literature and Psychoanalysis...*, p. 385.
14. Ernesto Laclau, 'Psychoanalysis and Marxism', *Critical Inquiry*, vol. 13, no. 2 (1987), p. 330.
15. Louis Althusser, *Lenin and Philosophy and Other Essays*, Ben Brewster (trans) (New Left Books, London, 1971), p. 177.
16. Ibid., p. 161.
17. Fredric Jameson, *The Political Unconscious: Narrative as Socially Symbolic Act* (Methuen, London, 1981), p. 86.
18. Pierre Macherey, *A Theory of Literary Production*, Geoffrey Wall (trans) (Routledge & Kegan Paul, London, 1978).
19. Terry Eagleton, *Criticism and Ideology: A Study in Marxist Literary Theory* (New Left Books, London, 1976), pp. 90–2.
20. Jameson, *The Political Unconscious*, p. 294.
21. Fredric Jameson, 'Postmodernism, or The Cultural Logic of Late Capitalism', *New Left Review*, no. 146 (1984), p. 71.
22. 'Introduction', in Mary Wollstonecraft, *Vindications of the Rights of Women*, Miriam Kramnick (ed.) (Penguin, Harmondsworth, 1975), p. 70.
23. Lilian S. Robinson, *Sex, Class, and Culture* (Indiana University Press, Bloomington, 1978), p. 115.
24. Juliet Mitchell, *Psychoanalysis and Feminism* (Allen Lane, London, 1974), p. xv.
25. Juliet Mitchell and Jacqueline Rose, *Feminine Sexuality: Jacques Lacan and the école freudienne* (Macmillan, London, 1982).
26. Mitchell, *Psychoanalysis and Feminism*, p. 416.
27. Michèle Barrett, *Women's Oppression Today: Problems in Marxist Feminist Analysis* (Verso, London, 1980), pp. 46, 56, 58.
28. Jameson, *The Political Unconscious*, pp. 19–20.
29. Jacqueline Rose, *Sexuality in the Field of Vision* (Verso, London, 1986), p. 90.
30. Cora Kaplan, *Sea Changes: Essays on Culture and Feminism* (Verso, London, 1986), pp. 152–3.
31. Jane Gallop, *Reading Lacan* (Cornell University Press, Ithaca, 1985), p. 315.
32. Angela Weir and Elizabeth Wilson, 'The British Women's Movement', *New Left Review*, no. 148 (1984), p. 97.

33. Perry Anderson, *In the Tracks of Historical Materialism* (Verso, London, 1983), p. 91.
34. Gallop, *Reading Lacan*, p. 316.
35. Toril Moi, *Sexual/Textual Politics: Feminist Literary Theory* (Methuen, London, 1985), p. 166.
36. Weir and Wilson, 'The British Women's Movement', p. 97.

10

The Reader in Analysis

Elizabeth Wright

My title is a pun. On the one hand it can mean the Reader subjected to analysis as a key element in literary theory, on the other the Reader as equivalent to the analysand in a psychoanalysis, making discoveries as a result of her or his analytic text. This chapter has two emphases corresponding to these two aspects – the first being reader-response in general, the second a particular species of the first, namely psychoanalytic reader-theory.[1]

There are three questions that the reader-response theorist might want to ask: (1) How does a reader process texts? (2) Why do readers read differently according to their place in history? (3) How does the text affect a reader? Now, very conveniently these three questions coincide with three positions occupied by the leading innovators in the field of reader-response criticism, namely Wolfgang Iser, Hans Robert Jauss, and Norman Holland.

PROCESSING TEXTS

First, then, how does a reader process texts? Or, to put it another way, what happens when we are reading? This is a theoretical question, one that was not asked two hundred years ago. It requires a very rapid overview of the scene in order to bring out the historical relevance of the move from author to reader. It is only over the last two hundred years that literature has been subjected to theoretical analysis as literature *per se*. Throughout the nineteenth-century readers and critics were mainly interested in the author, in how he or she came to write this work of genius. This led to studies of Goethe's or Shakespeare's genius, or, with the advent of

Romanticism, to an interest in the phenomenon of genius as such. Then, at the beginning of the twentieth century, there was a revolution in literary studies, starting with the Russian Formalists, who concentrated on the text itself and made a radical break from the author-centred tradition – a political reaction against the conformism of Tsarist ideology. But after the revolution, the Russian Formalists became unpopular with the Bolsheviks because of their detachment of form from content in a state in which content was meant to subserve the particular aims of the Party. The work of the Russian Formalists survived in that of the Prague Structuralists, and traces of the same formalism can be found in the work of the New Critics, though they conceived of their activity as apolitical. The New Critics were the last group of scholars to share one set of common text-centred beliefs: after them, in the 1960s, the theoretical scene suddenly exploded with many different schools. There was one group, however, known as the Constance School, who saw themselves as heirs to this tradition. Where the Formalists had moved from author to text, they began to move from text to reader, while insisting that a formal element remain at the core of the theory. Their aim was to take account of all three positions; author, text and reader. The Constance School regard other reader theorists, including the deconstructionists, as beyond the pale. One reason is that the deconstructionists discount philosophy, whereas the Constance School relies on it.

Wolfgang Iser uses a phenomenological approach in order to answer the question how a reader processes a text.[2] There was no theoretical concept of reading before phenomenology. The phenomenologists were interested in how the mind brings assumptions to bear upon experience, how it produces a continuing adjustment of percepts and concepts. *Gestalten* – unities of understanding – are projected onto experience, and these are capable of endless adjustment according to the new experience that results from their employment. Phenomenologists have noted that looking at a picture involves a number of rapid eye movements so that much more than one glance is taken up. Similarly, a reader fills out his experience of a book, continually adjusting his anticipation of what is to come and his retrospective gestalt of what he has already read. The problem is, how do I take in information over a period of time, moreover a span of time that will change my perception of a book? Once I close it and deal with something else, I will have a different memory of it than at the time when I am actually in the text.

The Constance School applies itself to this problem of perception, of how a text gets decoded over a period of time. Iser uses the terms *Projektionen*, the anticipations of what is going to happen, and *Retentionen*, the retrospective re-enactments that take place three pages or two chapters on. A reader's retrospective enactments, his *Retentionen*, will be different at every single page of the text, as more information is added; and also his *Projektionen* will change according to the information he takes up. Hence the reader cannot but adopt a 'wandering viewpoint': the information he takes up builds up a certain figure in his mind, but this figure is constantly in the process of change. The reader endeavours to close this gestalt, to turn out one interpretation, but the literary text refuses to do this. It leaves gaps for the reader to fill in. For example, in Fielding's *Joseph Andrews* Parson Adams is presented as an innocent exposed to the attacks and depredations of a wicked world. Whereas Adams is naively trusting, spontaneously brave, and selfless, he encounters the cunning, the cowardly and the selfish. Fielding, however, manoeuvres the reader by means of the absurdity of Adams's various mishaps and failures into laughing at his lack of worldly wisdom, thus seeing him as a narrow-minded fool. This has tricked the reader into siding with the worldly-wise hypocrites and cheats who have scored over Adams, an ironic equation which the reader is forced to reject. A gap opens – not only the obvious one between the reader's worldly wisdom and Adams's ingenuousness, but also between the reader and the hypocrites he finds himself aligned with.

> With the worldly wise lacking morality and the moralist lacking insight, the negative poles taken together reveal the virtual identity of their meaning, and the reader must measure himself against this, because it is a balance which is produced by *his* insight and which he himself must not fall short of.[3]

This ironic schema forces the reader into an uncomfortable moral position in which he is faced with a gap that he himself must now close. It subserves Fielding's declared aim, which is to make this private vicarious mortification into an experience which will enable the reader to judge the better in his own encounters with the world, avoiding not only the ingenuousness of Adams, but also the hypocrisy of his tormentors. Here a stable ironic schema is provided by Fielding, and the reader, according to Iser, obligingly responds by 'filling up the empty mould'.

Iser is thus able to argue that his theory allows for an interaction between text and reader. The problem is, however, that Iser's phenomenological approach leads him to make anthropological statements about readers. In this he takes his cue from the phenomenologist Roman Ingarden, whose key-work, *The Cognition of the Literary Work of Art*, published in Polish in 1937, was translated into German in 1968, and thus Iser was able to make use of it in advance of the English-speaking world;[4] Ingarden could not then be read and assessed in America, where it would have had considerable influence. According to Ingarden, a text consists of structures, devices and schemata, and this structured entity must be properly decoded. For Ingarden the work originates in the intention of the author and what reading produces is only a 'concretisation' of a predetermined form. The gaps, the places of indeterminacy, may be filled in by 'permissible elements', actualisations appropriate to the author's design. Hence the reader's role is no more than to complete the schematised structure. The gap is to be deleted so that harmony is re-established. Iser took from Ingarden the principle of the filling in of indeterminacies, the 'adequate' concretisation of the text, but for him the gap is what is interesting, because its filling in will depend on the reader's 'wandering viewpoint', dependent on a temporal process, as I explained above. It is in this way that he has endeavoured to turn the one-way process going from text to reader into an interaction between reader and text.

The great problem with his approach is that it makes the reading process into a constant: it assumes that everyone reads in the same way. Not only does it take for granted that a reader starts at page one and works through a book in the given order, but also that he will never use a text to bring his or her own fantasies into play. Iser is interested exclusively in how one deals with information intellectually, and how in the process one polishes up one's faculties and becomes a more resourceful reader. His concept of the 'implied reader'[5] indicates a reader who lives up to the text's cultural expectations of her or him, even though the aesthetic potential of the text, the continuous challenge posed by the gaps, is such that it can provoke a variety of 'adequate concretisations'. It is this interaction between an idealised text and an idealised reader, which is at the core of Iser's *Wirkungsaesthetik*, his aesthetics of response. It is also how the majority of students are taught to read when they first come up to University, with the further addition of historical 'background' in the hope that it will help them to fill in the gaps. But this cannot turn a potentially a-historical theory into a historical one.

DIFFERENT READINGS

This brings me to the second eminent theorist of the Constance School, Hans Robert Jauss, who coincides with my second question: why do readers read differently according to their place in history? Where Iser is the proponent of an aesthetics of response (*Wirkungsaesthetik*), Jauss is that of an aesthetics of reception (*Rezeptionsaesthetik*). Both Iser and Jauss are interested in reader-response, both work with a phenomenological approach, both were pupils of Gadamer (who taught them Ingarden). But there the common ground ends. Where Iser's aesthetics of response is profoundly ahistorical, Jauss's reception theory is a historical theory. In his key article, 'Literary History as a Challenge to Literary Theory', Jauss proposes a new kind of literary history.[6] His main question is: how can one account for the fact that texts are read differently in time? Why did so many young men commit suicide after reading Goethe's *Werther*? Reading *Werther* today might produce a variety of responses but suicide would be most unlikely to be one of them. So how does Jauss deal with this problem? He comes up with the term 'horizon of expectations' (*Erwartungshorizont*).

This is a phenomenological term; it is like a 'frame of reference'. Jauss's horizon of expectations, however, is basically historical: it consists of different kinds of information that are available at a given moment in history; for a contemporary reader of *Werther* the horizon of expectations would be constituted by all the texts written at the time, scientific, philosophical, literary, literary-critical, and so on. As I understand it from students of the Constance School, Jauss's PhD students are asked to make '*Querschnittsanalysen*', that is, to take a cross-section of information samples at a particular synchronic moment. Jauss chooses one year, say 1823, and selects four students: one will be writing about every novel published in that year, another about every play, another about all the poems, and yet another about all the philosophical writings. Jauss's ultimate aim, his *Lebenswerk*, is to write a new kind of literary history which gives all the information at that given moment in history.

What theoretical conclusions does Jauss draw from his investigation? He attacks conventional literary history on two grounds: its *linearity* (that of one work reacting against another work), and its focus on the *author* rather than the reader. His aim is to establish as precisely as possible the horizon of the reader. And here one obvious distinction can be made between Iser's reader-response theory and Jauss's: where Iser's theory postulates a reader prestructured by the devices of the text, a reader *in* the text, Jauss's theory postulates a real reader, one that exists empirically outside the text.

Jauss sees what happens between reader and text as a continuing process, which works not only synchronically, at a given moment in history, but also diachronically, that is through time and history. A literary history based on a history of the work's reception will reveal the process whereby a merely passive reception by readers and critics can stimulate an author's active reception and production. It will make plain how the work solves formal and moral problems left unsolved by the previous one, and how it poses new problems in its turn. For it is Jauss's contention that the more distance there is between a new work and its horizon of expectations and the more it challenges its readers and contributes to a change of horizon, the greater will be its aesthetic value and its ethical consequences. As an example he cites Flaubert's *Madame Bovary*, arguing that the new narrative device of free indirect speech drew the then historical reader into Emma Bovary's world with a sense of shock and forced him to reconsider the moral issues raised in the novel.

As in Iser's theory, then, it is the change of perception produced in the reader which is seen as the main criterion of aesthetic value. The problem with such a theory is that it cannot account for the supposedly lasting value of the literary canon, which can then only be read against the grain if it is to disrupt our horizon of expectations if it is to have any shock value. Neither can there be an adequate reading for so-called trash literature, a related embarrassment, this time for Iser. Trash literature turns out ideal readers, ones that respond perfectly to the structures of the text, doing exactly what the author has intended them to do, reading from cover to cover, and perfectly adjusting their responses as they go along. What the theory of the Constance School does not allow for is the question of what kind of text might provoke a reader to read against the grain, because their model precludes giving the reader this kind of freedom.

AFFECT

The main element that both Iser and Jauss ignore is the affective side of reading. My third question – how does a text affect us? – begins by looking at what the text does to the reader. A theorist who concerns himself with this question is the American critic, Norman Holland, who investigates reader-response with the help of psychoanalytic theory.[7] He was not the first psychoanalytic critic to make the move from author and text to reader and text – that was another American, Simon Lesser[8] – but Holland was the first to produce a consistent psychoanalytic reader-theory, the first systematically to put the reader in analysis rather than the author.

Holland focuses on the subjective experience of the reader, on the unconscious factor in *reading*, whereas it had been the practice since Freud (whose 'reader-theory' is really only in embryo) to focus on the subjective experience of the author, the unconscious aspect of his or her creative activity. Basic to psychoanalytic theory is that neither author nor reader can understand all that moves them because the text evokes repressed material. Reader-response, in the early passive version of psychoanalytic reader-theory, is a kind of re-cycling of the unconscious fantasies of the author by the reader, in the process of which the formal skills of the author act as both veil and lure for the forbidden material from the unconscious. The analogy to clinical practice in this model of reading lies in the 'free-floating' attention the reader/analyst gives to the author/analysand, listening with a 'third ear' for the compulsive patterns produced in the so-called 'free' associations of the 'text'. The analytic concept of transference is transferred to the reading situation: transference responses are the unconscious attitudes we bring towards other people because we cannot help but repeat our loves and hates of those first significant others who helped make us what we are. In the analytic space, to which the reading space is seen as analogous, this intense relationship is re-created.

In author-centred theories of reading, a reader, say like Marie Bonaparte, believes she is analysing the author's transference to his material and thus gaining access to his unconscious.[9] In reader-centred theories, such as Norman Holland's, it is the reader's transference to the author's transference that is at stake, what is known as the counter-transference, because it is a reaction to another's transference: in other words, it is not the author's fantasies that are the issue, but the reader's. The text produces turbulences in the reader which the reader has somehow to cope with. So, where in Iser's theory the gaps of non-sense which appear in the text are the result of a consciousness which cannot keep in step with the flux of time, in psychoanalytic theory gaps are the consequence of censorship, places where unconscious meaning gets dis-placed. And where in Iser's theory the reader fills the gaps via an understanding based on reading competence, general erudition and imagination, all function of the intellect, in Holland's latest theory the reader fills in so as to negotiate as painlessly as possible – 'transact' in Holland's terminology – the dominant unconscious fantasies which the text evokes in the reader. Unfortunately Holland's theory hardly allows for any productive activity on the part of the unconscious. In keeping with his adherence to ego-psychology, it is the rational part of the mind which performs feats of transformation by means of certain classical defensive operations, the principle being that the reader will use a text in order to turn unacceptable private fantasies into socially approved aspirations in ways typical to his or her particular 'identity theme', that is to say, the reader uses a text as he or she would a life situation, as material for the continuing formation of his or her identity. Like Jauss, Holland conducts experiments with empirical readers, analysing their different associations to a single text – their transference responses to it – and then analysing his response to their response in terms of counter-transference. But in this theory of reading, the unconscious is tamed rather than allowed to participate in the process of making new meaning (since all the emphasis is on the mastering of anxiety). For instance, Holland describes 'Sandra's' reaction to a poem by the American Imagist, Hilda Doolittle, and writes that it 'seemed quite different from H. D.'s characteristic concerns. Sandra interpreted the images in terms of strength and power .. very different from H. D.'s associations ... We are seeing Sandra achieve the poem in her own individual style.' Her own individual style, however, is that of maintaining her identity theme, not of producing a persuasive reading which she is recommending to others.

Although both Iser and Holland claim to have established an inter-subjective theory of reading and pay lip-service to the notion of text-structure exerting a pull on the reader, Iser privileges the author as the ultimate God of the Gaps and Holland does likewise with the reader. Holland's answer to the question 'How does reading affect us?' takes us too far away from the text to make reading anything but a highly subjective activity, with little change wrought in the reader, though it may not be an inaccurate description of how readers in general deal with books. Iser's theory, on the other hand, makes no allowance for a real reader at all. Holland's and Iser's theories complement each other one-sidedly in an interesting way, but the two theorists show little sign that they could learn from each other.[10]

So could there be a different answer to the question 'How does the text affect us?', one that gives the text a more active role in the reading process? One of the difficulties of psychoanalytic reader-theory has been the problem of assigning an unconscious to the text. Texts, it is said, do not have an unconscious, only people, and psychoanalysts have been the first to scoff at the idea of a textual unconscious, thinking it was some foible of the literary critic who is thus poaching on the analyst's preserves. The notion of 'the text' developed in the wake of Saussurean linguistics, to be later revised. Despite the revolutionary effect of Saussure's doctrine of the arbitrariness of the sign, of the arbitrary link between signifier and signified (i.e. sound and concept), which did away with any simple notion of referentiality, of some pre-existent object out there, ready to be named, it was none the less obvious that what remained to be accounted for was the Real that lies under all the objects referred to in a text. Although it is signifiers which divide up the Real (the fundamental contingencies of nature), what lies between those divisions is not necessarily completely defined. Signifiers refer to signifieds as various sortings of the Real, but there remains an excess which lies outside the recognised definition. It is at these margins of language that the unconscious takes effect. The reader can hence be seen as at the mercy of the text, since he or she does not know what referential effects will be brought into play in the course of his or her reading. But the text is also at the mercy of the reader, because of the mediating effects of his own unconscious. Language is the node where there is an intersection of cultural and personal interpretation.

For a textual theory of the affective side of reading which privileges neither author nor reader I finally want to turn to the reader-theory implicit in Jacques Lacan's reading of Freud, although Lacan is often accused of neglecting the emotions. Lacan might indeed want to put the question 'How does a text affect a reader?' more in terms like 'How does the unconscious read?'; nevertheless, the two questions are intimately related. Whereas for Holland transference to the text involves the re-working of certain prominent fantasies by the reader, whereby the text and its characters are treated as figures of the past on which one transfers one's dominant fears and wishes, for Lacan transference is a process which goes on in language. The same mechanisms which characterise the dream – Freud calls them condensation and displacement – function in all human symbol-systems, in particular in language.

The unconscious reads via verbal associations and sounds that attach themselves to networks of images coming out of early concrete experience, bodily effects in relation to early love, hate, knowledge and truth. These images continue to resonate like a text of the premature self, in Freud's terms as primary-process logic, in Lacan's as the Imaginary, in Kristeva's as the Semiotic, the difference in terminology implying a different value judgement. Whatever the case might be, this 'text' brings the unconscious into the supposedly objective and rational secondary-process language. Therefore, in a psychoanalytic theory of knowledge there will always be an excess of meaning, which may also be experienced as meaninglessness, and it is this excess which is left out of Saussure's theory of language and out of other objectivist theories, such as Speech Act Theory. Lacan calls this inherent duality of language 'the discourse of the Other': on the one hand, the first Other, the early sounds of the 'Mother tongue', on the other hand, the second Other, the Father's language, the Symbolic Order, forbidding incest and determining gender. Hence the subject is split, because the visible subject of perception and representation is unconscious of its source in the Desire of an Other. What concerns the Lacanian reader is the unconscious truth of the text, the desire of the text which has an effect both on author and reader. For Lacan the focus is on textuality, the condensations and displacements (metaphors and metonymies) of language in the production of desire.

It is the conscious speaking subject, the 'I', which Iser and Holland deal with in their supposedly intersubjective theory of reading: Iser is not interested in an unconscious at all, and Holland, in so far as he deals with an unconscious, wants it to be under the control of the 'I', which for him is the stable ego. For Lacan, however, the 'I' is the subject of language, trying to fit into conventional 'false' discourse, while the 'true' subject can only make itself known via the narcissistic manoeuvres of the 'mirror stage', the Imaginary fusion with its first Other. The Imaginary and the Symbolic will continually fight over the interpretation of the lived (Real) experience the subject has. It is this struggle which is embodied in language – hence another of Lacan's dicta, 'the unconscious is structured like a language'. Both writer and reader get caught up in these structures; the experience of attaining subject-status in and through language reveals itself in the repetition of sounds, words and themes. The desire of the text is here not a search for identity in Holland's sense, not 'How do I maintain myself?', but 'Tell me what to do with my desire'. This is the author's appeal to the reader as much as the reader's appeal to the author. There is thus a move from the production of regressive fantasies to the production of future-oriented desire. In this view it is neither the reader who is the prime maker of meaning (Holland) nor the author who controls the reader via the gaps in the text (Iser): both author and reader are controlled by the strategies of language. Subjective (private) meaning is mediated for both by the effect of an (intersubjective) Other – the public language shared by all.

With what, according to this theory, is language really concerned? Only with the subject's desire for knowledge, a knowledge which it hopes the text will produce. The text structure is desired on the one hand as Law, the language of the Symbolic which gives the subject its sexual identity, and on the other hand as the continued search for the lost union with the first Other. Thus meaning is continually deferred, and textual analysis, like life-analysis, is interminable, the gaps in the text being its refusal to yield a final meaning. In a Lacanian psychoanalytic reader-theory, gaps occur because of the elaboration of desire under the impact of (oedipal) Law, and they are as much an enigma to the author as they are to the reader. 'The pleasure of the text' (Roland Barthes) can give a double satisfaction, rather than a single one of mastery as in Holland's theory: it can play out the movement from Imaginary to Symbolic ('cultural pleasure'), or it can do the reverse, from Symbolic to Imaginary ('non-cultural bliss').

But, if one accuses Iser of having produced an a-historical reader-theory, where does history come into the Lacanian view? This is also the question asked by those who accuse Lacan of harbouring a patriarchal theory. Interpretation, however, is not only affected by the rules and conventions of the Symbolic Order at a given moment in history, but also by our subsequent re-readings of those rules. That is why we shall never be able to read a text of the past as if we were a contemporary reader, however hard we try with all the scholarship at our disposal. Even so, the material of the text will continue to have a Real effect on modern readers, in that they will go on feeling the gap between the Real of the world (contingent nature) and the referentiality of language. It is the filling in of *this* gap which poses such a threat to our desire, unless it be that we take the opportunity of re-reading the rules and intervening with a new authority upon the old.

Notes

My thanks to Evelyne Keitel for a lively discussion on the work of the Constance School.

1. Accounts of reader-response theories can be found in Robert Holub, *Reception Theory: A Critical Introduction* (Methuen, London and New York, 1984); Ann Jefferson and David Robey, *Modern Literary Theory: A Comparative Introduction* (Batsford, London, 1982) (contains chapters on Russian Formalism and modern psychoanalytic theory); Rudolf E. Kuenzli, 'The Intersubjective Structure of the Reading Process: A Communication-Oriented Theory of Literature', *Diacritics* (June 1980) (issue discussing Iser and Holland); William Ray, *Literary Meaning* (Basil Blackwell, Oxford, 1984) (chapters on Ingarden, Iser, and Holland); Susan R. Suleiman and Inge Crosman (eds), *The Reader in the Text: Essays on Audience and Interpretation* (Princeton University Press, New Jersey, 1980) (essays by Iser and Holland); and Jane P. Tompkins, *Reader-Response Criticism: From Formalism to Post-Structuralism* (Johns Hopkins University Press, Baltimore, 1980) (essays by Iser and Holland). Elizabeth Wright, *Psychoanalytic Criticism: Theory in Practice* (Methuen, London and New York, 1984) contains chapters on Holland and Lacan.

2.   Wolfgang Iser, 'The Reading Process: A Phenomenological Approach', in Tompkins, *Reader-Response Criticism*.

3.   W. Iser, *The Act of Reading: A Theory of Aesthetic Response* (Johns Hopkins University Press, Baltimore, 1978), p. 218.

4.   Roman Ingarden, *The Cognition of the Literary Work of Art* (Northwestern University Press, Evanston, Ill., 1973); originally published in Polish in 1937.

5.   W. Iser, *The Implied Reader: Patterns of Communication in Prose Fiction from Bunyan to Beckett* (Johns Hopkins University Press, Baltimore, 1974).

6.   Hans Robert Jauss, 'Literary History as a Challenge to Literary Theory': originally delivered as a speech in Constance (1967); published in *New Literary History*, no. 2 (Autumn 1970); collected in Jauss, *Towards an Aesthetic of Reception* (University of Minnesota Press, Minneapolis, 1982). The latter contains an Introduction by Paul de Man.

7.   Norman H. Holland, *The Dynamics of Literary Response* (Oxford University Press, Oxford, 1968).

8.   Simon O. Lesser, *Fiction and the Unconscious* (Beacon Press, Boston, 1957).

9.   See, for example, Marie Bonaparte, *The Life and Works of Edgar Allan Poe* (Imago, London, 1949); originally published in French in 1933.

10.   See the discussion in *Diacritics* (June 1980).

11

Psychoanalysis: Telepathy, Gossip and/or Science?

John Forrester

Some brief introductory remarks are in order to place my chapter in the context of this series, and also to give some idea of the links between the enigmatic words in my title. I shall not be applying cultural theory to psychoanalysis, nor shall I be deriving cultural theory from psychoanalysis. Rather, I shall be giving a psychoanalytic account of the culture of psychoanalysis: a psychoanalysis of psychoanalysis. I should also add that when I use the term 'psychoanalysis', I am referring to a discursive *practice* – a practice guided by and infused with theory: the practice of two people talking to one another, within the rules laid down in order to define that practice.

The technique of speech known as psychoanalysis requires one to examine the frame of discourse as much as the so-called meaning. What aim does this discourse have, over and beyond what it says? Is it my role here to give us something to gossip about over dinner? Am I speaking so as to elicit all those stories of telepathy, the occult that everyone has experienced, or at least heard of through the grapevine, so that we can all collectively analyse these stories, only to realise that, as Derrida so aptly puts it, we realise that the question of telepathy is not one of knowledge or non-knowledge. In his article 'Télépathie', he intimates this on two levels: firstly by writing in the first person – a first person which is recognisably that of Freud's, so that we are tempted into asking how Derrida has come to be in a position to be able to write 'Freud's' 'I' for him: by divination, by psychoanalysis, or by telepathy? And then, amongst the things he writes, we find the following:

> There's no knowing (and on this point I'm in a strong position because here there's no question of 'knowledge'. Everything in our conception of

knowledge is so constructed that telepathy is impossible, unthinkable, unknowable. If there is such a thing, our relation to Telepathy won't belong to the family of 'knowledge' or of 'non-knowledge' but to another genre). So I will do everything I can so that you can neither believe nor disbelieve that I myself believe or don't: but you will never know precisely if I'm doing it on purpose. The question of *on purpose* will lose all meaning for you.[1]

If the question of telepathy leads us to an epistemological impasse, such that it is best to leave the question of belief or knowledge entirely to one side, so also does the question of gossip, but this time in both the epistemic and the moral spheres. Knowledge had by gossip only barely maintains its claim on that word, sketching out the no man's land of fiction which equally constitutes the social knowledge by which we live. In addition, gossip only appears as such when there is a transgression of rules of discourse. Talking about someone who is not present is the rule, not the exception, in conversation: but that is not gossip. It only becomes gossip once the talk implicitly or explicitly addresses moral questions concerning them, or moral questions raised by their actions. And of course to think of gossip as a form of moral discourse makes as much sense as talking of telepathy as a form of knowledge.

To give you a sense of the sort of approach I have been using in my studies of psychoanalysis, some semi-autobiographical remarks may be of some help. For some years I have been engaged in what I am obliged to call a psychoanalysis of psychoanalysis. If there is one cultural artefact that can be exhaustively subjected to the discipline of analysis then that artefact is analysis itself. The procedures I have adopted are both historical and conceptual-analytic, and both these kinds of procedure turn around the questions: what are the limits of the analytic object? What defines the border territory between the analytic and the non-analytic, or the extra-analytic? How did the social practice we call psychoanalysis come into being, and what are the effects of its existence on the ensemble of other discursive practices?

Some years ago I wrote two papers, one on Dora, the other on Freud, Lacan and Derrida in which these themes are explored. The paper on Dora, prepared for the first time I spoke at the ICA, drew its inspiration from listening to Aria 12 from *The Marriage of Figaro* – the scene where Suzanna and the Countess are dressing up Cherubino as a woman. In this aria, in listening and looking, we cannot forget that Cherubino is a woman singing a man's part.[2] Halfway through this aria, just when Suzanna makes an aside to the Countess about how handsome Cherubino is, there is a bridge passage of dialogue between violins, voice and cellos: a sublime procession of chattering violins, with cellos gliding gently up and down, with keys descending, then ascending, redescending and reascending, all evoking the hint of a *perpertuum mobile*. Mozart is saying – this could go on for ever, this delicate game, so delightful and touching, so gleeful and gay! It is clear that this music is depicting Cherubino walking up and down, as Suzanna appraises the cut of [her]/his/her dress. But at the same time, the music depicts the secret talk of women in the boudoir. As Suzanna says in her aside:

> Isn't he handsome,
> What roguish glances,
> What airs, what graces!
> If women fall in love with him,
> They have good reason why.

For me, this scene came to depict the delights of feminine gossip. Now these delights are ones that men are prone to feeling excluded from, indeed even paranoid about. For instance, take the following passage from P. D. James's *A Taste for Death*:

> Now, above the tinkle of kettle lid and crockery, he [Adam Dalgliesh] could hear their voices, conversational, almost ordinary. From the few phrases he could catch, they seemed to be discussing the merits of a make of electric kettle which both possessed. Suddenly he felt that he shouldn't be there, that he was redundant as a detective and as a man. They would both get on better without his male, destructive presence. Even the room seemed inimical to him, and he could almost persuade himself that the low broken sibilants of female voices were in conspiracy.[3]

It was the perception of the fascinations of feminine gossip, when combined with the male horror of exclusion from its mysteries, that underpinned my account of the case of Dora: in their conversations, Freud refused to take up the position of woman in his sessions with the young hysterical girl, precisely because it would have meant that his precious psychoanalysis might turn out to be just a version of gossip, of women chatting amongst themselves, the seemingly inconsequential chat of Dora with Frau K., or of Dora with her grandmother.[4] If I and others have been speculating that Freud refused to acknowledge the feminine transference in his analysis – which seems plausible, given some of the other things that went on in, say, his 'A Case of Female Homosexuality' – then we are still obliged to ask what exactly in his masculine identification he was not prepared to give up. To say: he was not prepared to give up his phallus, his penis, would overlook the fact that for Freud, his phallus was so transparently identified with his power as talker and writer, as word-magician. The symbolic castration that Freud feared might well have been the deprivation of the word as identified with the penetrating observation, the interpretation that uncovered the secret hiding-place of the repressed –but an observation and interpretation that could be translated into the form of the written. The art of feminine gossip, especially as seen from the outside, might well have seemed to him to leave no room for these masculine powers of conversational magic.

This view of Dora takes psychoanalysis itself to be akin to gossip. In the second paper, entitled 'Who is in analysis with whom?',[5] I asked this eminently gossipy question of psychoanalysis itself, viewing it as a thing to be gossiped *about*. I adopted the masculine position of being 'outside', and, in order to find out what the cultural effects of this strange form of discourse were, I gave up the temptation to 'look inside'. Instead, to understand it, I used, without making it explicit, a very crude model, in part derived from Lacan and Derrida, which it will be my business today to outline for you.[6]

Psychoanalytic practice is a specific form of discourse between two people, defined by rules of asymmetry: the patient agrees to obey the fundamental rule, namely to tell the analyst everything that enters his or her mind, while the analyst abstains from such free discourse. Instead, he or she offers interpretations of what the patient has said. Certain rules govern the relation of this discursive dyad to the outside world: the analyst gives the patient an implicit or explicit assurance that anything said will be treated with absolute confidentiality.[7] The patient, however, does not offer such an assurance, but is implicitly or explicitly encouraged to refrain from discussing the analysis much with people 'outside'.[8] As a cultural artefact, the investigation of this discursive dyad should, I conclude, concern itself as much with the semi-permeable membrane that is as a consequence of these rules placed *around* the two people talking as it does with the *content* of the talk.

So, we have a model of two people talking, according to certain rules, with a boundary limit operating as third term. Psychoanalysts themselves, following Klein, Winnicott and Bion, have referred to this limit, this membrane, as the container, and the themes of the inside and outside brook large in Kleinian theories of projection and introjection, as they do in Lacanian theories of the topology of analytic space.

How are we to investigate the functioning of this semi-permeable membrane? The first thing to be said concerns the fact that the very existence of the membrane gives gossip and psychoanalysis something in common: they are both conversations taking place in the *absence of the real*. Gossip always takes place in the absence of the parties being gossiped about, although naming them is crucial to the activity. Similarly, the rules of analysis require that all participating parties be absent, *including those addressed in the second person*. What I mean by this strange formulation is that even the analyst is absent when addressed in the transferential mode of the second person, the 'you'. The analyst achieves this through the technique of transference interpretation: sentences containing 'you' are treated as if they were passing him by, as if he were passing them on. In Lacan and Derrida's formulation, he acts as a postman, relaying or redirecting all the messages that come to him.[9] He tries to act like the lost and found department of the Post Office, ascertaining to whom these communications are addressed. In this way, a declaration of love or the heaping of abuse can be interpreted as being about someone who is not there. One consequence of this peculiar stance of the analyst is that the patient finds it possible to gossip about him- or herself – something that in everyday life is impossible. It is this gossiping about oneself that people in analysis often find so repulsive and fascinating about their own activity; it also means that they find it difficult to recognise the charge of self-centred, narcissistic preoccupation that those 'outside' often level at those 'inside' analysis.

The consequent professional absenteeism of the analyst allows one to see the similar structure of gossip and the joke as analysed by Freud: both concern three parties, where one is necessarily absent, and the pleasure of the talk conducted under these circumstances has as its condition this absence of the third party.[10] What is more, besides this similarity, there is an interesting opposition between jokes and gossip. In Freud's theory of jokes, a dirty joke is told by one man to what Freud calls the third person (also a man), in the absence of the woman, the second person, who is the original target of the seduction aimed at in the joke. In contrast, gossip is traditionally a feminine art – or vice, as the moral opprobrium directed at women's chat for centuries testifies – and as we saw in the passage from P. D. James, it is the absent man, the man as rendered structurally absent, who is the fundamental precondition of gossip. Hence Freud's fright at catching himself gossiping with Dora. . .[11]

Gossip and joking thus seem to have complementary – inverted and homologous – gender structures. In addition, they both inhabit a sharply contoured space of the forbidden and the enticing. The discursivity of gossip in particular also helps to *define* the margins of the licit, whereas the punctuality of joking *celebrates* the existence of the cut-off.

Joking, however, is explicitly fictional. Jokes are first and foremost *stories*, whether about Englishmen, Scotsmen and Irishmen who are more fictional, and therefore 'made more real', than any existing national types, or about supposedly real characters, such as Gorbachev or Reagan. Any supposedly true stories that are also jokes immediately lose their quality of verisimilitude, of plausibility and instead became true, *irrespective* of their verisimilitude and plausibility. However, one can see a common root of gossip and joke in children's stories and jokes about adults: they often have the character of being crude fantasies which eventually climax in an imagined scene, at that moment provoking great hilarity.

Whilst the gossip of adults differs from joking in its avowed relation to the real, it shares with psychoanalysis what I will call the *fiction of the real*, alongside the already mentioned requirement of the absence of the real: in order to be a successful gossip, or a non-resisting patient in analysis, you must be seen to name names, you must tell stories earmarked as *true*, about real, live people. The patient who refuses to reveal his parents' names is a figment of the imagination, the analyst's nightmare. None the less, we have been forcibly reminded recently by the scurrilous, and by no means previously unnoticed, stories that Masson tells in his book *The Assault on Truth*[12] about the early history of Freud's relations with his patients that the real of analysis is an ever-receding one. Masson finds this outrageous and morally blameworthy. For the psychoanalyst, on the other hand, what defines the rules of the discourse is that there is no moment when the analyst decides: 'This actually happened'. None the less the fiction of the real is not touched by this technical procedure.[13]

If the semi-permeable membrane which constitutes analysis allows one to draw analogies between analysis and gossip, an eminently psycho-analytic way of further investigating the membrane's properties is to ask: what happens when the membrane is broken, and the high levels of osmotically concentrated contents leak out? For the moment, let us consider the two participants in the analytic conversation as separate parties: it is clear that it is either the analyst or the patient who can do the leaking. The analyst's communications with the outside world fall into two categories: first, the so-called 'scientific communication' – the case-history of the patient. Secondly, the analyst may gossip about the patient. Stanley Olinick has devoted a paper to considering what he calls the gossiping psychoanalyst, employing the following definition:

> By 'gossip' I refer to an indiscreet type of loose talk, with or without the use of names or other identifications. This entails impromptu, casual case vignettes that are brought up during social encounters with col-leagues and others. They are not intended as scientific exchanges, but as social talk.[14]

So one of the questions implied by my title emerges: under what conditions does talk about an analysis qualify as a scientific communication, rather than as gossip?

Analysts have taken this question very seriously, as is demonstrated by a paper on the significance of the sex of the analyst for the course of the analysis by the aptly named Ethel Person. Person illustrates part of her argument by referring to two male analysts who had slept with their patients. The re-analysis of these analysts prompted Person to point out two factors. One was the self-destructive urge these seductions manifested: the male analysts knew they would be 'found out', when their female patients/lovers talked (gossiped?) to their next analysts; however, they expected that this would not become '*public* knowledge', but would be confined to the world of rumour. In the course of their re-analyses it also became clear that the seduction of their patients had been, for both of them, a repetition of what each of them had felt to be a betrayal, indeed a 'rape', to use their word, by their own analysts, who had used material from their analyses in scientific communications without asking their permission.[15] Notice how the original sin[16] of analysis here gets transmitted, transferred from analytic cell to analytic cell, with rumour and scientific communication doubling up as the means by which the piercing of the membrane operates.[17]

If we consider the patient as the source of leakage through the semi-permeable membrane, we also find two categories: first, those analytic communications that have been displaced from *within* the analysis, which should have been spoken to the analyst, not to someone outside: what analysts call acting out (here the act in question is the act of communicating, and hence acutely uncomfortable for the analyst, devoted to the purification of communication of its aspect of action). Secondly, there is the category of gossip in the ordinary sense of the word – gossip about the analysis, gossip about the analyst, the sort of self-revealing chat that analysands sharing a psychoanalytic culture indulge in. This sort of gossip is very common, and it is clear that it is the uncanny kinship with analysis, as well as the sense of potential analytic relevance and analytic power that this gossip engenders that often makes it even more interesting and dangerous than ordinary gossip about work, friends, children and so forth. Putting this another way, we all feel that gossip is dangerous, that it is illicit and exciting, but for analysts and analysands, that dangerous pleasure is compounded by the awareness that gossip is remarkably akin to analysis, both in its powers of revelation of the truth, and in its revelation of the power of the truth.

It is not clear that the first category of the analysand's gossip, 'acting out', and the second, 'ordinary gossip', can be kept apart. Purist analysts – and on this point any analyst worth his or her salt is a purist – would regard *all* communication about the analysis to a third party as being misplaced communications *to* the analyst. Or rather, to be more precise – and this is the source of the value of the salt I just mentioned – the rules of interpretation that analysts are following lead them to regard such gossip as misplaced communications: it is their *job* to regard gossip as misplaced communication, meaning roughly that this is what the patient is paying them to do, namely to *analyse* the gossip about analysis, as they would anything else. However, it seems to me that if one can identify and distinguish the *analyst's* gossip about the analysis, it seems unduly mean and absolutist to argue that the *analysand's* gossip about the analysis does not count as such. And, of course, to the outsider, to anyone other than the gossip's analyst, it simply *is* gossip. And this outsider might be tempted to ask the question: what are the consequences of retaining the symmetry of

assimilation, so that where the analyst assimilates gossip to acting out, the
theorist of gossip assimilates acting out to gossip?

So far I have separated out three categories of leaked communication:
scientific communications, acting out, and gossip. But there is also another
means by which the membrane might allow unregulated passage across it:
the case of telepathy. One of my arguments in this chapter is that telepathy
came to have such an important part in Freud's psychoanalytic theorising
precisely because once the psychoanalytic situation has been conceptual-
ised as a semi-permeable discursive membrane, telepathy becomes a threat
to that situation. The aim of the rules of analytic discourse are to regulate
the flow across the membrane; telepathy represents a direct threat to this
attempt at discursive regulation.

The form of telepathy that would be most obviously significant would be
one in which a thought from 'outside' enters into the analytic dyad, rather
than emanating *from* it. In the former case, telepathy and gossip work in
opposite directions. Rather than placing the accent on the direction of
passage across the membrane, it is plausible that what is at issue here is the
membrane and its permeability. To illustrate this, let me quote at length
from Freud's lecture on 'Dreams and occultism', not only to give you a
sense of the 'membrane' model I am using, but also to indicate Freud's
surprising thinking on this subject.

> If there is such a thing as telepathy as a real process, we may suspect
> that, in spite of its being so hard to demonstrate, it is quite a common
> phenomenon. It would tally with our expectations if we were able to
> point to it particularly in the mental life of children. Here we are
> reminded of the frequent anxiety felt by children over the idea that their
> parents know all their thoughts without having to be told them – an
> exact counterpart and perhaps the source of the belief of adults in the
> omniscience of God. A short time ago Dorothy Burlingham, a trust-
> worthy witness, in a paper on child analysis and the mother, published
> some observations which, if they can be confirmed, would be bound to
> put an end to the remaining doubts on the reality of thought-transfer-
> ence. She made use of the situation, no longer a rare one, in which a
> mother and child are simultaneously in analysis, and reported some
> remarkable events such as the following. One day the mother spoke
> during her analytic session of a gold coin that had played a particular
> part in one of the scenes of her childhood. Immediately afterwards, after
> she had returned home, her little boy, about ten years old, came to her
> room and brought her a gold coin which he asked her to keep for him.
> She asked him in astonishment where he had got it from. He had been
> given it on his birthday; but his birthday had been several months earlier
> and there was no reason why the child should have remembered the gold
> coin precisely then. The mother reported the occurrence to the child's

analyst and asked her to find out from the child the reason for his action
[is this gossip or scientific communication? – JPF]. But the child's
analysis threw no light on the matter; the action had forced its way that
day into the child's life like a foreign body. A few weeks later the mother
was sitting at her writing-desk to write down, as she had been told to do,
an account of the experience, when in came the boy and asked for the
gold coin back, as he wanted to take it with him to show in his analytic
session. Once again the child's analysis could discover no explanation of
his wish.[18]

The telepathic question par excellence, one which reveals its kinship to
psychoanalysis immediately is: 'Whose thoughts are these, inhabiting my
inner world?' The fundamental rule of analysis has as a strict corollary that
the patient ignores questions concerning the provenance of the thoughts
'heorshe' has. Children think their parents know all their thoughts;
analysands often think that their analysts know all their thoughts – the
after-image, one suspects, of the fundamental rule. So whose thought is it?
Such questions are expressly put to one side in analysis, to be dealt with
later, you might say. Under these circumstances, telepathy, or thought-
transference as Freud rebaptises it, seems the natural state of affairs. As
Derrida so wittily puts it:

we won't have taken a single step forward in our discussion of the
despatch [*envoi*] (the adestination, the wandering of destiny, of destina-
tions, of clandestination) if amongst all these telethings we don't touch
on telepathy in person. Or rather if we don't allow ourselves to be
touched by it... The truth which I find so difficult to get some grip on is:
that non-telepathy might be possible. It is always difficult to imagine that
one might be able to think of something in separation, within one's
interior space, without being surprised by the other, without his being
already in on it, as easily as if he had within him a giant screen, just when
speaking, with a remote control unit to change the channel and play with
the colours, the discourse being repeated in large letters to avoid all
misunderstanding... This puerile belief of mine, in part mine, can only
stem from the foundation – sure, let's call it unconscious, if you want –
upon which has been erected objectivist certainty, this so-called pro-
visional system of science, the discourse which is linked to a state of
affairs in science which has made us hold telepathy in some respect. It is
difficult to imagine a theory of what they still call the unconscious
without a theory of telepathy. They can be neither confused nor
dissociated.[19]

The fundamental rule of psychoanalysis requires the patient to put to one
side the question, 'whose thoughts are these?', in order to allow these
thoughts to emerge as anonymous, almost collective[20] – *already* in the

form of hearsay. The distance between what I say of myself as garnered from hearsay and what is said of me by gossip or telepathy is thus, once again, bracketed off by psychoanalytic *technique* – again, I should emphasise this is not so much a question of theory. But the theory that is then elaborated on the basis of the material thus furnished, the theory of the unconscious, and in particular of the dream in its regal relation to the unconscious – or is it rather the unconscious in its regal relation to the dream? – all this theory furnishes out a new form of reality, which Freud calls psychic reality. This new reality, which goes beyond anything which I can call simply mine, cannot truly distinguish between the voices of rumour, of gossip, of telepathy, and those voices which are unconscious. Just take the well-worn example of post-hypnotic suggestion: whose thought is it, which emerges, telling me to put up my umbrella while giving this lecture? If the super-ego is the voice of my parents, in so far as I have forgotten what they said to me, then why cannot those other voices, whether I feel at ease in their presence or sense them as alien, as foreign, as voices from another world, why cannot these voices be the voice of my neighbour, my *Mitmensch*, even my analyst or fortune-teller,[21] come to haunt me when I'm best defended against ghosts?

Of the four means of breaching the membrane that I have mentioned – science, gossip, acting out and telepathy – two of them are already theorised by psychoanalysis: the scientific communication is the form of leakage *permitted* to analysts, and acting out is the form of leakage *expected* of patients. They form a pair. But both gossip and telepathy are not allowed for: they have not been adequately tamed by theory, and maybe cannot be tamed by theory. Not even Freud's papers on telepathy attempt to *tame* it: quite the contrary, in fact, which is one reason why they are so interesting. For Freud, telepathy often represents another *competing* category of phenomena to those psychoanalysis deals in. If the patient's communications come from 'outside' the analysis, from someone else, what sense will it have to talk of his specific unconscious? It is also no accident that he deals more with what he calls 'thought-*transference*' than telepathy proper.[22] The question implicit in all of his papers on the topic is: is the transference psychoanalysts deal in similar to thought-transference, and, if so, which is the more fundamental category?

So we have two illicit modes of transmission or communication: gossip and telepathy. Gossip is the underbelly of analysis, telepathy its shadow. However, there is another way of approaching the analytic dyad, which treats them analytically: that is as a dyad, not as two individuals. Then the question of the permeability of the membrane leads to the question: how does psychoanalysis itself get transmitted across this membrane? What guarantees that the discursive dyad is engaged in analysis, rather than the gossip that Freud feared Dora was seducing him into?

There is a very straightforward answer: the analyst brings with her her own experience of a similar dyad that she had herself experienced. Analysts bring with them the fruit of their own transference to their own analysts. That is, analysis is not transmitted from one dyadic 'cell' to another either via gossip or via the scientific communication: it is transmitted via the transplanting of the conditions for generating a transference-neurosis – the essential experience of analysis.

However, this chain of the analytic discourse, passed down from analytic parent to analytic child, has as its point of origin the original analysis: Freud's own analysis. Everyone claims analytic descent from Freud. And what some see as a complicating factor in training analyses, but which I regard as an essential factor, like the transference itself, is the question of the analysand's relation to Freud – what Granoff calls the transference to Freud.[23] It has enormous consequences for the cultural characteristics of psychoanalysis, which I will now explore.

What I am about to discuss will, to some of you, seem like gossip. Culturally, both critics and defenders of psychoanalysis behave as if they were dealing with a whole series of skeletons locked up in cupboards – skeletons that throw revolutionary or unwanted new light on the lives and practices of the early analysts. They treat what other people would regard as material for gossip as if it were truly the repressed secret, the hidden motor of their science. Let me mention some examples. Masson's book, *The Assault on Truth* tries to paint Freud as an intellectual coward who refused to look reality in the face when confronted with it, and dressed up the evidence so that he could conceal the horrible reality he had discovered. One part of the horrible reality was connected with the near fatal surgical error that Freud's friend Fliess perpetrated on one of Freud's most important patients, Emma Eckstein, and Masson traces, with little comprehension, the interesting way in which she became the first person to cross the analytic Rubicon by switching from patient to analyst.

Where Masson thinks the moral of this story is that Freud from then on repressed the real causes of neurosis, the sexual assaults on children, I judge it far more pertinent to point out that the other features of the analysis of the dream arising out of the Emma case which Freud left unmentioned were to do with his sexual feelings for his patients.[24] The indeterminacy of knowing whether it is past seductions by the parents, or present seductions by the analyst is what is interesting – because unspoken – when it comes to these skeletons in the closet.

The theme continues into the next piece of gossip, which concerns Freud's relation to his daughter, Anna. Rumour has it that Freud analysed his own daughter, Anna – and that this piece of analytic incest is meant to explain how and why she and the other guardians of the Freudian legacy have acted in order to protect his memory from being besmirched. The gossip runs: how could the founder of analysis think he could analyse his very own daughter?

When we turn to Anna Freud's great rival, Melanie Klein, we find similar gossip. Phyllis Grosskurth's biography reveals how the first child patients Klein had were her own children.[25] And the tantalising ethical and epistemic problem raised – and all gossip is addressed to both sorts of questions – by this gossip is: is this connected with the fact that Klein's most virulent and passionate analytic critic for many years was her own daughter, Melitta Schmideberg? And with respect to questions concerning the *internal* space of analysis: what connection might this practice of the mother analysing her own children have with the theoretical disputes Klein was famous for as to the irrelevance for analytic purposes of the child's 'real' relations to its parents?

This sort of gossip, gossip by analysts about other analysts, in particular about the founding analysts, seems to me to be more than just gossip. It points to that which is unanalysed in analysis itself. This sounds like the attitude of the more purist analysts themselves: yes, Freud should not have analysed Anna, Melanie Klein should not have analysed her own children – they obviously 'needed' more analysis! As if the unanalysed, the unconscious, could be *done away with* by more analysis. Instead of this blind prescription, I am suggesting that there is always an irreducible residue of each analysis, which is passed on through the genealogy of analysts, manifesting itself in those symptoms that now masquerade as theory.

Even without knowing the gossip about Freud and his daughter, or about Klein and her children, we would know that the central analytic question raised by their work revolves respectively around the father–daughter relationship,[26] or the mother–child relation. In this sense, the gossip amongst analysts is exactly what one might expect it to be: the making explicit of the unconscious of their psychoanalytic theories, through it being the discourse of their other, as Lacan defines the unconscious. The discourse of Freud's other is the gossip about his daughter; the discourse of Klein's other is the gossip about her children. In this sense, this gossip is the *analysis* of their respective psychoanalytic parents/theories.

Lacan meditated very deeply on these questions, and I wish to quote to you a long passage from his Seminar II that makes some theoretical points pertinent to these considerations of analysis in general and gossip about analysts in particular. He also makes the link with Freud's interest in telepathy:

> Think back on what we said in preceding years about those striking coincidences Freud noted in the sphere of what he calls telepathy. Very important things, in the way of transference, occur in parallel in two

patients, whether one is analysis and the other just on its fringes, or whether both are in analysis. At that time, I showed you how it is through being links, supports, rings in the same circle of discourse, agents integrated in the same circle of discourse, that the subjects simultaneously experience such and such a symptomatic act, or discover such and such a memory.

Here we rediscover ... that the unconscious is the discourse of the other. This discourse of the other is not the discourse of the abstract other, of the other in the dyad, of my correspondent, nor even of my slave, it is the discourse of the circuit in which I am integrated. I am one of its links. It is the discourse of my father, for example, in so far as my father had made mistakes that I am absolutely condemned to reproduce – that is what we call the super-ego. I am condemned to reproduce them because I am obliged to pick up again the discourse he bequeathed to me, not simply because I am his son, but because one can't stop the chain of discourse, and it is precisely my duty to transmit it in its aberrant form to someone else. I have to put to someone else the problem of a situation of life or death in which the chances are that it is just as likely that he will falter, in such a way that this discourse produces a small circuit in which an entire family, an entire coterie, an entire camp, an entire nation or half the world will be caught.[27]

The discourse in which my life, my thoughts, my desires are caught up is what Lacan calls the symbolic order: the stories that I hear as a child, stories of the sins of my fathers and mothers, the uncle who tells me that my mother really wanted a girl, all these stories which Freud called the family romance, all of this is the discourse of gossip – when seen from a particular perspective of being a subject outside the circuit who becomes implicated through the very fact of the existence of the circuitry. Gossip may not be a very grand name for Lacan's grand vision; but we are referring to the same thing: the phenomenon in which the discourse of the other, which is what the analyst says to me, is my unconscious – in the end the analyst only echoes back the gossip that inhabits the subject without him knowing it. And it is the specific circuit of discourse that analysts inhabit in their gossip about their forebears that is the unconscious of analysis.

Having mentioned Lacan, it is only fair to do some gossiping about him. And here we encounter a most curious fact: when it comes to Lacan's clinical practice, the only form of knowledge we have is gossip. Lacan's so-called scientific communications were never, with one exception I will come to, about his patients – they were always reflections on other people's cases, or on analytic concepts in general. Yet there has never been an analyst whose practice has been so discussed, interrogated. In 1962, the London Committee investigating Lacan's suitability as analyst went to Paris, were installed in the Westminster Hotel there, and spent days interviewing Lacan's analysands about his way of conducting analysis. As well as telling this story in her recently published second volume of the history of psychoanalysis in France, Elizabeth Roudinesco gives page after page of transcribed interviews with ex-patients of Lacan. One piece of gossip about Lacan will suffice to back up my Lacanian claim about the discourse of the other.[28]

The gossip concerns the one exception to Lacan's practice of never recounting case-histories from his practice. Lacan's medical thesis of 1932 was based upon his study of one woman patient who had been psychiatrically interned after she had stabbed a famous actress backstage. This paranoid woman, christened Aimée by Lacan, was his analytic muse, just as Anna O. was to Breuer, or the crowd of female hysterics were to Freud. Roudinesco goes so far as to claim that Lacan's 'analysis' of her was more constructive for his own personal development as both patient and analyst than his own, roughly contemporaneous, training analysis with Rudolph Loewenstein. This magnificent lengthy thesis, devoted primarily to Aimée, is certainly testimony to her importance to him.

Some twenty years later, Aimée's son – who, after her hospitalisation, had been brought up by an aunt – entered analysis with Lacan, without knowing that he was his mother's analyst. Nor, Lacan afterwards claimed, did he (Lacan) recognise Didier Anzieu as the son of his patient, having either never known, forgotten or failed to recognise the family name as that of his ex-patient. For an analyst who became celebrated as the advocate of the importance of the name-of-the-father, this is an extraordinary fact – but it fits in perfectly with my claim that the unanalysed residue, pinpointed here by gossip, is the motor of psychoanalytic theory. Indeed, the story does not end there. At about the same time as Anzieu completed his analysis with Lacan, in 1953, his mother, who had been released from hospital during the war, and had since become a cook, entered service with Lacan's father in Boulogne. On meeting her former analyst and psychiatrist, when he came to visit her employer, his father, she asked him to return the writings of hers which he had used to construct his thesis about paranoia. He refused. Certainly one is tempted to interpret this refusal as an intervention – or a refusal to intervene – within the circuit of discourse now established between mother, son, analyst, analyst's father, theses, writings and so on. Meanwhile, Lacan supplied the son, Didier Anzieu, with help towards the project he, Didier, was engaged upon: answering the question whether self-analysis is possible. Published in a first edition in 1959, enlarged in 1975, this work, now entitled *Freud's Self-Analysis*, has recently been translated into English – it is the definitive work on the subject, and I recommend it to you all.[29] None the less it bears the traces of its genesis, in that various ideas and arguments which are clearly based upon Lacan's seminars, which Anzieu attended in the 1950s, are presented there without any mention of Lacan's influence. Telepathy, plagiarism – certainly the circuit of analysis – what question is this? you might well ask.

I hope these examples will give you a sense of the importance of the gossip about analysts, in so far as it throws light on the unanalysed residue of analysis, and is thus absolutely essential to the writing of a history of psychoanalysis. Given my model of cells of discursive dyads, connected together at the official level by scientific communications between analysts, by gossip by analysts and patients, it is clear that it may well be as much the gossip that goes on between and within these cells that constitutes a psychoanalytic culture as the diffusion and acceptance or rejection of the 'science' of psychoanalysis. And this is in addition to the suggestion I have made that psychoanalysis be seen as, in part, the science of gossip. These two levels – gossip mediating *between* analytic dyads, and gossip as what goes on *within* those dyads – emerge clearly in a remark of Serge Leclaire's.[30] He notes that, in a sufficiently psychoanalysed culture, such as contemporary Paris, the question as to what is being said by friends and lovers on their respective couches can take on a greater analytic significance than the traditional Oedipus complex. The structure of gossip here replaces the family structure, the structure of blood and lineage, which is the norm assumed by psychoanalysis. This remark connects up neatly, you may say too neatly, with the history of the word 'gossip'. 'Gossip' stems originally from 'God-sib' – siblings in the sight of God. From the fourteenth century on, there developed three primary senses of gossip:

1. godparent: third party that oversees the future moral development of newborn babe;
2. gossip: women who gather together at the lying-in of a woman;
3. gossip: light hearted and idle talk, especially of women (by implication, of women gathered at a lying-in).

An explanation which isn't in the *Oxford English Dictionary*, and for which I am grateful to a friend working on the history of midwifery,[31] is the following. In the seventeenth century, the gossips who attended the lying-in were all women, men being barred. The gossip was then called on to bear witness in church to the fact that this baby being christened was the baby she had seen born; in doing so she became the god-parent.[32] In this way the gossip mediated between the all-female mystery of birth and the patrilineal world of the church, of the christening. Not a bad lineage for a word which I take to describe the cultural unconscious of psychoanalysis.

Notes

1. Jacques Derrida, 'Télépathie', in *Cahiers Confrontation 10* (Automne 1983), pp. 210–30; this passage from p. 216.
2. All translations are from Lionel Salter's version. The aria runs:

> Come...kneel down...
> Stay still here...
> Keep quiet; now turn round...
> Bravo... that's very good.
> Now turn and face me,
> Here! your eyes towards me...
> Look straight in front at me...
> My lady isn't here [1].
> That collar a bit higher,
> Those eyes cast down,
> Your hands folded before you...
> Then let's see how you walk
> When you're on your feet.
> (*aside to the Countess*) [2]
> Look at the little rascal,
> Isn't he handsome?
> What roguish glances,
> What airs, what graces!
> If women fall in love with him,
> They have good reason why.

Note also that Cherubino has already sung his/her famous aria,

> Voi che sapete,   You ladies
> Che cosa è amor,   Who know what love is,
> Donne, vedete   See if it is
> S'io l'ho nel cor.   What I have in my
>   heart.

3. P. D. James, *A Taste for Death* (Faber & Faber, London, 1986), p. 258.
4. John Forrester, 'The Untold Pleasures of Psychoanalysis: Freud, Dora and the Madonna', in Forrester, *The Seductions of Psychoanalysis: Freud, Lacan, Derrida* (Cambridge University Press, Cambridge, 1990), pp. 48–61. Other accounts arguing similar views are referred to in this paper.
5. John Forrester, 'Who is in analysis with whom? Freud, Lacan, Derrida', in *The Seductions of Psychoanalysis*, pp. 221–242.
6. The problems of being Lacan's translator over the past few years have led to a singular intellectual phenomenon for me: an incapacity to remember whether certain ideas, when expressed in English, are 'mine', my version of Lacan's ideas, or my translation of Lacan's French. Perhaps it is not surprising that this has been my lot, given that the act of translation is specifically aimed at repressing the original and replacing it with an exact replica. On the psychoanalytic theme of the 'exact replica' see my '"... a perfect likeness of the past"', in Andrew Benjamin and David Wood (eds), *Writing in the Future* (Routledge, London, 1990) and in Forrester, *The Seductions of Psychoanalysis* pp. 90–6.
7. Sigmund Freud, *An Outline of Psycho-analysis*, SE, vol. XXIII, p. 173: 'The analytic physician and the patient's weakened ego form a pact with each other. The sick ego promises us the most complete candour – promises, that

is, to put at our disposal all the material which its self-perception yields it; we assure the patient of the strictest discretion and place at his service our experience in interpreting material that has been influenced by the unconscious. . . This pact constitutes the analytic situation.'

8. The idea that the analyst encourages the patient, *in any way*, either implicitly or explicitly, may seem to some unduly interventionist; the issue forms part of the substance of the debates concerning active technique instigated primarily by Ferenczi. It is clear that Freud agreed with many of the techniques Ferenczi created, for instance, forbidding certain actions within analysis which had the function of substitutive masturbatory activities, or encouraging phobics to place themselves in situations which elicited the anxiety associated with the phobia. But avoiding discussing the analysis 'outside' is not the only question here; there is also the analyst's working assumption that the family and friends of the patient will, at some point in time, prove to be enemies of the treatment.

9. See my paper cited in note 5 above, and Lacan's 'Seminar on *The Purloined Letter*', translated in *Yale French Studies*, no. 48 (1972), pp. 39–72, the sections devoted to *The Purloined Letter* in Jacques Lacan, *Le Séminaire. Livre II. Le moi dans la théorie de Freud et dans la pratique de la psychanalyse*, translated as *The Seminar. Book II. The ego in Freud's theory and in the technique of psychoanalysis*, edited by Jacques-Alain Miller, translated by Sylvana Tomaselli, with notes and index by John Forrester (Cambridge University Press, Cambridge, 1988), pp. 175–205, and Jacques Derrida, 'The purveyor of truth', *Yale French Studies*, no. 52 (1975), pp. 31–113.

10. Freud, *Jokes and their Relation to the Unconscious*, *SE*, VIII pp. 181–6. It is also plausible to argue that gossip and joking are tools of the oppressed; on this, and other analogies with Freud's discussion of jokes, see Patricia Meyer Spacks, *Gossip* (University of Chicago Press, Chicago, 1985).

11. This may give a further insight into Dora's putative intentions; for a similar line of thought concerning these, see Michel Foucault, 'Introduction' to Ludwig Binswanger, *Le rêve et l'existence* (Desclée, Paris, 1954).

12. J. M. Masson, *The Assault on Truth* (Chatto & Windus, London, 1984).

13. This is the solution to so many of the quarrels about whether or not analysis deals with real or fantasied events. Again, Derrida's Freudian musings are exactly on target: 'An event can take place which isn't real. My usual distinction between reality and external reality is perhaps not quite adequate at this point. It gestures towards the event which no idea of "reality" can help us think. But so what, I'll say to you, if what is announced in the announcement indeed bears the index "external reality"? Well then, treat it as an index, it can signify, telephone, telesignal another event which takes place before the other, without the other, in accordance with another time, another space, etc. That's the *a*, *b*, *c* of my psychoanalysis. When I speak of reality, it's so as to send them to sleep, otherwise you won't understand any of my rhetoric. I've never given up hypnosis, I've simply transferred one mode of induction to another: one might say that I've become a writer and have poured all my powers and hypnagogic desires into the writing, into the rhetoric, into the staging and into the composition of texts' ('*Télépathie*', p. 219).

14. See Stanley L. Olinick, 'The gossiping psychoanalyst', *International Review of Psycho-Analysis*, vol. 7 (1980), pp. 439–45. This passage from p. 439.

15. Ethel Person, 'Women in therapy: Therapist gender as a variable', *Int. Rev. Psa.*, vol. 10 (1983), pp. 193–204. 'Although neither had reacted negatively at

the time of the discovery, in re-analysis each expressed the feeling that he had been "raped" ' (p. 201).

16. It is not feasible to justify in this paper calling the seduction of a woman patient the 'original sin' of psychoanalysis. See my 'Contracting the disease of love: authority and freedom in the origins of psychoanalysis'; 'Rape, seduction and psychoanalysis' and 'The true story of Anna O.', all in Forrester, *The Seductions of Psychoanalysis* (see note 4 above). For an account of the early history of Freud's theories explicitly in terms of 'original sin', see Marie Balmary, *Psychoanalyzing Psychoanalysis. Freud and the Hidden Fault of the Father*, trans. with an introduction by Ned Lukacher (Johns Hopkins University Press, Baltimore, 1982).

17. This point is expanded upon in the paper cited in note 5.

18. Freud, 'Dreams and occultism', *New Introductory Lectures on Psychoanalysis*, Lecture XXX (1933 [1932]) *SE*, XXII, pp. 55–6. The brief paragraph which then follows – 'And this brings us back to psycho-analysis, which was what we started out from' – ends the lecture.

My thinking on the topic of telepathy is very much in line with that of Wladimir Granoff in *Filiations* (Paris: Editions de Minuit, 1975), and the more detailed studies, by Granoff and Jean-Michel Rey, *L'occulte, objet de la pensée freudienne* (PUF, Paris, 1983), and by Jacques Derrida in a series of papers, including 'Télépathie' *op. cit.*

19. Derrida, 'Télépathie', pp. 209–10; my translation. Cf. also the passage on p. 211: 'Because here is my last paradox, which only you will fully understand: it is because there will have been telepathy that a post card may not arrive at its destination. The final naivity would be to think that Telepathy guarantees a destination that the "Post Office" [*postes et télécommunications*] fails to assure.'

20. See Lacan's discussion of the acephalic subject and the 'collective unconscious' in *The Seminar. Book II* (cited in note 9 above), esp. pp. 170–1.

21. For the story of the fortune-teller and the analyst, see Freud, 'Psycho-analysis and telepathy', *SE*, XVIII, pp. 185–90, and my paper cited in note 6 above.

22. The distinction he draws between them is a fine one: telepathy is the report of an *event* coming to the consciousness of a person in a different place (and perhaps time), by means of some mysterious process of transmission; thought-transference is the transmission of a *thought* from one mind to another. Note that this may be transmission to the *unconscious* mind of another person – which is where psychoanalysis is in a privileged position to investigate the phenomenon.

23. Granoff, *Filiations* (see note 18 above).

24. This is explored in detail in my *The Dream of Psychoanalysis*. See also a series of fine books by Monique Schneider, including *La Parole et L'Inceste. De l'enclos linguistique à la liturgie psychanalytique* (Aubier Montaigne, Paris, 1980, and *'Père, ne vois-tu pas ...?' Le père, le maître, le spectre dans l'interprétation des rêves* (Denoël, Paris, 1985), and also Michel Schneider (no relation), *Blessures de Mémoire* (Gallimard, Paris, 1980).

25. Phyllis Grosskurth, *Melanie Klein. Her world and her work* (Hodder & Stoughton, London, 1986), esp. pp. 95–100.

26. This relates to the material alluded to in note 16 above.

27. Jacques Lacan, *Seminar II*, cited in note 9 above. Chapter entitled 'The circuit', p. 89.

28. See Elizabeth Roudinesco, *Histoire de la psychanalyse en France. 2, 1925–1985* (Seuil, Paris, 1986), pp. 135–6.

29. Didier Anzieu, *Freud's Self-Analysis*, trans. Peter Graham (Hogarth Press and the Institute of Psycho-analysis, London, 1986).
30. Serge Leclaire, *Démasquer le Réel* (Seuil, Paris, 1971), esp. pp. 33–41. I discuss Leclaire's argument at greater length in the paper cited in note 5.
31. Dr Adrian Wilson, Wellcome Unit for the History of Medicine, University of Cambridge.
32. This fact also adds a surprising twist to the claim that paternity is always subject to a doubt that is never at issue when dealing with questions of maternity. At a time when a sizeable proportion of children born became foundlings, abandoned to various institutions, this is perhaps not so surprising.

Notes on Contributors

Parveen Adams lectures in psychology at Brunel University. She co-founded and co-edited the feminist journal *m/f*. She is the editor of *Language in Thinking* and has published numerous articles on feminism; she is working on a book of essays on perverse sexualities.

Homi K. Bhabha is Lecturer in English Literature and Literary Theory at the University of Sussex. He has published essays in a number of journals including *Critical Inquiry, New Formations, October* and *Screen*. A collection of his essays is due for publication, and he has edited the anthology *Nation and Narration*.

Victor Burgin is Professor of Art History at the University of California, Santa Cruz. He has published *Thinking Photography, The End of Art Theory* and *Between*.

Elizabeth Cowie teaches film studies at the University of Kent, Canterbury. She co-founded and co-edited *m/f* from 1976 until it ceased publication in 1986; a collection of articles from the journal is forthcoming. She has published in *m/f, Framework, Camera Obscura* and *The Oxford Literary Review*, and has an article in the anthology *Feminism and Film Theory* edited by Constance Penley. She has recently completed a book on representing women: psychoanalysis and feminist film theories.

James Donald teaches at the Open University. He has edited the journals *Screen Education* (1978–80) and *New Formations* (1987–9). Among the books he has edited are *Formations of Fantasy* (with Victor Burgin and Cora Kaplan), *Politics and Ideology* (with Stuart Hall), *Subjectivity and Social Relations* (with Veronica Beechey) and *Fantasy and the Cinema*. He is currently working on a book about education, popular culture and government.

John Forrester is Lecturer in History and Philosophy of Science, University of Cambridge, translator of Lacan's *Seminars* (volumes 1 and 2), and author of *Language and the Origins of Psychoanalysis, Who is in Analysis with Whom? Freud, Lacan, Derrida* and *The Seductions of Psychoanalysis*.

Mary Kelly is an artist, writer and teacher currently based in New York. Amongst her works are *Post-Partum Document* and *Interim*.

Laura Mulvey is Senior Lecturer in Film at the London College of Printing. She has directed six films with Peter Wollen; her book *Visual and Other Pleasures* was published in 1989.

Elizabeth Wright is Lecturer and Fellow in German, Girton College, Cambridge. She is author of *Psychoanalytic Criticism: Theory and Practice* and *Postmodern Brecht: A Re-Presentation*.

Robert Young is Fellow of Wadham College, Oxford. His most recent book is *History and Colonialism*; he is joint editor of the *Oxford Literary Review*.